Mrs Despard and The Suffrage Movement

This book is dedicated to Makenna Matheson–Pollock (born 2016) and all the girls of her generation, in the hope that they will grow up in a fairer world.

Mrs Despard and The Suffrage Movement

Founder of The Women's Freedom League

Lynne Graham-Matheson and
Helen Matheson-Pollock

PEN & SWORD
HISTORY

First published in Great Britain in 2019 by
Pen & Sword Military
An imprint of
Pen & Sword Books Ltd
Yorkshire – Philadelphia

Copyright © Lynne Graham-Matheson and
Helen Matheson-Pollock 2019

ISBN 978 1 52673 112 8

A CIP catalogue record for this book is
available from the British Library

Printe[d] ... [Internationa]l [Ltd],
[Padstow, Cornwall.]

Pen & Sword Books Limited incorporates the imprints of Atlas,
Archaeology, Aviation, Discovery, Family History, Fiction, History,
Maritime, Military, Military Classics, Politics, Select, Transport,
True Crime, Air World, Frontline Publishing, Leo Cooper, Remember
When, Seaforth Publishing, The Praetorian Press, Wharncliffe
Local History, Wharncliffe Transport, Wharncliffe True Crime
and White Owl.

For a complete list of Pen & Sword titles please contact

PEN & SWORD BOOKS LIMITED
47 Church Street, Barnsley, South Yorkshire, S70 2AS, England
E-mail: enquiries@pen-and-sword.co.uk
Website: www.pen-and-sword.co.uk

Or

PEN AND SWORD BOOKS
1950 Lawrence Rd, Havertown, PA 19083, USA
E-mail: Uspen-and-sword@casematepublishers.com
Website: www.penandswordbooks.com

Contents

Charlotte Despard

W e came across Charlotte almost by accident, when we were researching notable women from Kent. Not nearly as well known as Millicent Fawcett or Emmeline Pankhurst, she has two roads and a public house in London named after her, and the suffrage organisation she co-founded – the Women's Freedom League – existed until 1961, long after the other suffrage organisations had disappeared.

Charlotte is usually described as a suffragist but she was so much more. She did not enter public life until she was widowed in her forties. She was wealthy and left her beautiful home in Surrey to live in a tiny flat in Battersea, fighting for better lives for the poor, particularly women and children. She was a pioneer, introducing school meals and medical checks for children in school. She was a member of the Independent Labour Party (ILP) and the Women's Social and Political Union (WSPU) led by Emmeline Pankhurst. Charlotte was a social reformer – she fought for votes for women but also for votes for all men, and better working conditions for all.

After the constitutional issues and the split in the WSPU, Charlotte was instrumental in the founding of the Women's Freedom League (WFL), and became its first president. She was firmly behind the non-violent militancy of the suffragists, leading the tax resistance policy and the boycott of the 1911 census. She went to prison for her cause, as did her close friends Kate Harvey and Maud Gonne.

Just after the First World War Charlotte decided to go back to her Irish roots and moved to Ireland to fight for Sinn Féin and an independent Ireland. There are those who say that if she had not stood against the British government in this way, she would have been honoured as Millicent Fawcett and Emmeline Pankhurst have been.

Even today some of her activities would be considered amazing – she was aged 95 when she died and in the last years of her life she stood for parliament and travelled to Russia. Charlotte died in Ireland, lonely and poor, having used all her wealth to try and help others less fortunate.

She was never known as Charlotte, always Mrs Despard, but to us, in the less formal twenty-first century, she is Charlotte. We wish we had been able to meet her.

Lynne Graham-Matheson
Helen Matheson-Pollock

Acronyms Used

AGM	Annual General Meeting
COS	Charity Organisation Society
FOSR	Friends of Soviet Russia
ILP	Independent Labour Party
IRA	Irish Republican Army
IWFL	Irish Women's Franchise League
IWP	Irish Workers' Party
MP	Member of Parliament
NEC	National Executive Committee (of the WFL)
NUWSS	National Union of Women's Suffrage Societies
NWSPU	National Women's Social and Political Union
SDF	Social Democratic Federation
WFL	Women's Freedom League
WPDL	Women's Prisoners Defence League
WSPU	Women's Social and Political Union
WTRL	Women's Tax Resistance League

Chapter 1

Early Life

London, 1892

A slender, middle-aged woman dressed in widow's black, with an unconventional lace mantilla and leather sandals, waits nervously at the bottom of the steps to Wandsworth Town Hall. Beside her is a short man in the uniform of an army officer. 'Remember,' he says to his sister, 'it's only the nervous who are of any real use.' Taking a deep breath, she climbs the steps and Charlotte Despard makes her first public speech.

*   *   *

Charlotte French was born on 15 June 1844, the third of seven children, not in Kent as other writers have stated, but in Edinburgh, Scotland. The reason for this is unclear – her mother was Scottish, so perhaps they were visiting relatives. Her father, Commander John Tracey William French, having lost an eye in the battle of Navarino, retired from the navy in 1836. He was energetic, forceful and frustrated by the lack of action in the peacetime navy. At the age of 32 he had married Margaret Eccles, fourteen years his junior, who brought piety and an unstable temperament, which suggests their marriage may have been difficult. Margaret also brought a significant dowry – she was a very wealthy heiress, from a family with a substantial property portfolio around Glasgow. Captain French was Deputy-Lieutenant of Kent and a magistrate, his behaviour on the bench making him an object of fear. He ran his estate in Kent with fanatical efficiency and attention to detail. 'He was,' wrote his son, 'a man of great strength of character, firm will and self-reliance, and these personal qualities were hardened and developed by eighteen or nineteen years of strenuous service.' Charlotte clearly inherited some of her father's characteristics.

Charlotte and her siblings spent their childhood in Ripple, Kent, on an estate that had come into the family two generations earlier. Of more significance to Charlotte in later life, however, the Frenchs were also of Irish descent, although they had not lived in Ireland since the eighteenth century. When English law arrived in Ireland in 1635 the Frenchs, and many others, were dispossessed. Later the new nation suffered from the destruction of James II's kingship by William of Orange in 1690. John French, also known as Tierna Mor, sided with William and, through backing the victorious cause, managed to restore the family fortunes. When he died he owned 47,000 acres and £1,000 was spent on his funeral. Charlotte's great-grandfather, who settled in Kent, was the grandson of Tierna Mor, descendant of the greatest chieftains in western Ireland.

Margaret née Eccles had five daughters – Mary, Caroline (Carrie), Charlotte (known as Lottie in her youth), Margaret and Sarah (Nellie) before giving birth to a son, John, and then Katherine (Katie). She spent most of her adult life pregnant or recovering from childbirth, having had several miscarriages in addition to her seven children. Her husband excluded her from his activities and she gradually became a recluse. Exhausted, she immersed herself in the devotional literature of the Presbyterians, leaving her children to their own devices.

Little concrete information survives about Charlotte's early life but what we know suggests a fairly typical, if eccentric, Victorian upbringing of benign neglect in pursuit of gentility. Her early life seems to have been happy, perhaps wilder than was usual, with Charlotte herself reflecting:

> Looking into the dim past I see a little company of girls in a beautiful old Kent garden … The show garden was kept in trim order. We were not allowed to run about on the lawns. That however was a matter of small moment to us, for we had a wonderful playground of our own – a wild corner, hidden away behind a large and imposing rockery with which the superior and alien race never meddled … Through the summer days we enjoyed ourselves, planning out houses, planting gardens and digging deep holes which served the purpose of robbers and smugglers.

There seems to have been little adult involvement in the children's lives and few governesses or tutors stayed very long. When Charlotte was 10 things changed swiftly and dramatically. Her father died and her mother was incapable of caring for the family so Captain Smith, a friend of her father, became their guardian and imposed stricter supervision on the young children. Rules were put in place and freedom swiftly curbed:

> Some interfering superior person reported that we were entering into friendly relations, by means of holes in a tall hedge, with some village children outside. We were then given prim, box-hedged gardens in full view of the library and morning-room windows, and told to cultivate them. I never cared for my new garden and deeply envied the happy village children who could run about as they liked and did not seem to be troubled by those superior persons, nurses and governesses.

Charlotte gathered up the money she had been given by generous relatives, ran the three miles to the nearest station and tried to buy a ticket to London, where she planned to earn her living as a servant.

> Needless to say, I was stopped, but I had gone so far that I could not return that night, and I spent it alone in a little awe and some importance at a station inn. After that, lest I should infect my sisters with my spirit of insubordination, I was kept in solitary confinement for three or four days, and then sent away to school.

She hated the imprisonment of school and worked herself into a series of illnesses. She was finally sent home through ill-health after a year and said later, 'That is a hideous time which I never like to remember.' Years later she summarised her feelings:

> One day I was taught to sing a little hymn by my governess. It went like this:
>
> > I thank the Goodness and the Grace
> > That on my birth hath smiled,
> > And made me in these happy days
> > A happy English child.

> I was not born a little slave
> To labour in the sun
> And wish I was but in the grave
> And all my labour done.

That hymn was the turning-point. I demanded why God had made
slaves, and I was promptly sent to bed. Oh, how I hated the nurses
and governesses, and I stood at the gates of my home and envied the
little village children. They were free. They had liberty.

As Charlotte grew older reading became her escape. She loved poetry,
particularly Milton's *Paradise Lost*, and the romantic poetry of
Wordsworth and Keats. Charlotte's campaigning nature also showed
itself from an early age. Supporting the Italians in their struggle for
independence, she was among the cheering crowds at Dover when
Garibaldi arrived in England, and she adopted Mazzini as her 'master
and mentor'. The *Risorgimento* (the campaign for Italian political unity)
coincided with her adolescence and showed her lifelong enthusiasm for
political rebellion and democracy.

John's maleness set him above his many sisters and he became their
spoiled pet. Eight years older, Charlotte became his willing slave,
pandering to his whims, and setting a pattern of behaviour which did
not change – whatever he did she adored and forgave him. Even when he
was a field marshal commanding British forces in a world war, she still
thought of him as her baby brother and wrote to him accordingly. She
was responsible for teaching him his letters and numbers though, which
she found very dull.

Her persistent rage against authority comes perhaps from a childhood
lacking in parental love, affection and attention. All Charlotte's sisters
married autocratic men who possibly provided some of the guidance
they lacked as children. John had a life within military discipline but was
known to assert that 'the absence of a powerful, directing mind brought
to bear on my childhood has had a certain influence on my life.' In 1860
Margaret French was committed to a lunatic asylum. At that time in
a wealthy family harmless lunacy could have been managed at home;
possibly she was violent and needed to be restrained, therefore needing

more care than her household could provide. It may have been from Margaret that her children inherited their fiery tempers and strong wills.

Before Margaret was committed to the asylum, in 1857 the family trustees had decided to send the children to live with their mother's relatives in Edinburgh. The Eccles family were strict Presbyterians and saw it as their duty to instil in these wild children the values of their faith. 'Unless we were converted there was no hope of safety in the future, and converted people kept themselves apart from the world,' Charlotte was told.

> Operas, theatres and dances were sinful. Light literature, everything indeed that was interesting and human, must be accepted with great reserve. It was sinful to sew or knit or open a book of fiction on a Sunday, and anything like pride in dress or appearance was treated with suspicion.

Charlotte was sent to a school for young ladies in Atholl Crescent where she memorised passages of prose and poetry, developing an excellent memory. The years in Edinburgh left a mark on her speech – she would say 'forenoon' rather than morning and 'haar' instead of sea mist. She was also left with a strong sense of duty and belief in self-improvement, which were in conflict with her 'undisciplined' mind. She felt strongly her lack of education and said later, 'I had not been taught to do any one thing thoroughly [and] I may say that throughout my life this has been my great drawback.' As was her nature, she 'taught and drilled' and was proud to have 'succeeded in partially overcoming the disadvantages of an inferior, slipshod education.'

This education was typical of that for a Victorian girl of her class, whose vocation was a suitable marriage. Charlotte and her sisters were taught 'a little music, a little drawing, no science or mathematics, but a little literature, geography and history. Manners of course!' Considering her education against the backdrop of the education reform she later pursued, Charlotte commented 'the impression left on my mind is of incompetent teachers and indifferent learners – nothing thorough.'

The Eccles family cut all ties between them and their foster children in 1863: when Mary French turned 21 and became legally independent they lost no time in transferring all responsibility to her. The French children moved into a large house on the edge of York, where Mary was responsible for five girls aged 10 to 20 and a 12-year-old boy. Charlotte again went to school but at 18 she stayed at home to help her older sisters run the house. Now an heiress she had the prospect of £2,000 a year (approximately £240,000 today) when she married.

This may have been the first time that Charlotte really understood that she came from a wealthy family, with a social standing that set them apart from many people around them. Just after she moved to Yorkshire, Charlotte had visited a rope factory and there saw sweated labour, and more poverty and misery than she had come across before. Women and young children, aged up to about 8 years old, sitting before huge piles of rags, picking at the cloth to make rope from the threads. She fiercely resented the injustice, and could not see how the way that the people themselves must feel had not put things right. She was learning about the expectations of the adult world and the harshness of the rules; the conflict between her private ambitions and society's expectations left her angry and confused. Recalling the experience she claimed:

> That was a strange time, unsatisfactory, full of ungratified aspirations. I longed ardently to be of some use in the world, but as we were girls with a little money and born into a particular social position, it was not thought necessary that we should do anything but amuse ourselves until the time and the opportunity of marriage came along. 'Better any marriage at all than none,' a foolish aunt used to say.

Charlotte had fought against attempts to discipline her and curb her temper but now felt powerless against the social norms that were pushing her towards what was expected of her. She reflected later:

> The woman of the well-to-do classes was made to understand early that the only door open to a life at once easy and respectable was that of marriage. Therefore she had to depend upon her good looks, according to the ideals of the men of her day, her charm, her little drawing-room arts, and the frills and furbelows with which fashion decreed she should disguise herself. MAN would have it so.

As a young woman Charlotte was not classically beautiful – her nose a little too big, her jaw a little too heavy – but she was not unattractive, with striking blue eyes and heavy waves of chestnut hair. Despite her often prickly manner, she was likely pursued by many young men (her income alone was of great appeal) but seems clear that she was looking for an older, father figure, to compensate for her lack of affection and guidance as a child.

Across the 1860s while Charlotte was living in London she had fallen hopelessly in love with a young man. When he ended their brief relationship he recommended that she read Shelley, as he would suit her, leading her towards the great passion of her life. She knew some of Shelley's work, but not the poems deemed unsuitable for a young lady. She traced much of her inspiration to Shelley, the poet of rebellion. She was taken up with his praise of the independent woman, but also picked up on his ideas about fairness, socialism and revolution. Charlotte was very innocent and unworldly and when she first came across the poverty and squalor of the East End: 'I longed to speak to these people in their misery, to say, "Why do you bear it? Rise as the men of Argolis did under Laon and Cynthna. Smite your oppressors. Be true and strong."' Fortunately some instinct prevented her doing so but this was a reflection of Shelley's views on rebellion for all parts of society.

In Shelley's opinion men were imprisoned by factories, women by marriage. He wrote that men and women should have to stay in a marriage only as long as they loved each other, that there was nothing wrong with women having sexual appetites. For Victorian patriarchal society women were dangerous, liable to turn to prostitution and therefore needed the strictest supervision. The stability of society depended on the denial of women's independence, and the attack on marriage was scandalous because it threatened the very fabric of society.

'I remember how, even in those days,' Charlotte wrote, 'I felt with hot indignation the disabilities of women.' She was being pushed towards marriage, and wanted affection, but wanted her freedom too. 'A system could not well have been devised more studiously hostile to human happiness than marriage,' Shelley had written, and Charlotte had taken notes.

Around this time the family began to break up – sisters Margaret and Mary married, Katie went to school in Brighton and John went off to prepare for the naval exams. With no responsibilities the other three sisters – Charlotte, Caroline and Nellie – engaged a chaperone and travelled around Europe, mainly Switzerland, Bavaria and the Tyrol, concentrating on the countryside and avoiding cultural centres. At 23 Charlotte was already 'on the shelf', although later she said 'that gibe would not worry the modern girl too much!' They stayed in Venice for two months before returning to London, where Nellie was married. Charlotte and Caroline, her favourite sister, decided to continue their travels, travelling alone because at 28 and 26 they were now old enough to chaperone themselves. The sisters began their trip with a visit to Paris, but Bismarck's Germany was trying to extend its empire and having fought the French at Metz and Sedan, the German army was closing in on Paris. The two women delayed their departure from Paris until it was too late to go on and they had to return to England, although a different version of the story says that John Lydall (Mary's husband) had to go to Paris to rescue them.

Upon her return Charlotte went to stay with friends and there met a young Irishman called Maximillian Despard who had just returned from the Far East. Although only a few years older than Charlotte he was calm and self-assured, with the authority of an older man. They met frequently at his house in North London and she discovered he was amusing and had radical views just as she did. When he asked her to marry him she was pleased to accept. It was a short courtship – they met in the late summer of 1870 and on 20 December that year they were married.

Although generations of Max's family in Ireland had served the British Crown, there was one exception which caused the name Despard to become associated with rebellion. The founder of the family was Philippe d'Espard, a Hugenot refugee sent by Queen Elizabeth to Ireland as a land commissioner. His descendants inherited an estate and a Protestant faith. In 1792 Colonel Edward Marcus Despard, who had had a distinguished career as a soldier in Central America, was removed from his post as governor of a British settlement on the Yucatan following complaints from some of the colonists. He disappeared for a while but it seems that some of his time was spent with Irish revolutionary Wolfe Tone, who shared his enthusiasm for the French Revolution. By 1796 they were in communication about the prospects for revolution in Ireland. The name and principles of Wolfe Tone are still sacred to Irish Republicans because he united Presbyterians and Catholics under the banner of Liberty, Equality and Fraternity. In 1798 the United Irishmen launched three uprisings in Ireland while Edward Despard was to rouse the mob in London. The government put down the insurrection and detained Despard without trial: by the time he was released in 1801 Tone was dead and Ireland had become part of the United Kingdom. Despard plotted to secure the independence of Ireland and the overthrow of the government – the Tower of London, the Bank of England and the Houses of Parliament were to be seized and the king assassinated. With five others, Despard was found guilty of treason and for the last time in British history the men were sentenced to be hanged by the neck until not quite dead, then cut down, their bowels removed and cast into the fire, their heads removed and bodies quartered. In the event the drawing and quartering was not carried out.

The remaining Despards were extravagant, litigious and eccentric, but most confined their lives to within the family estates at Mountrath in Central Ireland. They married Wellesleys, Pakenhams, and each other. Three successive generations of George Despards married three successive Gertrude Cardens, the last of which unions produced Max. The Cardens suffered from chronic ill-health and the marriage of Max's parents was considered unwise as the Carden and Despard lines were then so interwoven as to bring concerns about inbreeding. Max did not escape – he was always a delicate boy and at an early age caught scarlet fever, from which he never fully recovered. As was often the case the fever developed into nephritis, or chronic kidney disease, from which he was to suffer all his life and which eventually killed him.

Max was born in 1839, the seventh of eight children. While his brothers went to school and university in Dublin, Max was kept at home with only his tutors and two elder sisters for company. He grew up quiet and self-absorbed and like many of his family had a gift for figures. He joined a shipping firm in London and was sent to Hong Kong as their agent in the early 1860s. There was money to be made in Hong Kong for those with the right qualities, which Max had. He was not reckless and made money quickly, trading in his own right in tea and precious stones. In 1865 when a group of men proposed founding the Hong Kong and Shanghai Bank he invested £6,000 – a shrewd investment, which was worth about £30,000 when he died – and he developed a taste for luxury. Money and marriage went together and Max was wealthy enough to marry whomever he chose.

Charlotte and Max made frequent visits to Ireland but most of their early marriage was spent in London or at their house in Sussex. They enjoyed boating on the river. Details of their life together were kept private but she said she had an ideally happy marriage because they understood each other and Max respected Charlotte's individual identity and intelligence. Charlotte herself wrote, 'I married happily, in the sense that my freedom in that relation, often so difficult, was always respected.' She may have had a degree of freedom and happiness, but descriptions of the marriage do not suggest much laughter or great passion. Max's judgment for good investments perhaps hints at coolness and precision, and Charlotte described him as having a much better head for law than many a trained lawyer. He did not impose his views on his wife, though for the duration of their marriage she took his political, spiritual and social principles as her own. Within a couple of years of his death, however, she had rid herself of them all.

Like Charlotte, Max supported the idea of fundamental reform in society, from a wider franchise to safer working conditions. They thought that the logic of their views would prevail, and were frustrated when it did not. 'Like many other women,' Charlotte wrote, 'I soothed my disappointment and expended my superfluous energies in taking up all sorts of causes – sweated women workers, crèches in poor districts, inspection of factories, temperance.' One of her causes was the Nine Elms Flower Mission. Nine Elms in Battersea was one of the poorest parts of London, where people lived in slums and children suffered from malnutrition and illness. Kind ladies with country gardens distributed flowers, so the Londoners would have a touch of colour. Charlotte, a keen gardener, was happy to help and sent flowers from her garden.

Charity work was a common activity for middle- and upper-class women – some felt it was their duty, others wanted to help those less fortunate than themselves – and Victorian widows particularly would often fill their time with 'good works'. It was regarded as a perfectly respectable activity, being an extension of their domestic responsibilities, so it was a way of getting involved in activities outside the home. Providing flowers to brighten the homes of those living in slums, rather than giving them money – which was thought to encourage feckless spending – or even food and clothes, shows how misguided some of their efforts were, however well-meaning.

Although Max was willing to give advice he did not want to get involved in work with the poor and Charlotte followed his example, probably with some reluctance. Before her marriage Charlotte had longed to do something useful, to serve or have some kind of career. At that time there were few suitable careers for a married woman but being a writer was one of them. With Max's agreement and guidance, Charlotte directed her energy towards writing.

The circulating libraries of the later Victorian era preferred novels to come in three volumes, so subscribers had to pay three times to read a single work. It could be difficult to fill the necessary 700–800 pages so authors had to resort to sub-plots, long sections of description and moralising and many, many characters. This did not, in the majority of cases, lead to page-turning literature. Charlotte's novels are wildly romantic, populated by stereotypes, with cardboard characters who go through a series of unlikely events until they have a happy ending where lovers are reunited and fathers rediscovered. In her writing, her own search for spiritual certainty is frequently blurred with a search for lost parents. Years later an unnamed admirer described her work as 'brilliant' and suggested that had she kept writing she would have become 'one of the foremost literary figures of our time', but this seems very unlikely, although one year she earned £300 from her writing. A review of her first novel, *Chaste as Ice, Pure as Snow* in *The Atheneum* reads: 'it occasionally nearly rises to tragedy but it is never pathetic [meaning moving], and is seldom either humorous or absolutely dull.' An exception was *A Voice from the Dim Millions*, a political novella about a factory girl and her family living in poverty, clearly based on Charlotte's observations of life in Nine Elms, but even here her passion and sense of wrong does not come across as it might. Focusing on poverty, disease and the early death of factory workers, it allegedly tells the 'true history of a working-woman.' One by one the woman's family members fall prey to problems such as the sweatshop system, disease, unemployment and prostitution.

God knows this is no fiction I am telling. God knows that lives sadder than ours are being lived out every day. Here – in this rich, and free, and prosperous country – men and women groan daily in a slavery from which there is no rescue but death.

This story too has a happy ending, however, with the working-woman becoming co-manager of a sewing shop.

We are told by some that we are spoiling the labour market. I may be very unphilosophical, but whenever I hear that said, I am seized with an ardent wish to have a large enough business to spoil it for good and all.

When Gladstone was returned to power in 1880 the Despards looked forward to far-reaching reforms to eradicate sweated labour and slum housing and extend the franchise to male rural householders – they were not interested in including the franchise for women as, like most radicals, they saw it as a way to increase the Conservative vote by including wealthy middle-class women, when it was more important to extend the vote to agricultural labourers. Hopes quickly turned to disappointment – with a large majority the Liberal government was not concerned with radical change. Home rule for Ireland dominated matters but there was one important development. The Married Women's Property Act was passed in 1882, allowing wives to own property independently of their husbands. Charlotte would have been pleased by this as she had been very upset by a case in Nine Elms where a drunken husband, long separated from his working wife, had twice broken into her house and stolen her savings. When Charlotte went to the police she found that 'stolen' was not correct, as he had more right to his wife's money than she did.

In 1879 the Despards moved to a new home, Courtlands, an estate in Surrey, out of line with their political views but in keeping with Max's taste for luxury. He was continuing to trade in tea and jewels very successfully. His friends were mostly colleagues and other men who had done well. Charlotte had little in common with them and her friends tended to be children – the children of friends and neighbours as she had none of her own.

Charlotte was 26 when she married and presumably realised quite quickly that there would be no children, a situation made worse because her sisters, except Carrie who married late, all had several. She later wrote of 'the thousands of women [who] … have passionately craved for the sweetness of motherhood of which an inexorable fate has betrayed them,' but otherwise said nothing about her disappointment. Much later she was careful to point out that motherhood was just one option open to women. Her sister Margaret is reported to have told one of her grandchildren that Max was impotent, possibly caused by his illness – or generations of inbreeding. Whatever the reason, Charlotte's love of children is evident in the way she cared for so many. They were not always comfortable with her, but she behaved as if they were sensible people who could be given responsibility and with whom she could discuss the issues of the day. Fifty years later her favourite nephew recalled the serious conversations they had when he was about 10 concerning the poor wages paid to road-menders.

Soon after moving to Surrey, Max's health worsened. The cold winters of England were very difficult and for the rest of his life the Despards went abroad from autumn until early summer. They made one visit to the Mediterranean but otherwise always went to India, moving on from there perhaps to Australia, Hong Kong or America. While they were in India Max was content to stay in the heat of the plains while Charlotte went up into the hills to explore the Buddhist temples. Charlotte's last novel, *The Rajah's Heir*, written at this time and clearly inspired by her travels, has a heroine reaching for spiritual fulfilment, like Charlotte.

Max's illness did not follow a steady course. There were periods of despair followed by hope as he seemed to improve, but each period of improvement was a little shorter than before. Most of the time he was silent and turned in on himself, so Charlotte kept herself busy with her writing. In 1889 they went to India for the winter, but on the journey home Max's condition suddenly grew worse. The ship diverted to Tenerife and he was taken ashore, accompanied by Charlotte and his younger brother Fitzherbert. When it became clear that there was little time left they took Max aboard the next England-bound ship that called at the island so that he could die at home. As the SS *Coptic* entered the Bay of Biscay he fell into a coma and on Good Friday, 4 April 1890, Max Despard died and was buried at sea. Charlotte was widowed at the age of 45.

Chapter 2

Entering Public Life

After Max died in 1890, Charlotte hid away with her grief at Courtlands for several months, refusing all visitors. She had filled her time travelling with Max, pursuing a career as a writer with his approval and following his values and beliefs. After his death, without children or family close to her, she must have felt very alone. Her only interest was the planchette (from the French for 'little plank') popular in Victorian séances, which she used to try and communicate with Max. Forerunner of the Ouija board, the small, flat piece of wood, often heart-shaped, had castors and an aperture for holding a pencil, for automatic writing. For the rest of her life Charlotte wore the black clothes of a widow, with a black lace mantilla and leather sandals, standing out at a time when there was a fashion for enormous hats crowned with ostrich feathers, and women in her social circle would sometimes have changed their clothes several times a day.

The nearest house to Courtlands was Claremount, owned by Queen Victoria and occupied by the Duchess of Albany, widow of the queen's youngest son, Prince Leopold. When the duchess, patron of the Nine Elms Flower Mission, heard that Charlotte had become reclusive, she was summoned to Claremount, which she described later as having the power of a royal command. The duchess suggested that Charlotte should take up charity work again, as a way of getting back into public life. This was an activity of which Max had approved, and it was difficult to refuse a request from a member of the royal family, so in the late summer of 1890 Charlotte again crammed her carriage with baskets of flowers for the poverty-stricken houses of Nine Elms. 'It was,' she said later, 'my friends of Battersea who best helped me bear my desolation.'

It was soon clear, however, that sending baskets of flowers was not enough for Charlotte. She wanted to be more involved in improving the lot of the poor. Fellow suffragist Teresa Billington (later Billington-

Greig) wrote that Charlotte was not a believer in official public service but 'held very strongly that there must be personal relations between those who served and those who stood in need of service.' Max had left her financially independent, with share dividends of £500 annually from his investment in the Muir Mills in Cawnpore and an income of about £3,500 per year from his investment in the Hong Kong and Shanghai Bank. £3,500 in 1890 is worth approximately £427,410 today. Her marriage settlement produced a further £2,000 a year and in addition to Courtlands she owned property in Sussex and Croydon, so she was a very wealthy woman. She was not just financially independent – being a widow in Victorian times gave her a social status and a degree of freedom.

At the turn of the twentieth century Britain was one of the richest and strongest nations in the world and a leading industrial power, producing more than half the world's iron, coal and cotton cloth, but industrialisation brought problems as well as wealth. In 1801, at the time of the first census, 20 per cent of the population lived and worked in urban areas and 80 per cent in rural areas. By 1911 the situation had reversed and 80 per cent of the population was crowded into the towns and cities. Over the same period the population of London grew from under a million to over six million people. Providing housing and sanitation for so many people meant much of the urban population lived in poverty, with terrible living and working conditions. Overcrowded housing led to disease and in the burgeoning towns and cities alcoholism and violence were real problems. Charles Booth's *Inquiry into Life and Labour in London (1886–1903)* survey produced a series of maps coloured street by street to show levels of poverty and wealth. The area of the Nine Elms Flower Mission was black, indicating extreme poverty.

Nine Elms is the low-lying stretch of Battersea from the Lambeth border to Battersea Park. Nicknamed 'the island', the area has long been an industrial community and dependent on the river. It was said that you could smell Nine Elms long before you arrived there, the air heavy with the product of the gasworks, railway works and factories. At the end of the nineteenth century the majority of the population of Nine Elms was Irish. Employment for men was mainly from the gasworks and the railway depot, for women laundries or factories. It was in this district, one of the poorest areas of London with some of the worst slums, in which the wealthy middle-class Charlotte decided to live. In many ways she had nothing in common with the people of Nine Elms, but there was clearly something about the women and children she met that made her think this was where she wanted to be. Perhaps they gave her a purpose. She and her brother felt close to their Irish roots, and the large Irish population of Nine Elms may have strengthened this.

At the end of 1890 Charlotte rented a house at 95 Wandsworth Road, near to Nine Elms, although she continued to live at Courtlands. In 1891 she purchased 2 Currie Street, Nine Elms. She seems to have been catapulted into living there – her brother, now a lieutenant colonel, was posted to India and did not want to take his young children with him but could not afford a separate house in England. The obvious thing was for his family to move into Courtlands and for Charlotte to make her home in London, although she kept a cottage on the Courtlands Estate.

Children quickly became the focus of Charlotte's attention. Although elementary schooling had been available to all children since 1870, the charging of fees did not stop until 1891. For the poorest families education was a luxury even when it was free – girls could be needed at home to help with younger children, boys to help their fathers. Childhoods were very short – children of 8 or 10 could be working a seventy-hour week, and the lucky ones who were to learn a craft would be apprenticed at 13 or 14. As many families lived in one or two rooms, older children would be pushed out into the streets to make room for the babies. Poor diets, through ignorance and lack of money, left them weak and susceptible to illness and infections, and families could not afford medical attention. It was these children, who had to grow up so quickly, that she urgently wanted to help.

Charlotte hired a nurse to make regular visits to her house and then swept up from the streets the children who looked most in need of care. Soon there was a queue of parents and children at her door so Charlotte opened up the ground floor for them, her personal comfort and convenience were not important. Toys were provided and later newspapers, as many of the children were really young adults. Not surprisingly the children enjoyed being there so wounds took longer than usual to heal and ailments were invented to make more visits necessary. Charlotte was delighted, writing: 'Soon even the youngest realised that the slightest ailment was a chit which allowed them to enter the club.' Another woman was employed to play with the children and other activities were introduced. A small hall at the back of the house was taken over and gymnasium equipment installed. The fiction of being 'patients' was dropped and the first Despard Club was in operation.

The effects of a poor diet were clear – the children lacked energy, were pale and listless, with rickety legs and small bodies. Charlotte produced milk puddings and vegetable broths and tried to teach their parents about nutrition but was met with indifference, even resentment. Mothers felt that not even a trained nurse could teach them anything – the very high infant mortality rate had led to feelings of powerlessness and fatalism. Charlotte battled on and did what she could but it was the feeling that one person could not change anything which led her first into Poor Law reform and later into suffragism; it was her involvement in what she called 'the child movement' that began her work in social reform.

Knowing the benefits of country air, in the summer of 1891 Charlotte organised a trip for the children and their parents, and in horse-drawn charabancs they trekked down to Courtlands. Her nephew Gerald French later wrote:

> It certainly was amusing to some extent, but it had its trying side. For instance, they came equipped with several barrel organs, which of course they never ceased playing from the time of their arrival until their departure. Their women-folk accompanied them, and dancing went on during the greater part of the day on the lawns and on the drive. My father, if I remember rightly, threw himself nobly into the breech and helped to organise sports for the men. He possessed a most acute sense of humour and I think he was more amused than anyone at the extraordinary antics of the invaders of our peace and quietness. They swarmed all over the place, and when evening came and they set on the return journey to London, we at any rate were not sorry that the entertainment had at last come to an end.

The parties that she organised for children, with 'large scale organisation and tremendous provision of food and drink' (Ryder) earned her the family nickname of 'The Quartermaster General'.

In 1892 Charlotte made her first public speech at Wandsworth Town Hall; before she came to live in Battersea she had felt unqualified to speak out, but now she was a participant – and she was angry. She was not a confident speaker and could only go ahead when her brother accompanied her to the steps of the hall and gave her encouragement. When later she became known as a speaker, she forced herself to overcome her fear of the speaker's platform, accepting a growing number of invitations to speak to charitable and philanthropic societies. For the rest of her life she did not lose her nervousness – she could not eat beforehand, while speaking she was conscious only of her audience and at the end of her speech it was the enthusiasm, or not, of the audience which led her to be elated or exhausted. She was, perhaps, not a charismatic speaker, but her need to 'get my message through' gave her speeches a driving force which drew in her audiences.

When Charlotte started public speaking, her concern was the children, and the appalling conditions in which so many of them had to live. This was partly due to the ignorance of their parents and she talked about the importance of education. As she became more involved in their problems, however, she became more aware that it was not the failings of the parents that were the issue, but the cruelty of the system and the low wages that barely kept families from starvation. She found herself wanting a role where she could make a difference.

The population of Battersea had doubled between 1870 and 1891 to 258,000 and was still increasing by about 5,000 a year. There was very high unemployment. A dramatic fall in wheat prices had led to a fall in the number of rural jobs and a surge of unskilled people moving into towns to find work, many from Ireland. A man would hope to earn enough during the summer to keep his family out of the workhouse in the winter when there was little work. Perhaps one job in three was on a casual basis, for a day at a time, and the main employer in Nine Elms was the gasworks, which did at least have work during the winter. A crowd would collect around the gasworks gates at first light and the foreman would select the workers needed. Often the gates would close on around 200 disappointed men, many of whom had walked miles to be there, and by the time they knew they had no work for the day it would be too late to try anywhere else.

Victorians had a fear of pauperism, which they thought could engulf society, and charity had to be strictly controlled so it could not encourage a feckless attitude. The aim of the 1834 Poor Law Amendment Act was to make the able-bodied poor self-reliant – the only assistance available was to enter a workhouse. The aim was to make being a pauper less appealing than having a menial job, but it became the policy to encourage a dread of parish charity and over the years the punitive intentions of dealing with the poor became stronger. The deserving poor – those who lost their jobs through no fault of their own – were helped only with suspicion. The undeserving poor could not be allowed to starve, but were punished for a lack of thrift and want of social responsibility. After 1834 parishes were grouped together into Poor Law unions (larger parishes became Poor Law parishes), with centralised workhouses built to standard designs. Conditions in the workhouse were deliberately harsh so that only the truly destitute would apply for relief – the assistance offered was worse than the living standards of the lowest paid independent labourer – and working-class people dreaded the grim workhouses. Those in the workhouse lost all rights to their personal possessions, and if they had the vote were disenfranchised. Husbands and wives were separated, so they could not add to the burden of the poor by breeding.

Each Poor Law union was managed by a board of guardians elected by local ratepayers, with magistrates belonging to the boards by virtue of their office. Boards were dominated by farmers in the country and wealthy tradesmen in towns: policies tended to reflect the attitudes of these social groups. Radical opponents of the new system saw it as an attempt by ruling elites to reduce wages and place working people at their mercy. There was resistance by many well-to-do people who had traditionally taken responsibility for the disadvantaged members of their communities and saw this as unnecessary interference by central government in local affairs. The Poor Law boards managed the local workhouse, an infirmary, vaccination officers (smallpox), registrars and doctors and part-funded local voluntary groups. The public face of the Poor Law was the relieving officer, who assessed applicants' needs. In many places lady visitors managed visits for children who were discharged from public care at the age of 13 and kept an eye on children where there were reports of neglect, or chased up recalcitrant fathers.

Charlotte was elected to the Kingston Poor Law Board as guardian for Esher, a post which required her to supervise the running of the workhouse, in April 1892. This was one of few elected posts open to women, and she found herself working with retired generals and vicars. There was little real poverty in Esher and it cost around £800 to finance the Poor Law generously. Charlotte retired after a year, believing that the real poverty was in the cities, and her ambition to be of some use in the world did not work in wealthy Surrey.

In May 1893 Charlotte joined the ranks of ladies who visited women in the workhouse to read to them. Speaking to the women she learned that many of the elderly had been abandoned, had no visitors and were unable to leave the workhouse. She started to befriend them and take groups of women outside for tea; once outside they were more vocal about their complaints. They talked about their diet of stringy half-cooked meat, thin gruel and rotten potatoes; having one towel for two dozen women; only having coarse, ill-fitting clothes and heavy boots to wear; a lack of ventilation so rooms were stuffy and smelly; the rudeness of those in authority. Asked why they did not complain to the guardians, they told Charlotte that the guardians ignored complaints and the master put those who complained on a diet of bread and water, so it was better for them not to say anything as they were too old to cope with this. Charlotte began gathering evidence to confirm their stories and then wrote to the guardians, concluding

> I have had occasion several times lately to think that the present management of the workhouse is deficient, and that the aged inmates are given neither the comfort nor the respect that is the due of misfortune.

The guardians replied that her accusations were groundless – the food was excellent, the workhouse well managed. Charlotte took in a few of the most bullied women but could do nothing for the others. One who complained was transferred to another workhouse. Charlotte realised that change could not come from outside and in December 1894 stood for election as a guardian for Vauxhall. As her name and work were well known her election was a foregone conclusion. Her first board meeting in January 1895 marked the beginning of nine years working in Lambeth, and the start of her public career at the age of 50.

In 1895 Charlotte bought the corner shop in Everett Street, which backed on to her house. This became the headquarters of the Despard Club, her social enterprise where children and young people could come for basic health care, education and support. By knocking through the dividing walls she created an enormous room on the ground floor, and she lived in a flat above. Charlotte's house at 95 Wandsworth Road was within the boundaries of Lambeth, the biggest Poor Law union in London, with one of the worst reputations for ill treatment and corruption. Two workhouses were designed to hold more than 1,800 people, with another 600 in hospital and a further 4,000 receiving relief outside the workhouse. The annual cost was almost £200,000, at a time when the turnover of a large factory would be around £50,000 so it was a huge undertaking. Its affairs were controlled by thirty unpaid guardians who met for three hours a week. Rumours of corruption circulated – there was a story from an Anglican curate published in the local newspapers in 1892 that the guardians were ensuring jobs and contracts for their relatives. The curate was forced to retract the story but the rumours continued – that the relieving officers, in charge of outside relief, fiddled their accounts, that the workhouse master gave the inmates inadequate rations and sold the surplus food for his own profit, that the taskmaster had inmates making furniture for his own benefit. Charlotte heard these stories at the Despard Club but was more concerned about issues of inefficiency and ill treatment. For example, one of her children came to her for help when his father was sick and his mother could not work because she had a week-old baby so the family was in danger of starving and the relieving officer had refused to help. When Charlotte went to see him she was ordered out of his office. It was four weeks before he would give any relief and during this time she kept the family alive herself. She sent off an angry letter to the guardians complaining about his inaction and he was censured – but for fiddling his expenses, but not for inefficiency. More and more stories were brought to her attention and the attitude of the receiving officers towards the poor infuriated her more than the worst corruption, because the poor were demeaned and lost their self-respect.

The Lambeth board was no different to others in its amateur, casual approach to its duties.

George Lansbury, also a Poor Law guardian summarised the extent of cronyism and abuse in the system, writing:

'You scratch my back and I'll scratch yours' was the basis of policy where jobs and contracts were concerned ... the slum owner and agent could be depended upon to create the conditions which produce disease: the doctor would then get the job of attending the sick, the chemist would be needed to supply drugs, the parson to pray, and when, between them all, the victims died, the undertaker was on hand to bury them.

At their weekly meetings the Lambeth guardians approved reports without discussion and ratified decisions already made by the secretary. Charlotte did not fit in easily with such a group and wasted no time in trying to implement change. She was a minority of one in opposing the re-election of the long serving chairman, Mr Howlett, who owned slum property in Nine Elms. The male guardians were not pleased with her suggestion that the six female guardians should become the domestic committee, to supervise expenditure in the workhouse and infirmary. Her most important task, though, was to change the treatment of the workhouse inmates.

Charlotte focused on Samuel Ayles, master of the Renfrew Road workhouse which housed some 1,250 people. It briefly held Charlie Chaplin, with his mother and brother. She already knew that Ayles punished elderly inmates by placing them on a bread and water diet. He admitted this but said he always consulted the medical officer first, to ensure that their health could stand it. The guardians accepted this explanation until Charlotte persuaded them to find out what the practice was in other workhouses. They found that such punishment was rarely used against the elderly but they refused to take action against Ayles. Charlotte appealed over their heads to the Local Government Board, stating that they allowed the bread and water diet to be

inflicted on persons ... who are wholly unfit to bear it, and in fact would not bear it did not others supply them with part of their own food. I cannot, moreover, feel comfortable in leaving this matter in the hands of the master, Mr Ayles, a man not at all gifted as an administrator, and to my mind too young for the important and onerous post.

The Local Government Board asked the guardians to comment. Angered by Charlotte's actions they repudiated her allegations and informed Ayles that they were satisfied with his behaviour. The board replied to ask whether there had been compliance with the appropriate regulations, specifically requiring the medical officer's agreement in writing. The required certificates were eventually produced and although Charlotte had not succeeded in getting rid of Ayles, the bread and water punishment ceased.

But Charlotte had set her sights on Ayles and continued to hunt him. When she found a pile of stale, but edible, loaves that was about to be removed from the workhouse she said to the guardians 'I am compelled to believe that someone connected with the workhouse obtains payment for this valuable property.' Ayles denied any involvement, but Charlotte subsequently discovered that more bread was apparently being consumed in the workhouse than in the previous year, although there were fewer inmates. Waste was an important issue for the guardians and they began to find fault with Ayles, reprimanding him when Charlotte found irregularities in his distribution of tea and when she discovered that prayers were not said at breakfast in his workhouse. They were shocked when she produced evidence of his immoral behaviour – he had employed a girl from the workhouse as a servant. When she became pregnant, allegedly by the bath-house attendant, although there were other rumours, he allowed her to take furniture from the workhouse to furnish her flat. The guardians then used committees to investigate Ayles' every move and when he retired shortly afterwards many of them said that he had been a 'profligate ... unfit to be in charge of a workhouse.'

Other officials suffered for not being sufficiently respectful of the inmates, according to Charlotte. A former policeman was brought to the infirmary suffering an epileptic fit and an attendant remarked 'All policeman go up the pole when they get their pension.' Charlotte persuaded the Board to censure him, and she was responsible for the dismissal of a nurse who made a group of inmates carry out menial work.

These various incidents show Charlotte's moral code and her capacity for sticking with a course of action but these individuals were not her real targets – she was aiming at the guardians. They had control of the Poor Law in their area and Charlotte aimed to reform the system. As an example, Poplar had the toughest workhouse in London in 1870 but after a group of Independent Labour Party reformers under George Lansbury and Will Crooks won control of the guardians in 1895, it became one of the most liberal boards in the country.

For a long time the guardians had left the running of the workhouse to the paid employees and had very little idea what was going on. Charlotte persuaded them to think of individuals rather than cases and to keep a closer eye on the day-to-day running of the workhouse and schools. She doubled the length of time spent at committee meetings and trebled the number of committees. Charlotte proposed that four call-over committees should be set up to look at the circumstances of everyone under the guardians' care. There was little enthusiasm for this but the Ratepayers' Association had decided that the Lambeth workhouses housed more than their share of paupers from outside the parish and in the call-over committees they saw a way of unearthing the 'foreigners' and sending them back to their original parish, so with the backing of the ratepayers the committees were established.

The information collated by the committees gave Charlotte a basis for educating the guardians. Some ten families a week were returned to their parishes, pleasing the ratepayers, but also helping the guardians to understand that many of those who had been forced into the workhouse could be better helped in other, cheaper ways. Life also became better for those who remained in the workhouse, with small touches like personal combs and brushes, bedside lockers and packets of tea. Elderly ladies who were allowed out were given black dresses to wear instead of the humiliating workhouse rags. The women were put to sewing and dressmaking rather than picking oakum (plucking threads to use in making rope) and some of the men started painting, gardening, milling flour and baking. Various practices were unearthed under Charlotte's watchful eye, such as blind inmates being left unattended without any entertainment or anything to do, and how groups of inmates could be moved between workhouses at any time at the whim of the master, so no one knew how long they would stay with their friends. On Sundays preachers would descend on the workhouse and thunder out their sermons while the ladies of the Norwood Flower Mission would sing hymns all at the same time so the workhouse would become what Linklater described as a 'bedlam of religion'.

Public education at the time included responsibility only for teaching pupils in the classroom, but Charlotte saw a wider responsibility than this. Seeing the effects of rickets, consumption and chronic ill-health in the half-starved children, she was convinced that before education could begin, the children had to be properly fed and reasonably healthy; 'nourish the body and the brain will benefit' was her motto. Once she was elected a manager of the two Nine Elms elementary schools she lost no time in putting her ideas into effect. The board members had only been used to considering issues such as exam results and blocked lavatories, but the new member put forward her theory about nutrition and her idea that three unused rooms in one of the schools should be turned into a kitchen and dining rooms. The board said that money could not legally be spent on such a project. When Charlotte suggested that she would provide the saucepans, stoves, tables and benches herself, the board simply decided that it would neither aid nor obstruct her. Equipment was brought in and volunteers found and after 1899 Nine Elms had a school-meals service for the poorest children, seven years before the government first authorised education authorities to offer such a service. The School Board eventually set up a Committee for Underfed Children to raise funds and run the scheme officially and when unemployment soared in 1904 over a hundred children were being fed daily. When Charlotte also brought to the Committee's attention the number of children arriving at school without shoes, the board was better prepared to resist her proposal, saying it was a fact of life. Once again Charlotte was forced to act herself and, with the help of the Ragged School union, she set up a fund to buy boots. Two hundred pairs were distributed in the first year, either free or for a shilling each, depending on the family's circumstances, with money raised put aside for future emergencies.

In May 1900 Charlotte was interviewed by an investigator for the Booth survey. He met her at her home in Nine Elms, in the centre of 'this poor neighbourhood'. It was a rough area – so bad that Booth's investigators had to be accompanied by a policeman. He noted that:

> Mrs Despard is one in ten thousand, and hardly anyone that I have seen in the whole course of the Inquiry has left so strong an impression of a strong and gracious life. If I wanted to read a district with sympathy, I would be inclined to borrow her eyes, and if to influence it, I should be content with her heart. Catholic and socialist, the ideal is very strong with her.

Although she was working with some very tough and difficult boys, the investigator was struck by the mixture of discipline and freedom in the club

> The boys' club she has made her home, or perhaps one might better say, her home is their club. She does not find them unmanageable. They submit to her gentle force.

Clearly people could be dominated by her presence. Her once explosive anger had been tempered by age to a steely moral authority. Her hair had gone grey and her face was losing the soft contours of a younger age, above her blue eyes her heavy eyebrows were dark and expressive. She said she had known Nine Elms for twenty years – when living in the country she had 'beautiful gardens' and used to bring up flowers once a week but had been living there for three years, with two servants to look after her, and her absences were rare and short.

The interviewer asked if she saw herself as a socialist, and she said she did. He describes her as 'one of those who hope for a fundamental change in the social and industrial structure of society', with 'completer recognition of the demands of the common welfare'. 'But I always think', she said, 'that the change will have to come from the top. If it does not meet with a general welcome, it will bring more harm than good.' The investigator reported that she tries to use her own 'comfortable' income in the best way she can but brushes aside advice that its retention is inconsistent with her opinions. 'She makes good stewardship her duty, rather than the shifting of responsibility, which would be the result of alienation.' She was impatient of the indifferent rich and scornful of smart society.

The investigator found that the overcrowding was not as bad as it had been, due to stricter supervision, but housing conditions were still poor and on hot summer nights the streets were a common sleeping ground. In her house the servants had to take great care to keep it free from vermin and the smell from the gasworks, and even more the dust 'make[s] the place a very unpleasant one to live in.' Drink and gambling were great local vices but Charlotte denied the suggestion of professional vice and of serious crime. Petty larceny and the quarrelling and violence that are apt to follow excessive drinking made up the greater part, she thought, of the issues in the district and considered it was too 'black' on the Booth map.

'Loaning is a curse, and some of the very worst people in the district are women who make this their business, and who in order to increase their business tempt women, generally younger than themselves, first to drink, and then to borrow.' Charlotte's next-door neighbour was a 'horrible old person of this kind'. The Crown, a local pub, was known as the Ladies' House, the recognised drinking place for women, and hated by all but a few of the local men – Charlotte was hoping she could get hold of the pub for other uses.

'Her first cares are perhaps the boys and the children, but she has a large mothers' meeting and appears to move about a good deal among the people'. She had a clothing club connected with the mothers' meeting and gave subscribers some credit and 'the benefit of the farthing on the draper's prices.' So a woman buying 6 yards of cotton at 2 pence 3 farthings would only pay 1 shilling, and that in instalments. This had rarely been abused and was very popular. Charlotte said it was a form of disguised giving, that had led to better clothing of the children.

Naturally, I think, of a strong, although of an intensely sympathetic nature, more than once while we were talking, her voice broke and her eyes seemed to fill with tears, and this happened when she spoke of the children. She loves them, and finds them 'adorable' in Nine Elms, using that much-abused word in no conventional sense.

The problem of how to deal with the boys growing up was obviously an issue for her. A particular difficulty was trying to integrate the two clubs because, the report says 'she finds the difference in class too great. Her rough boys may go there for gymnasium practice … but that is all.' The boys from Nine Elms were tough, but the youths at the Wandsworth Club refused to have anything to do with them. Wandsworth had

about 50 members, mostly van-boys, from just over school age to about 18. The problem of drafting off the elder members is beginning to loom ahead of her, and her hope that she might be able to move them on to the Despard Club is seen to be a mistake. The difference in class is too great, and at first even the use of the room behind the Despard Club, which she controls herself, was resented. Now, however, the feeling has changed for the better, and some of the Despard members even help her, when the lads from Nine Elms come over to the big room in Lambeth for their gymnasium nights but this is quite a different thing to welcoming them as members.

There was no question that the work Charlotte was doing was of immense value.

The Nine Elms Club seems to be open every evening and offers the usual pursuits – billiards and other games – but no cards because of the local weakness and the various ways in which the subtle virus of 'play' is spread. There are classes – carving, iron-work – too and on Sundays Mrs Despard's own conference, which is in the nature of a bible class but 'religion has to be run lightly'.

Charlotte's own skills as a storyteller – in particular her use of allegory – kept her audience's attention rapt and attendance was high. The boys paid a penny a week subscription and could buy refreshments and smoke. Ever the pragmatist, Charlotte recognised that if the boys could not enjoy their favourite pastimes they would not frequent the club. She was assisted by her servants and engaged several teachers, but otherwise ran the club single-handedly. She made it known, however, that she 'would gladly welcome the help of men, especially with cricket, football and boxing.' Continuing his review of the club, the interviewer recorded,

> The boys are an uncollared class 'I don't think that we shall ever wear collars in Nine Elms' but seem to be a good-hearted set of fellows, at least as far as Mrs Despard is concerned, and she never has any trouble unless, as sometimes happens, they are not quite sober. Then they can be saucy and quarrel but even then I think that she is their mistress, although a fragile woman. She recalled, with amusement, an occasion, when a big fellow who could have brushed her cruelly on one side, quarrelled, and she came in to quiet him. She took him by the arm, sharply, and all that the muscular young rascal did for himself, was to tell her she 'hurt' him! 'You hurt me' he cried, and she laughed when she thought of it.

This young man seems to have been well-grown, but she 'laments the stunted growth of most of them', which she attributed to the early age at which they start work, the long hours they work as van boys, the smoking etc. 'The rising generation of Nine Elms will be very poor in physique, I am afraid', she said. The neglect that children suffer when they leave school goes to her heart. Up to 13½, children are fairly certain to be under discipline and good influences at school, Sunday school 'or what-not' but after that age they are their own masters. They begin to earn money and the complete lack of control has the worst results, for both boys and girls. Mrs Despard 'explained bitterly' how easy it is for young lads to be served in a public house and how she had written to a Mr Thorne after she detected this in a pub in Nine Elms.

> In a hundred ways she gave me proof, if proof more than the fact of living there be needed, of her interest and care for Nine Elms, and it would be a benison for the people there if they could be made to realise how great her affection is for them and for their good. 'I am devoted to it' she said, in reply to a question that I put, because I wanted to know what she would say, and not because I had any doubt as to what the tenour of her reply would be. 'I can't think that I could live anywhere else.'

Little was said about her work as a guardian. She was doubtful as to whether she would stand again for the guardians, partly because the lease of the Despard Club, by which she qualified as living in Lambeth, was nearly up, and she was uncertain as to what would be done; and partly because there had been some wish that she would go on the School Board. As far as her public work was concerned, therefore, her plans were uncertain. Charlotte was clearly very open about, and critical of, people she worked with. She had 'no patience' for the Charity Organisation Society, thinking their tone 'hard, defective and unsympathetic'.

> Mrs Despard says that she can trace a distinct softening since she has been on the Board and, although at first they appear to have been somewhat antipathetic souls, they are now friends, and work well together. Mrs Despard condemned the use of paid agents at the local committees, especially in enquiry work and in dealing with applicants. Dr Whereat was mentioned with cordial liking, but the small staff at his mission was regretted, and she feared that Dr W was overtaxing his strength. She thought that Cardinal Vaughan had made a great mistake in running the big Westminster Cathedral scheme, as he has done, instead of trying to strengthen the hands of the poorer Missions. The under-manning of many of these was, she thought, a serious source of weakness to the Church.

The glowing and lengthy reports of Charlotte's work in the Booth survey made her name familiar to thousands of readers.

After women were brought into the workhouse to teach the blind to knit, and committees were formed to change various practices, Charlotte turned her eye to the many young people who each year were apprenticed, boarded out or sent to charitable institutions by the guardians and was appointed to the Council of the Association for Befriending Boys in 1901. The guardians knew little about the conditions in which young people lived, even though they were responsible for them, so more committees were formed and Charlotte produced reports on apprentices and boarded-out children with new ideas for employment of the jobless. Labour colonies and emigration were seen as effective solutions. The

Poplar guardians had bought land in Essex and were building a farm there but they had the backing of a millionaire and the Lambeth guardians were unable to follow their example through lack of money. Emigration seemed a good idea, particularly for orphan boys, so several hundred boys were sent to Canada through Dr Barnardo's Homes, who would place them with farmers for agricultural training. Charlotte decided that the guardians' responsibility did not end with placing them with Dr Barnardo's and in 1902 she set off on a six-week trip to see for herself. She travelled with members of the Catholic Emigration Society, but her visit was also political – like other activists she was concerned that the boys were just being used as cheap labour. Her trip took her by train, stagecoach and horse buggy from Quebec to Calgary, visiting Barnardo's in Quebec, Ottawa and Manitoba and farms along the way. The Catholic society had a clear system of inspection. Its children were always placed within easy reach of a church, a place of refuge, and received agricultural training. In contrast the Barnardo's agency in Toronto was found to be 'a very poor place'. Some of the boys had been moved several times, some were living very far away from school, one had been lost altogether. In the west there was no support network and households were often a hundred miles apart. Charlotte heard a number of complaints about the physical and moral condition of the children and their habits which 'seemed rather strange to me when I remembered the care that had been taken in selecting these children, and the healthy appearance they had presented when they bade us farewell.' This was in contrast with the earlier visit by Dr Barnardo's in 1900, meeting only with 'well grown, stalwart, muscular fellows, bronzed and bearded and altogether so changed that I usually quite failed to recognise in them the puny, half-starved, homeless waifs that had come under my care in England, twelve, fifteen or twenty years before.'

Charlotte was very disturbed by what she saw:

When I heard of the large parties continually going out, of the thousands of applications sent in by the farmers, and of the system of supplying the demand, it struck me that, in the nature of things, it was impossible for adequate inquiry to be made as to the fitness of the famers to train the children sent to them; and if they are not trained – rendered capable of doing good work in the future – we are simply cheapening labour and pouring a helot class into Canada.

(A helot being a member of a class of serfs in ancient Sparta, somewhere between slave and citizen in status.)

Another committee was formed to act on this report and in place of Dr Barnardo's the Church of England Central Society for Providing Homes for Waifs and Strays agreed to provide the services the guardians wanted for the Lambeth boys. Before Charlotte left for Canada, another guardian said that he would propose that the guardians call for statements reflecting on them and made by Mrs Despard at a meeting on 9 June to be either proved or withdrawn. Charlotte was not backing down. The hopelessness of everything associated with the Poor Law,

> and the ocean of misery through which I was compelled to wade made me search desperately for some remedy. Party politics held out no hope. I saw the terrible problem of the people's necessities played with. I heard promises made to them which I knew would not be fulfilled ... At last, sick of all these, I determined to study for myself the great problems of society. My study landed me in uncompromising socialism.

Charlotte had worked hard to change things for the poor in Lambeth – a colleague remarked that she had shown 'the supreme face of courage – never to falter when faced with overwhelming opposition.' Working as a Poor Law guardian had shown Charlotte that through her actions she could bring about change, but also although she had changed the way things were done in Lambeth she could not change the system. Seventy-two of every hundred paupers were women and children and to help them the patriarchal system of society had to change. Charlotte was not the only woman to be a Poor Law guardian who would later campaign for suffragism – others included Emmeline and Sylvia Pankhurst. Teresa Billington-Greigg later said of Charlotte:

> She was no trifler with service, no reformer of the platform only, no part time crusader, no rich woman scattering crumbs of benevolence. Her work for bettering the world became her life.

The 1894 decision to abolish the property qualification allowed women to stand for election as Poor Law guardians and although the number of women elected was nowhere near the number of men, it was nevertheless symbolic of women beginning to enter public life. There is little evidence of the arrival of women making a real difference, perhaps because national policy or local practice may have left little scope for radical change. King suggests that some historians have seen the scope of female guardians limited by gender conflict and Digby suggests that women involved in public welfare were caught in the 'borderland between public and private roles' and faced hostility when their language and actions took them too far out of the borderland. Others have supported this view. Hollis for example says:

> It took considerable courage to endure the snubs, smuttiness and cold shoulder treatment women met on many boards ... For the most part, women won grudging acceptance – it was seldom more than that – which they achieved by tact, persistence, silence and hard work.

This certainly seems to have been Charlotte's experience, as she battled against male committees. 'But for the Poor Law I might have remained an omnivorous reader with a literary interest in great ideas.' Later she said 'the Poor Law was my apprenticeship'.

Chapter 3

Causes

Working for a cause such as the poor, or votes for women would be enough activity and commitment for many people, but not for Charlotte. Throughout her lengthy widowhood she was attached to numerous causes, social and political, devoting her time and her funds to improve the lot of anyone who needed help. As well as suffragism she espoused pacifism, socialism, communism, Catholicism, vegetarianism, anti-vivisection, theosophy, tax resistance, anti-colonialism, and home rule for India and Ireland. She was also involved with the Women's Peace Crusade to oppose war and the Women's Prisoners' Defence League, and supported the National Canine Defence League. To Gifford Lewis, Charlotte exemplified 'a familiar clustering in the suffragist world of feminism, pacifism, vegetarianism and a working-class base', noting that in 1916 and 1917 she was 'on the councils of: the Women's Freedom League, the Women's International League, the No-Conscription Fellowship, the National Campaign for Civil Liberties, the Theosophical Society, the London Vegetarian Society, the Battersea Labour Party, the Women's Labour League, the Home Rule for India Committee and the Women's Peace Crusade.' According to Oakley she also became involved with 'trickier ideas' such as the transmigration of souls, which enabled her to seek political advice from the dead Italian politician and supporter of equal rights for women, Giuseppe Mazzini. The plot of her novel *The Rajah's Heir* is based on the Buddhist theory of the transmigration of souls. Charlotte wrote:

> Most, if not all, had given full credence to the assurance of their late rajah that, in the person of the successor he had chosen, he would himself return to them. To us of the West such a belief may appear childish. But we must remember the difference between our standpoint and that of the Asiatic. The doctrine of the transmigration

of souls from body to body, which to us seems unreal and fantastic, has, from the earliest ages, formed a part of the Eastern creeds. And, this granted, there could not surely be anything extraordinarily unlikely in one of high spiritual rank being permitted, if not to choose, at least to foresee, his next incarnation. In any case this was their belief ... (p.42)

Charlotte could not resist an invitation to join a committee, although as Helena Swanwick, president of the Women's International League remarked, 'she was no good at all on a committee where she found it impossible to bring her mind to bear on a resolution.' In 1916 and 1917 her various causes required Charlotte to attend between twenty and thirty public meetings a month, as well as her work at Nine Elms. Charlotte was valued because of the attention she gave; 'She is pre-eminently great,' Nina Boyle said, 'morally and physically, because she does not care what results come out of the things which she holds as convictions.' If she was asked to join a peace meeting she would be there, even if it meant a long and difficult journey. A journalist at a meeting in 1917 said 'She seemed to belong to an age of samplers, embroidery and wax fruit', but even then, when she was frail and elderly, she was not afraid of a crowd. Emmeline Pankhurst reported that when in 1932 Charlotte was speaking at a peace rally attended by around 50,000 people, men in the crowd shouted 'We don't want the German terms, we want our terms.' Charlotte replied 'You will have neither the German terms nor your own terms. You will have God's terms.' There was silence before someone shouted 'You'd better get out of this before you get hurt.' 'I am not afraid of Englishmen. None of you will hurt me,' she cried, and none of them did.

Charlotte became a vegetarian after Max died in 1890, his death giving her the freedom to follow her choice of diet. 'It was only after my husband's death,' she said 'that I was able to give full expression to my ideals.' Her vigorous old age was regarded as a good advertisement for vegetarianism. After Charlotte was selected as the Labour Party candidate for Battersea North in November 1918 the *Evening Standard* (27 November) commented: 'Regarding the election. "If fiery eloquence is an asset I will back the President of the Women's Freedom League against all comers. Her vigour and enthusiasm are the best and most convincing advertisement for vegetarianism I've ever struck.'"

Charlotte was initially drawn to vegetarianism through Shelley's work, becoming more committed in 1909 after contact with Gandhi, who joined the Vegetarian Society while he was a student in the UK. She became Vice President of the Vegetarian Society in London and then president in 1918. At that time the Vegetarian Society was based in both London and Manchester and although she lived in London she was also involved in the Manchester branch.

Vegetarianism came to prominence in the nineteenth century, when the reforming spirit, health reform, the temperance movement and the rise of philanthropy led to what would eventually become the Vegetarian Society. The first known use of the word 'vegetarian' was in an issue of *The Healthian* in 1842. Abstaining from meat appealed to educated people, to those who questioned the majority view on social and religious issues. The idea of eating meat as a brutalising force was strong and when social reform was gathering pace the question of whether abstaining from meat might bring order attracted attention. The Industrial Revolution had brought with it a number of social problems and there were some who saw a vegetable diet (vegetable then meant all kinds of plant food, including fruit, grains and beans) as a solution.

According to Twigg, enrolment figures for the Vegetarian Society during the 1880s show a membership of roughly four men to every woman, even though vegetarianism was thought of as 'feminine'. These figures may reflect the reluctance of women to join societies at a time when women were not generally active in public life, but some vegetarians bemoaned the lack of women, seeing female involvement as a way to advance vegetarianism, women usually being responsible for the household diet. By contrast there were a small number of titled women, but no titled men listed. Charlotte said:

Vegetarianism is pre-eminently a women's question. It is horrible to think that women should have to handle and cook dead flesh. The loathsome operations in the kitchen, the disgusting sights at butchers' shops, the brutalities of the slaughter-house, and the transit of cattle, are simply dreadful. If people themselves had to kill the animals there would be no meat-eaters.

Teresa Billington-Greig recalled festive meals and celebrations where socialists, suffragettes and family members munched on roast meat while Charlotte ate dry biscuits. Her lifestyle was frugal, at a time when vegetarian meant a traditional meal minus meat. Her vegetarianism was inspired by her commitment to 'slaying of the self' and the view that the slaughter and consumption of animals was a symptom of a corrupt and unjust society, although her famous sandals showed she was happy to wear leather. In her work with the poor she campaigned for them to be fed nutritious vegetable soup rather than the more usual bread or gruel. Charlotte recommended a vegetarian diet for general wellbeing and once for military efficiency – noting that the British Army during the First World War was marked by trails of empty beef cans, she suggested the beef contributed to constipation and skin troubles and to the deficiencies in vitamins and minerals that affected soldiers. All this, she said, could be remedied by a good vegetable soup 'such as any French housewife makes'.

One argument for vegetarianism was a practical one. Addressing the Vegetarian Society in 1907 Margaret Cousins gave a reason for women to switch to a simple grain/fruit/nut diet: the amount of time they would save by not having to spend hours in the kitchen preparing (or overseeing the preparation of) meat meals. According to Leah Leneman, Mrs Cousins was equally active in the Irish Women's Franchise League and the Irish Vegetarian Society, speaking and writing on both subjects and demonstrating the close connection she saw between them. The Irish Vegetarian Society was the source of hilarity with a president named Mr Henry Ham and vice presidents Mrs Maud Joynt and Mrs Jonathon Hogg. Women's emancipation, Margaret said, would come with freedom from the necessity of preparing complex cooked meals, but this did not mean 'the reign of idleness or the opportunity for all kinds of selfish pleasures.' She wanted to 'help women to free their hands and their minds in every possible way, for in the present absurd housekeeping arrangements a woman truly has 'no time to think ... and if she should get an hour of rest and quiet, she is physically so used up that she has no desire to worry her mind with intellectual and social problems.' By changing to a vegetarian diet women would have time

> to think over problems in life which their experience enables them
> to cope with better than men, and as a result there would be a more

spontaneous and all-pervading demand from all women for an equal opportunity with men for service in the state. Thus the Suffrage movements are more closely connected with the Food Reform movement than the enthusiasts of either are usually aware of.

As Leneman points out, this was a problematic argument, since labour-saving devices could have achieved that end as easily. Margaret Cousins also emphasised the effects on the 'fine and sensitive nature of a woman', of the preparation of flesh foods, taking this beyond the question of unpleasantness. A woman, she wrote,

> ... instinctively shrinks at first from having to touch raw meat, from having to disgorge the entrails of fowl, game and fish ... but through repetition of these unpleasant so-called duties, and through constant visits to the butcher's shop, a veritable veil of blood envelops us by degrees, which obscures the intuitions of our better selves from us, and at length causes us to be content with that against which we at first rightly rebelled.

In November 1913 Gretta Cousins, who would become prominent in the Irish suffrage struggle, was living in Liverpool on the first stage of a visit to India. She had what she described as the 'spiritual enrichment' of a visit from Charlotte, reported in the *Liverpool Express*:

> In recognition of her twenty years' labour for food reform, a luncheon was given today to Mrs Despard by the Liverpool Vegetarian Society ... Their guest, said Mrs Cousins, Mus.Bac. the president, was an arch-reformer and pioneer of the cause of freedom. Many of them looked upon her as being the real Queen Mother of Freedom, from the soles of her feet, where she wore sandals, to the top of her head, where she did not wear a hat (laughter and applause). She had as great a love for the freedom of the animal as for men and women, and as the freest woman she (the speaker) had ever met (applause). Mrs Despard expressed the opinion that vegetarianism was really at the base of a great many things. Food seemed only a humble thing, but if they realised what did and might go into them through the

body, then perhaps they would think the question of food was one of the greatest importance.

In 1923 Charlotte wrote a letter of condolence to Mrs Childers, whose husband had been executed in Ireland for having a gun. Planning to pay her a visit she said that she did not eat meat but 'anything else will suit me well'.

Vegetarianism attracted a number of feminists and suffragettes, including Annie Besant, Marion Wallace Dunlop, Miss Haig, Leonora Cohen and Lady Constance Lytton, partly through the influence of theosophy, which had explicit vegetarian links. Annie Besant promoted vegetarianism, writing *Vegetarianism in the Light of Theosophy* in 1913. Charlotte summarised the connection in her book *Theosophy and the Women's Movement* (1913 p.44) suggesting that theosophy and the women's movement both related to

> the other great movements of the world ... The awakened instinct which feels the call of the sub-human, which says: – 'I am the voice of the voiceless. Through me the dumb shall speak,' is a modern phenomenon that cannot be denied. It works itself out as food reform on the one hand, and on the other, in strong protest against the cruel methods of experimental research.

Both things, said Charlotte, were 'in close unison with the demands being made by women.'

Leneman cites evidence for the pervasiveness of vegetarianism within the Women's Social and Political Union (WSPU) from the diaries of the Blathwayt family, who lived in Somerset, and regularly entertained WSPU members. Mrs Blathwayt recorded on 30 April 1910 that Marion Wallace Dunlop (the first suffragette to adopt the hunger strike) and Florence Haig (who was several times imprisoned) 'like so many of them, never eat meat and not much animal food at all'. On 27 February 1911 she recorded that Mr Rogers (who worked for the Men's League for Women's Suffrage), and his wife came to lunch. Mrs Rogers was 'like so many suffrage people and did not eat the chicken, but she had vegetables, bread sauce, cream etc.' On 17 March Colonel Blathwayt recorded that Mrs Jane Brailsford (wife of H.N. Brailsford, an important Liberal journalist) 'like so many Suffragettes is a vegetarian, but she took Burgundy.' The Tollemaches (mother and two daughters) were suspected of burning down an empty house in Bath, and on 8 January 1914 Mary Blathwayt wrote in her diary: 'Tollemaches have advertised for their dog Bladud, who is in the habit of running away, but this time has stayed. I expect he would rather not live with vegetarians.'

A number of suffragettes became vegetarian when they were imprisoned. According to the Vegetarian Society's *Journal* of April 1907:

> It is interesting to see how vegetarianism becomes related to progressive movements. Quite a number of the leaders in the Women's Suffragist movement are vegetarians. On the whole they have been kindly treated by the prison officials, but they assert that the ordinary mixed prison food that is supplied is not of the most palatable kind, so that suffragists who now go to prison are advised to be vegetarian, as the food supplied to vegetarians is nicer in every way.

'It is a strange fact,' wrote Maud Joachim (*My Life in Holloway Gaol*, 1908) 'that the ranks of the militant suffragettes are mostly recruited from the mild vegetarians, and the authorities have allowed us a special vegetarian diet.' Vegetarian suffragettes included Eva Gore Booth, leader of the North of England Society for Women's Suffrage, who was a vegetarian from about 1906, and Leonora Cohen, a militant who smashed a jewel case in the Tower of London and went on hunger strike, and had been a vegetarian since the age of 5.

WSPU militant Margaret C. Clayton, in Holloway Prison during 1907–8 wrote:

> Dinner is supplied in two tins. In the deeper one lurk two potatoes in their skins; in the shallower, which fits into the top of the other, are an egg, and some cauliflower or other vegetable. Many of us are always vegetarians, and acting on expert advice, others are so pro tem., for the meat supplied is so generally disliked.

Mrs Blathwayt noted in March 1911 that Charlotte Marsh (a WSPU organiser who was imprisoned and forcibly fed many times) 'has begun the late custom of not taking meat or chicken. The prison diet was not always better than eating meat.' Victoria Lidiard, who spent two months in Holloway in March 1912, noted the prison authorities' total ignorance of a vegetarian diet, having been given the 'absurd' quantity of 'almost half a pound of butter beans.'

A number of women, such as Lady Constance Lytton, were vegetarians long before they became suffragettes. There was a belief – known as 'food reform' – that meat was responsible for many illnesses, and these conditions could be alleviated or cured by switching to a vegetarian diet. Constance suffered from what she called 'constitutional' rheumatism from a young age, and as a result of her aunt's investigations of 'theories of diet', she stopped eating meat and her condition improved. But she 'realised, too, that all these years I had caused untold suffering that I might be fed, and determined that in future the unnatural death of an animal should not be necessary to make up my bill of fare.'

Vegetarianism was an important part of the values of the WFL and as President Charlotte was a role model for members. In 1910 the WFL journal *The Vote* included a picture of Mrs Agnes Leonard, honorary secretary of the Sheffield branch, cooking a vegetarian dinner, with the comment that she was 'an expert vegetarian cook'. In January 1911, the Dundee branch heard a lecture on 'The Ethics of Food Reform' by 'Mr Dan Hamilton, a well-known vegetarian', and in 1912 the Edinburgh branch was given 'an exceedingly interesting demonstration of Vegetarian Cookery' by Miss MacDonald (Glasgow), assisted by members of the Edinburgh Vegetarian Society (reported in *The Vote*). In 1923 Dr Josiah Oldfield of the Fruitarian Society spoke to the Ashford branch of the WFL about the benefits of a diet consisting largely of fruit and vegetables, commenting that, 'It always gave him great pleasure to speak for the WFL, as he felt that when women bravely discarded high corsets and long skirts, they were opening their minds to a freer life of health and educational interests.' (*The Vote* 13 April 1923, p.119)

An unnamed speaker at a suffragette meeting in 1912 (possibly Marion Wallace Dunlop, suggests Leneman) said there are so many, whose hearts go out to the brave pioneers and leaders of our movement, whose souls are with them in their work, but whose duty lies essentially within the four walls of their home; and however much they may long to give a hand to those outside, feel that they have only very limited means of doing so.

But within the vegetarian movement a woman's ability 'to help the Suffrage Cause is practically unlimited. Vegetarianism aims so directly, as we women aim, at the abolition of the unregenerate doctrine of physical force.' In addition 'the Social evils which women are rebelling against, and hope ultimately to remedy through the power of the franchise would, in that community which is the ideal of the true vegetarian, cease to exist.'

Eating out was also important. The WFL opened vegetarian restaurants across the country during the First World War and the one in Holborn was praised in the popular press as 'a charming place' which was 'entirely inviting' (*The Star*). The International Women's Franchise Club held a dinner at the Criterion Restaurant, Piccadilly, on 26 October 1911. The president of the club was the Earl of Lytton. Membership cost a guinea a year with an additional guinea entrance fee for members who lived in London, so only well-off women could join. Diners were offered a choice of an ordinary or vegetarian menu, and 25 (of approximately 130) chose the vegetarian menu.

As the Vegetarian Society's *Journal* of April 1907 reported, suffragists released from Holloway would invariably breakfast at the Eustace Miles Restaurant, which was established alongside the suffragette movement, opening in 1906, just as the WSPU moved to London. It was located at 40–42 Chandos Place, at the western end of Covent Garden and Ellen Terry's daughter Edith Craig, who lived nearby in Bedford Street, used to sell the WSPU paper *Votes for Women* from a pitch outside. It was over a meal at the Eustace Miles in 1906 that Teresa Billington, with her background as labour organiser, persuaded Charlotte to join the WSPU. Eustace Miles, a Cambridge-educated health guru, opened the restaurant with his wife, Hallie, as a 'food reform' restaurant and some of the shareholders had suffragette connections. The Eustace Miles had a room to let for events, and audiences to lectures could enjoy breathing in 'ozonized air'. In January 1910 it was the venue for the inaugural meeting of the Men's Political Union for Women's Enfranchisement and in October 1914 it was the location for committee meetings of the United Suffragists.

Another venue much frequented by suffragettes was the Teacup Inn, opened in January 1910 in Bank Buildings, Portugal Street, just off Kingsway, now part of the London School of Economics. Although not a vegetarian café, it made sure its vegetarian meals were mentioned in its advertisements in *Votes for Women*. 'Dainty luncheons and Afternoon teas at moderate charges. Home cookery. Vegetarian dishes and sandwiches. Entirely staffed and managed by women.' The advertisements mentioned its location near the WSPU in Clement's Inn and in 1912 it moved to Lincoln's Inn House in Kingsway, making it the nearest café. The Teacup Inn advertised at least once in the Pankhurst paper, *The Suffragette* in June 1914.

The Gardenia Restaurant, at 6 Catherine Street, Covent Garden, was located in the centre of suffragette activity, with the WFL headquarters just south of The Strand in Robert Street, and those of the WSPU to the east of Aldwych in Clement's Inn. The restaurant hired out rooms to societies which coincided with their interests, such as a Vegetarian Club and the suffragettes. In *My Own Story* Emmeline Pankhurst refers to many WSPU breakfasts and teas held at the Gardenia and it was a favourite of the WFL, listed in *The Vote Directory*, the WFL newspaper's list of recommended retailers. The 6 May 1911 issue reports on a suffragist's day – the author has tea at the Gardenia: 'a fragrant cup of tea and some cress sandwiches made with Hovis bread.' In 1912 the WFL rented a room in the Gardenia in which to hold weekly discussions on subjects such as 'Jane Eyre and its relation to the Women's Movement', and on 17 February 1912 three of the Gardenia's rooms were hired by the WFL for a fundraising supper, with dancing and performances by the Actresses' Franchise League. The Gardenia management seems to have been very supportive of the suffragette cause; on 2 April 1911 – census night – they allowed the restaurant to be used by suffragettes trying to evade the enumerator. A census schedule for 6 Catherine Street shows the manager, Thomas Smith, in his flat with his wife and children and restaurant staff but a separate schedule, completed by the Census Office with information supplied by the police, shows that the restaurant was packed with 200 women and 30 men. These people had spent the evening at the Aldwych Skating Rink and moved to the Gardenia at around 3.30 am for breakfast.

In 1912 there was evidence that the Gardenia was being used as an ammunition arming station for the WSPU. Stones – on one of which was written 'Votes for Women' – were found in an upstairs room rented by the WSPU and police testified to seeing the suffragettes throwing stones to break shop windows on more than one occasion. The restaurant closed in March 1913.

The WFL held a pescatarian dinner to celebrate when some women were enfranchised in 1918. The menu included a shredded vegetable soup (*consomme julienne*), turbot with new potatoes and lentil cutlets with tomato sauce. 'With unflagging zeal we press on towards greater freedom,' the menu read.

Many suffragettes took a more ethically focused stance and were against the wearing of fur and feathers. In 1913 there was debate as to whether the NUWSS journal *Common Cause* should carry some kind of fashion column. Ada Nield Chew argued in favour, her argument being that guidance was much needed on the best and most practical clothing for campaigning, with advice particularly appreciated on 'how to look and feel warm in winter without swathing oneself in dead animals' skins.' The decoration of ladies' hats was a real concern for some. In February 1909, with regard to the millinery stall at the planned Women's Exhibition, a plea was made in the WSPU journal that women would 'take the opportunity of dissociating themselves from "Murderous Millinery,"' and that the hats and bonnets with 'ospreys and the stuffed bodies of birds' would be "conspicuous by their absence"'. Others wrote in to support this stance and to 'try to get a stop put to the cruel, inhuman and revolting fashion of using beautiful birds for the purpose of personal adornment.'

Many vegetarian suffragettes were concerned about cruelty to animals, some seeing a relationship between the treatment of animals and women. One day Constance Lytton saw sheep on their way to be slaughtered; one had escaped and was being mistreated by its handlers. The crowd laughed when the sheep was caught and beaten. In *Prison and prisoners* Constance says the sheep was old and misshapen but she could see how it should have been on the mountain side with 'all its forces rightly developed, vigorous and independent.' She said she had always been unhappy about cruelty to animals

> But on seeing this sheep it seemed to reveal to me for the first time the position of women throughout the world. I realised how often women are held in contempt as beings outside the pale of human dignity, excluded or confined, laughed at and insulted because of conditions in themselves for which they are not responsible, but which are due to fundamental injustices with regard to them, and to the mistakes of a civilisation in the shaping of which they have had no free share. I was ashamed to remember that although my sympathy had been spontaneous with regard to the wrongs of animals, of children, of men and women who belonged to down-trodden races or classes of society, yet that hitherto I had been blind to the sufferings peculiar to women of every class, every race, every nationality.

Anti-vivisection was a very strong movement in late Victorian Britain but the leading Victorian feminist anti-vivisection campaigner, Frances Power Cobbe, was not a vegetarian, and it seems that many women did not contemplate other forms of cruelty to animals. George Bernard Shaw described attending an anti-vivisection rally in London where 'the ladies among us wore hats and cloaks and head-dresses obtained by wholesale massacres, ruthless trappings, callous extermination of our fellow creatures' but the vegetarian suffragists were certainly anti-vivisectionists. One of the most eloquent speakers on the link between vegetarianism and feminism was Louise Lind-af-Hageby. She has become known for the 'Brown Dog Affair', in which Charlotte was involved.

Emilie Augusta Louise 'Lizzy' Lind af Hageby was a Swedish-British feminist and animal rights activist who became a prominent anti-vivisection activist in England in the early twentieth century, at a time when vivisection was very controversial. Her education at Cheltenham Ladies College and private income enabled her to travel the world as a political activist, first opposing child labour and prostitution, later animal rights and supporting women's emancipation. University College London was the main institution for vivisection in the UK. In February 1903 a live brown dog was laid on a table in a teaching room in front of students and was operated on to find out how certain procedures would affect it. This was legal at the time. Lind and Leisa Schartau had enrolled at the London School of Medicine for Women to gain the knowledge that would help them better understand vivisection and campaign against it. They witnessed various vivisections and presented a diary of their observations to Stephen Coleridge, secretary of the National Anti-Vivisection Society. From what the women had written, Coleridge suggested that in the case of the brown dog the rules and procedures put in place to protect animals had not been followed; the 1876 Cruelty to Animals Act forbade the use of an animal in more than one experiment. A case against a surgeon involving vivisection could only be brought with the approval of the Home Secretary, and the then Home Secretary was not supportive of anti-vivisection so Coleridge decided to speak out publicly against the procedure and the doctor, William Bayliss. Bayliss filed a lawsuit against Coleridge for libel (Old Bailey, November 1903) and after days of testimony Bayliss won. Coleridge was ordered to pay his damages and fees, helped by a London newspaper that launched a fund to raise the money.

The case was lost but the work of the anti-vivisection campaign received a lot of support. A statue of the dog was erected in Battersea in 1906; speakers at the event included Charlotte and George Bernard Shaw. A series of riots began over the issue and the inscription, organised by medical and veterinary students read:

> In memory of the Brown Terrier Dog Done to Death in the Laboratories of University College in February 1903 after having endured vivisections extending over more than two months and having been handed over from one Vivisector to another till death come to his Release.
>
> Also in memory of the 232 dogs vivisected in the same place during the year 1902–3.
>
> Men and women of England, how long shall these things be?

The statue caused much controversy and had to have a police guard. Medical professionals agreed that animal experimentation, though unpleasant, was necessary for medical research. They were angry that the plaque on the statue seemed to blame the entire medical profession for the cruelty to the brown dog and many others killed at UCL. Resentment grew and the first attempt by medical students to destroy the statue was in late November 1907. Riots on 10 December were the result of five days of increasing animosity between anti-vivisection campaigners and angry students. The statue was discussed by parliament and eventually it was decided by the local council that it would be removed. During the night of 10 March 1910 – so as not to cause suspicion – the statue was removed and melted down. In 1985 a new memorial to the dog was erected in Battersea Park, now standing for the issue of animal testing rather than vivisection.

Anti-vivisection has always been a contentious issue, but there are questions over whether it was enough to get medical students – mainly well-educated upper-class males – brawling in the streets and attacking police. One suggestion is that sexual politics and links with suffragettes were the cause. The anti-vivisection lobby overlapped with those advocating women's suffrage, though not all anti-vivisectionists were suffragists or vice versa. Medical students appealed to anti-suffrage views to gain support for their cause. At a public meeting on 5 December 1907, Millicent Fawcett was the speaker and the meeting was stormed by medical students carrying effigies of brown dogs on sticks.

Lind became a British citizen and was active in several women's organisations including the WFL. She argued the kinship she felt between humans and non-humans had implications for the education and enfranchisement of women and support for animals and women was connected to 'a general undercurrent of rising humanity'. Neither women nor animals were regarded as persons during her lifetime – she represented herself in court as women could not be admitted as lawyers in the UK because they were not regarded as 'persons' within the 1843 Solicitors Act. She regarded feminism and animal rights (particularly as regards vegetarianism) as strongly linked, seeing the advance of women as essential to civilisation and the tension between women and male scientists as a battle between feminism and machismo. In 1907 Charlotte was involved in Lind's Animal Defence Society and arranged rallies. Speakers at the meeting in February 1910 included Charlotte, Lind, and defeated socialist councillor John Archer, who would later become mayor of Battersea.

The monument to the dog itself, as opposed to what it represented, became invested with much power. Lind said its physical presence terrified the opposition – vivisectors hated it, she said, because through the story of one dog people were learning what happened to thousands of dogs and other animals – the statue of the dog had taken on the cause of the dog. According to Charlotte:

> It is 'lest we forget' that these memorials are put up. We see, here, the symbol and the evidence of what they are, and then we feel that this is a memorial to a martyr, a martyr to that which is falsely called science … when we see memorials to martyrs in a higher state of being we say 'there shall be martyrs no more'. We must not let these things happen again and we must make up our minds that each one of us in our own way will do what we can to stop it.

Lind broke a record in 1913 for the number of words uttered during a trial when she delivered 210,000 words and asked 20,000 questions during a libel suit against the *Pall Mall Gazette*, which had criticised her campaigns. The *Nation* called her testimony 'the most brilliant piece of advocacy that the Bar has known since the day of Russell [Lord Chief Justice of England], though it was entirely conducted by a woman. Women, it appears, may sway courts and judges, but they may not even elect to the High court of Parliament.'

Lind was a strict vegetarian and became a board member of the London Vegetarian Society. When the trial ended a vegetarian dinner was held in her honour; the chairman (Colonel Sir Frederick Cardew) said that 'The day that women get the vote will be the day on which the death-knell of vivisection will be sounded.' When Lind spoke to the Glasgow Vegetarian Society in 1914 a *Daily Mail* journalist wrote that he was 'almost converted to vegetarianism' by her 'straight hard logic'.

Craig Buettinger argued that in the UK, feminism and anti-vivisection were strongly linked, comparison between the treatment of women and animals at the hands of male scientists and husbands dominating the discourse. Some saw close links between suffrage and anti-vivisection, with the image of a dog strapped to an operating table like women being strapped down to be force fed. According to Oakley, for feminists images of the restrained dog blurred into images of suffragettes forcibly fed, women deprived of their ovaries or uteruses as a cause for hysteria or immobilised for childbirth and the interventions of medical men.

After Charlotte's death *The Vegetarian News* of November 1939 highlighted her vegetarianism, reporting that she was

> chiefly famous for the great part which she played in the movement for women's suffrage in the early years of the present century. She was a fine worker, however, both before and after, in many different fields. So full, indeed, was her life of other useful activities that she found but little time to devote to the vegetarian movement. None the less, the devotion of this venerable and valiant lady who was a sister of the first Viscount French to the cause for which the London Vegetarian Society itself stands was sincere, and with gratitude now claims to be recorded.

As well as deeply principled, Charlotte was very religious, converting to Roman Catholicism in 1892 and joining the Theosophical Society on 4 April 1899. In *The Herald of the Star* (February 1917) theosophist John Scurr describes her as 'the beneficent fairy of Nine Elms.' Before the Married Women's Property Act, 1882, husbands owned the earnings of their wives, often taking the money for alcohol or other personal use. The Act allowed women to designate Charlotte as trustee of their funds, protecting their earnings from their husbands. Scurr also discussed how Charlotte cared for children injured through work or play, asserting that 'It was a lesson to anyone who is leading a soft, comfortable existence to see how children of seven or eight bore unflinchingly and with a brave face the smarting pain when ointments and lotions were applied.' She seemed to embody theosophy's core principle of selflessness and Scurr ends his comments with: 'Love and service are the dominant passions of her life. When the history of this time is written no one will occupy a higher place than the beneficent fairy of Nine Elms – Charlotte Despard.' Charlotte was also interested in other religions and cults. She gave a speech about 'The new womanhood' to the London Spiritualist

Alliance and a lecture entitled 'The Spiritual Ideal of Womanhood' at the ninth national conference of spiritualists on 2 July 1911. The *Journal of the Society for Psychical Research* lists her as a new member in June 1905. Charlotte's best known theosophical publication is *Theosophy and the Woman's Movement* (1913). She transferred her membership from the English to the Irish society in 1922 and frequently lectured and wrote for *Theosophy in Ireland.* She left the society in 1934.

The WFL, or the League as members usually called it, was not as well-known as the WSPU or NUWSS and yet it continued until 1961, far longer than the other organisations, and played an important role in developing the wider feminist agenda. Some members, notably Bormann Wells, tried to move the WFL towards feminism, but others, including Charlotte, were less keen. Charlotte made a speech where she claimed to 'hate the very word,' stating:

> I am not a feminist – indeed I hate the very word. It is my earnest hope that the present women's movement will prove to be a passing phase and that the day is not long distant when it will merge with the men's movement.

Charlotte's interests were broader than votes for women – she wanted enfranchisement and better living and working conditions for all.

Many things changed for women during Charlotte's lifetime – women going to university and married women owning their own property, for example. Some historians argue that the militant action of the suffragettes was irrelevant because women would have been enfranchised anyway – the UK was behind many countries – but what was important was the way that women worked together for the first time. In 1934 the novelist Winifred Holtby wrote about the achievements of the suffrage movement in *Women and a Changing Civilisation.* It was no longer possible, she writes, 'to convince an intelligent girl that women cared nothing for impersonal issues, since women had been ready to jeopardise their lives for them.' It was also no longer possible to convince her that 'women were incapable of political acumen, since their leaders had shown powers of strategy and action unsurpassed in struggles for reform.' For Holtby the importance of the fight was not the vote but the part that the struggle had in 'shifting the public perceptions of women, and in changing how women were able to perceive themselves (Joannou and Purvis). According to Holtby, women had been enfranchised 'from more than their lack of citizenship. It had disproved those theories about their own nature that had hitherto constituted an obstacle to women's advancement.'

In pieces written for *The Vote*, Charlotte was not so vehemently against feminism. In an article (18 February 1911, p.201) she wrote:

> I see the Vote won and I see beyond it. I see our League settling itself through the instruments it has obtained to help in the great synthetical work of the opening century … My forecast is that in the Women's Freedom League one of these instruments is to be found. I see those who have been the most earnest students of social conditions – those who have felt most deeply the power of feminism and its part in the growing humanism of to-day refusing to loose the bands of comradeship that hold them together …

When the name of the Women's Freedom League was decided, it really pleased no one. Charlotte had privately thought of it as the League of Women for Freedom, which symbolised her ambitions. As she told the WFL at its first conference, 'Our cause is not only votes for women, but the binding together of all womanhood with human rights.' Linklater suggests that her feminism 'was sketched in broader terms than that of any other suffrage leader, and its starting point was the importance of self-discovery. In 1910 she summarised her position as:

> Hypnotised by a false presentation of morality, religion and duty, we women have been cajoled or forced into a false conception of ourselves. We ask first for enlightenment. We wish using our own capacities, seeing with our own eyes, and not with the eyes of men to understand our true position, to see clearly what are our duties and our rights.

She was interested in far more than votes for women. When women sweated workers went on strike for higher pay in 1910, she urged the WFL to support them because they were breaking the chains 'which woman has forged round her consciousness from the moment she permitted herself to be the instrument of man's pleasure.' After meeting Booker T Washington, advocate of equal racial rights, she used the example of Negro self-help to show that women must rely on themselves. She used as an illustration the claim of male workers to be paid more than female workers because they are the family breadwinners: 'A shoddy sentimentality. It is worse than stupid, it is dangerous because it fosters the fatal error that women are and ought to be economically dependent on men.' Charlotte also argued that the law, in cases of prostitution and infanticide, discriminated against women. 'Women are legal slaves,' she argued – the proof was that no male client appeared in court with a prostitute, nor did fathers when mothers were accused of murdering their children. She took up the case of Daisy Lord, an unmarried 19-year-old accused of murdering her newborn baby. Charlotte was alone in arguing that the father was equally guilty, and a young homeless girl who had given birth only hours before could not be deemed to be in her right mind except by an all-male jury. After attending the trial of another similar case she wrote, 'There was not one incident which did not force upon us the bitter consciousness that under the present law woman is held to be the property of men.'

This was too big an issue for many women at the time to deal with because 'women, trained through long ages to subjection, have even to learn to think independently.' Women needed a sense of solidarity – 'the common sisterhood of woman' that bound them. It also needed economic equality because, as Charlotte argued, 'Fundamentally all social and political questions are economic.' Equal wages would mean that a male worker would no longer fear being put out of work by a woman and 'men and women will unite to effect a complete transformation of the industrial environment.' In the home women needed economic independence to live as equals with their husbands. 'It is indeed deplorable that the work of the wife and mother is not rewarded. I hope that the time will come when it is illegal for this strenuous form of industry to be unremunerated.'

In 1918 Charlotte wrote the foreword to a book by L.A.M. Priestley *The Feminine in Fiction* in which she talks about what she calls the woman's movement:

FOREWORD

The modern Revolt of Woman has been expressed in many forms. Some, to whom it is repugnant the women who hug their chains and the men who fear to lose their power have altogether denied its existence. These put down certain strange phenomena to hysteria, general social discontent or failure on the part of the 'odd women' to gain woman's fitting place in the family.

Under these circumstances it is instructive as well as interesting to look over the literary records of her period roughly by what is called the 'Woman's Movement,' and to see how the men and women of genius, or even observation, have dealt with the world-old puzzle the relation of the sexes one to the other.

That is the service which the writer of this admirable series of sketches The Feminine in Fiction has rendered to the country.

The modern heroine and the heroine of the mid-Victorian era, as she shows us, are altogether different persons. They might belong to different races. The vapours; the abundant tears; the sweet submission; the tacit acceptance of a subordinate role which marked the belauded woman of a past generation have gone. If these are allowed to fill any space in the modern canvas, it is that their futility may be seen.

On the other hand in such a woman as Evadne in Sarah Grand's daring novel The Heavenly Twins and as Lyndall in Olive Schreiner's haunting record The Story of an African Farm we see woman in revolt one against the lies and conventions and deep-seated corruptions of Modern Society; the other against the moral and intellectual restrictions which surround the mind and soul of woman with an iron ring that in many sad cases can only break by the breaking of her body

Earlier still our author shows us Charlotte Bronte voicing in her valiant heroines her own passionate aspirations for freedom. In The Odd Women, one of the most tragic of modern romances, we have the girl Monica, sacrificing her liberty through terror of the humiliations of poverty-, and as a foil to her and her sisters, Miss Barfoot leading brave girl students along the path of knowledge and revolt.

Every one of these sketches has a deep interest of its own; but it is only when they are brought together and studied in combination that we begin to realise dimly that in the heart of society a great new force has been springing up, a force with which the future will have to reckon.

It is this that it holds up a mirror in which we see ourselves and our turbulent age that gives this little book its value. I have read it with deep interest, and I am certain it will make a peculiarly strong appeal to all who are taking their part in the Woman's Movement of to-day.

C. Despard

Revealing her enthusiasm for literature and learning, Charlotte's allusion to the *Mirror for Princes* genre of medieval literature speaks to her deep desire to advise and affect change through her devotion to her causes.

Chapter 4

Siblings

The Frenchs were a successful family, with three siblings, including Charlotte herself, in high profile roles. Charlotte had five sisters and one brother: Mary was the oldest, then Caroline (Carrie), Charlotte (Lottie), Margaret, Sarah (Nellie), John and then Katherine (Katie). Margaret married engineer Gavin Jones and went to live in India, where he was setting up the cotton industry in Cawnpore. Caroline married Augustine Whiteway and moved to Huntingdonshire, and Katie married Colonel Ernest Harley. Mary married solicitor John Lydall, who was much disliked – part of the reason for Charlotte and her sisters setting off for Europe. He was to figure very much in the fortunes of John French, with the families becoming more closely linked when Sarah married his younger brother, Wykeham. It is said that the historian of the Lydall family, Edward Lydall, found it hard to find anything pleasant to say about his grandfather John, a religious fundamentalist and fanatical member of the Plymouth Brethren. Every day started with prayers and he was a rigid Sabbatarian, against most forms of enjoyment. His religious beliefs had not stopped him amassing a considerable fortune, his wife's dowry adding to this. He was something of a snob, and the French genealogy was very much to his liking.

In adult life Charlotte had little to do with her sisters – her political views set them apart. Their differences made it difficult to talk to Carrie, her favourite sister, without a furious argument. 'It is the usual thing, she *cannot* understand my rebellion,' Charlotte wrote after one of these occasions. (Linklater p.96) She had little in common with Nellie, Margaret was still in India and Katie, whose husband had died in the Boer War, lived too far from London and was too busy with her children.

Charlotte and her brother had a close but complex relationship throughout most of their lives. They were diametrically opposed and profoundly misunderstood each other: he engaged in defending the constitution, she battling for its destruction. 'He took her opinions to be an eccentricity, forgivable in one who had devoted her life to the poor; while she, deeply though she had disapproved of the Boer War, could never quite believe that his soldiering was anything less innocent than the games of the little boy who had strutted about the Ripplevale lawns.' Of his sister's activities, French said 'we have tried all we could to keep her from mixing up with these foolish women.' (Linklater p.96)

John French considered himself Irish and was proud of his Irish ancestry, tracing back to fourteenth-century Norman settlers in Wexford through his grandfather, Fleming French, who moved to Ripple and died there in 1818. It is interesting that both John and Charlotte were very attached to their Irish heritage, even though their mother was Scottish. They both became involved in Irish matters later in life and shared Irish characteristics – warmth, generosity, physical courage, fierce temper, inclination to nurse a sense of injustice – although their adult lives could not have been more different. He led the largest army Britain had ever sent out, she opposed every war, particularly the one in which he was commander-in-chief, but they remained close despite their differences. Charlotte called him Jack and often helped him and his family with money. She also ignored his sexual activities, which other members of the family could not. For John, Charlotte was a mixed blessing – her husband had left her well off so she was a useful source of funds, but her dress was not suitable for the sister of an aspiring general and socially she became more and more of an embarrassment to him. She was a pacifist and socialist, campaigning vigorously for Sinn Féin when John French was Viceroy of Ireland.

John believed the loss of his father and mother so early in his life marked his character. When John was young, his sisters were concerned that the female environment at Ripple was not a good place for a small boy and he was sent to Harrow prep school with a view to entering Harrow later. He was not academic and his ambition was to join one of the 'fighting professions'. Realising he could enter the navy earlier than the army, he had a long battle with his sisters until they gave way and in spring 1866 he went to Eastman's Naval Academy in Portsmouth. In 1870 he resigned from the navy to enter the army which also did not please his sisters – the army was expensive, having private means was essential, and it seemed irrational to quit a promising career in the navy. He took a commission in the Suffolk artillery militia, a militia commission being a recognised 'back door' to an army career without the necessity of attending either Sandhurst or Woolwich. He was an accomplished horse rider and polo player and so joined the cavalry, the most costly arm. The income of a cavalry officer hadn't risen significantly since the reign of William III and a cavalry officer needed an income of £500–600 a year to make ends meet. This should have been fine – Ripple had been sold and John had an annual income of around £1,000 so he was much better off than many officers, but throughout his life he found it difficult to keep his expenditure under control and he was fortunate not to be asked to leave the army on at least one occasion. He had a keen interest in horse riding. He trained his own horses and won a number of races on his favourite mare, Mrs Gamp.

While horses were a very important part of the life of a cavalry officer, for John women were another. He was far from being the stereotype of a tall attractive army officer, being a 'short man with the bow-legged swagger of a cavalry officer', but his face and piercing blue eyes were not unattractive and his considerable success with women lay in his personality not his looks – he had a pervasive and compelling charm, with a generous and warm-hearted nature. He saw women as romantic heroines and, again mirroring his passion for horses, he loved the sport of the hunt.

In 1874 Gavin Jones, married to Margaret and settled in Cawnpore, persuaded John to invest in one of his schemes, the Muir Mills. He invested £4,000, the business prospered and he made a handsome profit, but this was only a temporary respite from his difficulties and he turned to his family for help. His brother-in-law, John Lydall (married to Mary) paid off his debts for Mary's sake. In June 1875 John French married Isabella Ireland Soundy. A married subaltern was rare then and this likely would have damaged his career even if Isabella had been well connected, which she was not. The marriage does not appear in military records or subsequent biographies – it seems likely it was kept secret from the military. Within two years he wanted to end the marriage but the scandal of divorce would have endangered his career. Lydall managed to arrange matters so Isabella was the guilty party and the decree absolute was granted in June 1878. George Wilson was named as the co-respondent and the suggestion is that Lydall's money brought them together, not mutual attraction. This soured relations with Lydall – shortly afterwards John went to Ladbroke Grove in search of cash and was told never to darken the door again. Years later Lydall described him as a 'sorry fellow'.

In 1880, aged 28, John married again, to Eleanora Selby-Lowndes, a very suitable match, one of eight sisters known as the Belles of Bletchley. Her father was a prosperous squire and a thrusting young cavalry captain would have seemed an ideal match. Eleanora was slightly older than John and by nature level-headed, steady and mature. She had a pretty face and a useful legacy. John was passionately devoted to her. They had four children, one of whom died in infancy from a tragic accident, and the first four years of marriage were probably the happiest in his life, but within ten years he was conducting spectacular affairs, giving her ample grounds for divorce. Eleanora was hurt but loyal and did not blow the whistle on his behaviour, which could have ruined his career, even when he was named as co-respondent in a divorce. One noted mistress was Mrs Winifred Bennett (née Youelle), a diplomat's wife. He became involved with her late in 1914, writing to her frequently while in France and seeing her almost daily when he returned to the home forces command in 1916. When he was Lord Lieutenant of Ireland Mrs Bennett's visits to Viceregal Lodge aroused considerable comment. When John was stationed in Egypt, his sister Nellie and the children moved to Buckinghamshire on the estate of Nellie's brother-in-law, Edward Hanslope Watts. John left his family there when he was stationed in Norwich 1886–8 and the marriage ties started to weaken. In 1888 he took command of the regiment; it and his family moved to Hounslow. At 36 he became a colonel despite issues with his lack of service and training. In 1891 the regiment was stationed in India. Eleanora did not accompany him, and French seemed to think her absence gave him a reason and opportunity for infidelity. He had at least one affair with the wife of a brother officer and became the subject of some scandal. When John returned to England in the summer 1893, his tenure of the 19th regiment completed, he did not slip straight into another appointment despite his success, perhaps because of the scandal, but was consigned to the half-pay list. This was not unusual for ex-commanding officers, but meant he had to borrow from Muir Mills against future profits and time on half-pay was time out of his career – two years on half pay meant automatic retirement. It is unclear why he was on half-pay when all signs seemed favourable.

Just before French left for India his wife and children moved to Courtlands, Charlotte's house in Esher, Surrey, and Charlotte moved into a cottage in the grounds. He joined them there in probably the most gloomy period of his career. He was desperately short of money. Even more humiliating, he tried to ride a bicycle as a cheaper alternative to a horse but never mastered it and was seen by fellow officers hopping down the road beside the bicycle, unable to mount. His spending continued and he had to pawn the family silver. Charlotte spent most of her time in London but made regular visits, often accompanied by members of the working men's club in Nine Elms.

In 1892 John accompanied Charlotte when she gave her first public speech at Wandsworth town hall as a Poor Law Board member. When she was overcome at the door by stage fright he encouraged her, but later he found it increasingly difficult to support her new public identity.

John's career eventually picked up. He was appointed as a colonel in August 1895 and major general in 1899, and was sent to South Africa. When he was appointed to the 1st cavalry brigade at Aldershot in 1899, his new brigade major was Douglas Haig. Haig loaned his superior £2,000 with which to pay off his mounting debts, in a transaction liable to misinterpretation. French was a very public figure – he had two knighthoods, the KCB and KCMG, honorary degrees from Oxford and Cambridge, the sword of honour, was a freeman of various cities and livery companies. While he had his faults, he was regarded as a good officer, 'I daresay that he is not the cleverest man, but he is the most successful soldier we could find. He has never failed' (Royal Archives, W39/21, Esher to Knollys, 16 January 1904). It was generally remarked that it was a comfort to find a leader who, whether right or wrong, invariably knew his own mind, and possessed the force of character to stick to his opinions, and the force of intellect to defend them, (ibid. W40/128, Esher to King, 26 September 1907).

After the Boer War John lived in London while his family lived in Hertfordshire. His children sided with their mother and he was not reconciled with them until his last days. His attitude to marriage is perhaps shown in a letter written to Winifred Bennett, then his mistress, on 15 September 1915:

> The husband is a very well known man – a rich man – and the wife very good looking. They've been married some 17 or 18 years. A few years ago they found out the same old story that they weren't *meant* to be in love with one another – so each went his and her way but they remained together and are the best of friends. The wife found what she thought was her '*alter ego*' in a Guardsman who is serving out here. About a year or two ago he gave her up and *married*. The husband then wrote to him and told him he had behaved like a cad to his wife and that he should always cut him in future and he has always done so. Now I call that husband a real good fellow.

By September 1913 he was Sir John French, field marshal and commander of the army. He argued against taking military action in Ireland, and in March 1914 he resigned from the army even though Asquith asked him to withdraw his resignation. Churchill described him as 'a broken man'. Although he was described as a 'political general' he was politically naïve. On 2 August 1914 French telephoned Ramsay MacDonald and Sir George Riddell, influential newspaper proprietor, answered the phone. 'Can you tell me, old chap, whether we are going to be in this war? If so, are we going to put an army on the continent, and, if we are, who is going to command it?' asked John. The response was 'Fancy you not having heard. Yes, you are to command all right.' He had already had a meeting and been led to believe this would happen. At midnight on 4 August, Britain was at war with Germany.

'News in the Paper ... makes one think that the class war has already begun' Charlotte wrote in her diary early in 1914. Sir John French had just been promoted to field marshal, the highest rank in the British Army. He still kept Eleanora and the children tucked away in Hertfordshire while he carried on his love affairs in a London pied à terre he shared with George G. Moore, a disreputable but wealthy American railway magnate and financier and the solution to his money problems. They shared a house at Lancaster Gate from 1910 until Moore's return to the United States in 1921, an arrangement conducive to the two womanisers.

Despite all this, Charlotte remained on friendly terms with 'my dear old Jack' and wrote in her diary he paid her a 'delightful' visit in spring 1914. A few months later he visited again, bringing his mistress with him.

John was a very emotional man with a mercurial personality, who tended to over-identify with his soldiers. By spring 1915 the pressures of high command were clouding his mind and he found it hard to forget that almost any action he took as commander-in-chief resulted, to some degree, in British casualties. His diaries and letters to personal friends reflect the anguish that growing casualty lists caused him. Later, French was reluctant to do anything that would put his forces at risk. 'This highly emotional aspect of Sir John's character sat uneasily beside its more rational elements, and it lends a distinctive, and not always comprehensible, aura to his generalship.' On 23 November 1915, French was told the strain of command meant he couldn't continue and he was offered a peerage and command of the Home Forces.

In January 1916 he returned from France to the newly created post of Commander-in-Chief Home Forces and became Viscount French of Ypres in February 1916. The Irish Home Rule Act of October 1914 was suspended until after the war, which damaged the Irish nationalists, who lost ground. They had supported Britain against Germany which also weakened their position. An index of failure was the poor performance of army recruiters in Ireland despite the backing of Home Rulers. Militant Sinn Féiners began to fill the vacuum – they were not interested in home rule but demanded complete Irish independence. French doubted whether Sinn Féin had much popular support and was certain Ireland would be given home rule after the war. He was confident enough to buy a house in Drumdoe in 1917 which was an unwise investment – he was rarely able to go there and the security situation deteriorated. He wrongly believed that his personal connection with Ireland gave him a special insight into its problems.

By spring 1918 French was re-established as one of the government's leading military advisers.

He became Lord Lieutenant of Ireland, one of the greatest challenges of his career. It is said that the fact he was appointed suggests the government was running out of options. There was no provision for Lady French to go with him, and his long-running affair with Winifred

Bennett continued. This was not a public scandal, but no secret to those in the same circle.

French now believed home rule the only realistic option for Ireland and set out to destroy the nationalist Sinn Féin in order to create the circumstances in which home rule could be safely introduced. On 19 December 1919 there was an IRA assassination attempt on his life and he retired on 30 April, aged 68. While French was recruiting the notorious Black and Tan troops to quell civil unrest, Charlotte was doing all she could to encourage it. Her brother never forgave her and refused to see her, even on his deathbed.

He remained committed to a peaceful Ireland and intended to live in Ireland after independence. His colourful private life continued – Mrs Bennett was still a regular visitor to his home and visited Cannes with him. He left official life in April 1921 and lived in London but wanted to move to Ireland – he purchased a second house, but conditions there meant he was unable to return. Early in 1923 Drumdoe was raided by a party of armed men who removed the contents. John could not live in either of his Irish properties and was unable to afford a property in London. Becoming an earl was not cheap and he did so with bad grace, protesting at having to pay stamp duty on his letters patent. Parliament granted him £50,000 in 1916 and he continued to receive a field-marshal's half-pay, but left only £8,450 net in his will – Irish properties and his expensive lifestyle, including lengthy stays at the Hotel Crillon in Paris, had swallowed up his money. In August he was offered the appointment of Captain of Deal Castle, which was purely honorary but gave him the right to live in the castle.

Lady French had not followed him to Ireland – the official excuse was it was too dangerous – and saw little of him when he returned. He had been estranged from his sons, but in 1922 re-established contact with Gerald, who had won the DSO and was deputy governor of Dartmoor prison. They grew close and it was Gerald who, until he died in 1970, defended his father's reputation. John's eldest son Dick, a talented artist whose military career was cut short by a riding accident, became the second Earl of Ypres.

John was 'very much the product of the nineteenth century and intellectually and temperamentally unsuited to meeting the challenges of the new conditions pertaining in warfare' (ODNB). His unreliable and very subjective memoir *1914*, first published by the *Daily Telegraph* in serial form and then as a book in June 1919, was the first such memoir from a serving officer. The book was largely compiled by *The Times* journalist Lovat Fraser from conversations with John French and was notable for its revelations about disputes at the highest level, attacking Kitchener, Asquith and Smith-Dorrien. Smith-Dorrien could not respond in public as he was serving as governor of Gibraltar, but French's version of events was savaged by royal historian the Hon. John Fortescue, who claimed *1914* was the work of a 'monomaniac' and French was dismissed as official historian. Smith-Dorrien was vindicated in the official history published in 1925. French's son continued to defend him but John's reputation had suffered considerable damage.

John's affair with Winifred Bennett diminished in intensity but he still enjoyed an active social life, staying in Paris and on the Riviera in winter. In 1924 he became ill in France, later diagnosed as cancer. He asked to be taken home to Deal Castle to die and did so on 22 May 1925. He was cremated at Golders Green and his coffin lay in state in the Guards Chapel, Wellington Barracks. An estimated 7,000 people, mostly old soldiers, filed past in the first two hours. His funeral took place on 26 May at Westminster Abbey and he was buried the following day at Ripple. Spectators were twelve deep outside the Abbey and the whole route was lined with people who came to pay their respects

Various works have been published and although Gerald worked hard to defend his reputation, John French remains a discredited man in military terms. Some feel this was too harsh – his failings have received more than their share of attention while his achievements have been ignored. According to Holmes (1981) he was not a great general, but a brave man and a good cavalry leader, and no other general could have held the army together as he did.

The other French sibling to gain some public prominence was Katherine (Katie) Harley (1855–1917), the youngest of the French siblings. Robinson describes her as coming from 'stalwart stock'. Katie was described as 'Wiry and energetic with a well-chiselled nose, pale piercing eyes, slight and graceful and a love for everything militaire.' She married Colonel George Harley and the family settled in Condover,

Shrewsbury. Like Charlotte, Katie changed direction after her husband was killed in 1907 during the Boer War. Like her elder sister she became a Poor Law guardian and joined the NUWSS in 1910, becoming president of the Shropshire Women's Suffrage Society and chairman of the West Midlands federation. It was Katherine's idea to organise a crusade for the vote, perhaps from her Christian beliefs – she was a member of the Church League for Women's Suffrage and saw the struggle for the vote in spiritual as well as political terms.

In 1913 the NUWSS had about 100,000 members. Katherine suggested the idea of the Pilgrimage at a meeting in April 1913, because she thought this would show parliament how many women wanted the vote and make it clear that their campaign was non-militant and peaceful. The *Common Cause* explained why this was such a good concept, and what it would mean to those who took part or witnessed it, using the old argument that women who were governed by the law should have some part in making the law. The Pilgrimage would spread the word across the country, and show that it was about ordinary working women and what should be a basic human right. Katherine had been inspired by the suffrage tours in caravans, taking the fight to everyone and explaining it to them, but the NUWSS could not afford caravans so the idea of a walking tour took shape. Members of the NUWSS set off on 18 June 1913, taking various routes across the country to Hyde Park, London.

Saturday 26 July 1913 was chosen as the date for the massed meeting in Hyde Park and working backwards from then, timetables were calculated for the six principal routes, several of which had multiple starting points. They were named the Great North road (which included East Anglia), the Watling Street route (with Wales), the West Country route, the Portsmouth road, the Brighton road and the Kentish Pilgrims' Way. A map was published showing routes and timings and those on the shortest route were to set off from Brighton on 21 July, but the longest routes from Carlisle and Newcastle would take six weeks. Newspaper editors were sent details in advance and asked to report on the pilgrimage as it passed and to publish a letter explaining its purpose and the difference between the law abiding suffragists and militant suffragettes.

Most of the women travelled on foot although some rode horses or bicycles and wealthy supporters lent carriages or even cars. It was not the intention that individuals would cover the whole route but that federations would do so. Katherine Harley was keen on the idea of uniforms and the pilgrims were urged to wear dark coloured coats and skirts or dresses, blouses to be white or to match the skirt. When there were arguments and some wanted to wear tweed, Katherine was clear that the press would soon ridicule them if they looked like 'a rag-tag bunch of maiden aunts'. Finally there was a compromise and she conceded that all pilgrims could wear whatever they wanted, but should raise the hem of their skirts to exactly four inches from the ground, to keep them out of the mud and look uniform, the cutting edge of fashion, mildly shocking. Hats were to be simple, white or dark colours, and a compulsory raffia badge was supplied for 3*d*, a cockle shell, traditional symbol of pilgrimage, to be worn pinned to the hat. Sashes were red, white and green; also available were a haversack in bright red, edged with green and with white lettering, and umbrellas with red, white or green covers. A lorry accompanied the walkers to carry their luggage, and Margaret Ashton brought her car and picked up those in difficulties.

Vera Chute Collum was working in the press department of the NUWSS and as a freelance journalist. Commissioned by the *Daily News*, in her first dispatch on 21 July 1913 she wrote about joining the pilgrimage:

> Your correspondent picked them up a few miles outside Banbury on Friday night. They were camped by the roadside taking their afternoon rest and had just held a meeting for the cottagers and been entertained to tea themselves in the rectory garden. A shrill whistle sounded, and the pilgrims scuttled to their places; the roll was called, the banners grounded ready to hoist aloft, and another whistle to stand to attention. Then a sharp word of command from the marshal [Mrs Harley] – a sister, by the way, of our most famous cavalry commander – and the pilgrims moved off, the leaders carrying a big blue banner with the words 'Law Abiding' blazoned on it.

On several occasions, when the Pilgrimage stopped for meetings and speeches, there was trouble and Katherine was injured.

It was estimated that 50,000 women reached Hyde Park on 26 July. *The Times* noted that the march was part of a campaign against the militancy of the WSPU:

> On Saturday the pilgrimage of the law-abiding advocates of votes for women ended in a great gathering in Hyde Park attended by some 50,000 persons. The proceedings were quite orderly and devoid of any untoward incident. The proceedings, indeed, were as much a demonstration against militancy as one in favour of women's suffrage. Many bitter things were said of the militant women.

The idea of a march was not a new one. In 1912 the 'Brown Women' (so-called because they wore russet tweed suits and matching hats decorated with emerald green cockades) marched about 400 miles from Edinburgh to London. It was the idea of Florence de Fonblanque, member of WFL, the New Constitutional Society for Women's Suffrage and the Conservative and Unionist Women's Franchise Association as well as the NUWSS and WSPU, who saw the idea of a long distance march as a demonstration of suffragette strength and determination.

In September 1912 all the suffragette societies were contacted to enlist support. On 12 October, headed by Charlotte Despard, some 300 women strode out of Edinburgh, with brass bands and thousands of spectators sending them on their way. They were beset by very bad weather and only six women walked the whole way. When they arrived on 16 November a band played in Trafalgar Square and the six original members received a silver medal. They had a petition to present to Mr Asquith. By the time they arrived in London it had thousands of signatures and was almost 800 yards long, each separate sheet mounted on linen and stored in a leather case. The petition read 'We, the undersigned, pray the Government to bring in a bill for Woman Suffrage this season'. It was taken to Downing Street and they were told the prime minister would be pleased to give it his consideration. A few days later the response was that he had nothing to add to previous statements, so the march had made no difference.

In July 1913 Millicent Fawcett wrote to Asquith 'on behalf of the immense meetings which assembled in Hyde Park on Saturday and voted with practical unanimity in favour of a Government measure.' Asquith replied that the demonstration had 'a special claim' on his consideration and stood 'upon another footing from similar demands proceeding from other quarters where a different method and spirit is predominant.' Again nothing changed.

The Pilgrimage though was considered a great success. In February 1914 Katherine was one of the founders of the Active Service League to build on this, to coordinate and undertake suffrage and welfare work. 'The Pilgrimage revealed to many of us the joy of working as one of many, rather than as units,' Katherine said. She wanted the pilgrims to come together again in groups, to dedicate between a week and a month of their time each year to good causes in the name of women's suffrage. The Active Service League was a forerunner of the Women's Royal Voluntary Service (founded in 1938) and acted as a conduit of energy, expertise and ideology leading directly from the Pilgrimage to all the different tasks to which NUWSS members could set themselves. During the war Active Service League members turned their hands to many things, including clearing vacant houses and fitting them out as hostels for volunteers and coordinating refugee relief work.

When war broke out in 1914, Katherine became part of the war effort. She sent a personal message to the women of Shropshire, asking them to take over men's jobs so they could go and fight, 'I ask this in the name of my brother, who so sorely needs the able-bodied men in the country.'

The Women's Emergency Corps, an organisation which helped women to become doctors, nurses and motorcycle messengers, was founded by Eveline Haverfield. With the financial support of the NUWSS Elsie Inglis, a founder of the Scottish Women's Suffrage Federation, formed the Scottish Women's Hospitals Committee. Other committees were formed in Glasgow, London and Liverpool and the American Red Cross helped fund the organisation. When Dr Inglis wanted to set up units on the Western Front she was told by the War Office 'My good lady, go home and sit still.'

Although it was opposed by the War Office representative in Scotland, Dr Inglis and the Scottish Women's Hospitals Committee sent the first women's medical unit to France three months after the war started, supported by the Active Service League. Katherine Harley was part of that unit. In April 1915 Dr Inglis took a group of women, including

Katherine, to Serbia. Over the next few months they established field and fever hospitals, dressing stations and clinics. Inglis and some of her staff were captured during the summer of 1915 but the British authorities negotiated their release, with the help of American diplomats. By the end of the war there were fourteen hospitals.

> Not only did they treat casualties with calm efficiency and conspicuous success (many never having had male patients before) but resident bacteriologists also conducted pioneering research into the diagnosis and treatment of gas gangrene. The death rate and number of amputations carried out at Royaumont [one of the hospitals] were among the lowest of any hospital in the theatre of war.

For her dedication and services to France, Katherine was awarded the Croix de Guerre, a military decoration awarded to those who carry out acts of heroism. She resigned in spring 1916 following a dispute and returned to England but was determined to rejoin the war effort.

When the Serbian government requested two more hospital units, supported by a motorised flying corps of ambulances, this was her opportunity. Accompanied by her daughter Edith, the unit opened in September 1916. The nearest allied hospital to the front, its role was to collect Serbian casualties from the front line and bring them to the hospitals for treatment. Within eight weeks of opening they had dealt with over 400 wounded. The unit operated in very difficult conditions but the women drivers had a reputation for being insubordinate and ignoring orders in their enthusiasm to help the wounded, even operating at night despite orders not to do so. They were criticised for lack of discipline, smoking and drinking. It was felt Katherine did not have a firm enough grip on their activities and, following an inspection by the Scottish Women's Hospitals, Katherine and her daughter agreed to resign.

In November 1916 Monastir (now Bitola in Macedonia) was occupied by the allied forces with other forces located on the surrounding mountains, so it was subject to enemy artillery fire and bombing. Katherine and Edith moved into the town to help the women, children and elderly. Katherine rented a house in the town and funded the establishment of an orphanage. On 7 March 1917 Katherine and Edith were having tea with Miss Mary L. Mathews, head of the American Girls' School, when a shell hit the street and Katherine was killed.

Katherine was described as not an easy colleague, and not one happy to take orders. Marjory Lees kept a notebook on the 1913 Pilgrimage with a tribute to Katherine Harley and added a quote at the end of her handwritten obituary: 'To die for one's country is fine ... but to die for another country, that is superb. That is something beyond us.' Marjory and Katherine's travelling companion, Lady Rochdale, was equally fulsome:

We have not sat at home while our men went out. We have gone out, too, and worked, some quite as hard as men. Only last week we heard of the death of a very keen suffragist who was killed by a shell as any man has been killed. We suffragists feel very proud of the woman who laid down her life as any man has done for her country. I knew her personally and walked by her side many miles in the suffragists' pilgrimage. We stood side by side one night when a great many men were hurling things at us. She stood her ground then as I am sure she stood it out in Serbia. We suffragists feel very proud of the name of Mrs Harley.

Suffragette Nina Boyle wrote 'Tell Mrs Despard that it was a real delight to see someone so like her, in person and in spirit.' It seems very sad that two sisters who in many ways seem so similar, and were fighting for the same cause, were not closer.

Chapter 5

Petticoats and Politics

Charlotte referred to her work with the Poor Law as her apprenticeship; before this she had naively believed that it was only necessary for society's wrongs to be pointed out and they would be put right, but soon found that this was not so. At her first board meeting as a Poor Law guardian in 1892, Charlotte was confronted by a group of unemployed workers who asked that, rather than being sent to the already full workhouse, a situation that happened every winter until spring meant more jobs, they be given work painting and repairing the infirmary. 'The hopelessness of the whole business and the ocean of misery through which I was compelled to wade made me search for some remedy,' she wrote. The unemployed men were members of the Marxist Social Democratic Federation (SDF) and argued that welfare projects were cheaper than workhouse projects and better for those concerned. Their explanation, and the worsening situation with the workhouse population soaring to record levels, made Charlotte seek alternative solutions.

> I had been brought up in the dear old superstition of my fathers that English men and women are free, and there is no need for revolution ... I had thought for a time to find the change I wanted in Liberalism.

In 1891 Joseph Chamberlain seemed to hold the answers with a programme for radical reform but it had minimal effect on Liberal policy and when little had changed by the 1895 general election, Charlotte had decided that 'Party politics held out no hope. I saw the terrible problem of people's necessities played with. I heard promises made to them which I knew would not be fulfilled. Hot with helpless indignation I beheld their urgent needs turned into party cries for election purposes. At last I determined to study for myself the great problems of society. My study landed me in uncompromising socialism.'

One of the main challenges for Charlotte, however, was how, as a woman, she might effect change. Women were active in political organisations during the nineteenth century, before their prominent involvement with the suffrage campaign. From the 1880s there was a movement of women into organisations that had been the sole province of men as women's usefulness as canvassers and organisers was identified and used by the two major political parties. Women were involved in the formation of the Social Democratic Federation (SDF) and the Independent Labour Party (ILP). These were the only organisations to admit women to the main party on equal terms with men but they were not treated equally – women were seen by some socialist men as a problem that needed to be addressed. In the ILP few women were involved in policy making in the early years but women did take a leading role in branch life and as public speakers.

The over-riding principle was that women had particular interests and concerns which they needed to address. From some women there was evidence of dissatisfaction with their assigned roles and a desire to engage in activity directly related to women's status in society. In the socialist parties women began to see the need to organise into separate groups; in the 1890s there were a number of women's ILP groups and in 1904 Women's Socialist Circles were formed by a number of SDF women. Women who were members of political organisations did not see this leading to separation from the larger male-dominated party, but the development of distinct women's organisations became more important as attention turned increasingly towards the single issue of women's suffrage.

From the 1880s women's particular interests in education, welfare and health led many towards a route into public policy by standing as Poor Law guardians, or joining school boards and other similar bodies. Women made a significant difference to local welfare services and they were able to learn more about women's exclusion from male-dominated policy making. Campaigns accelerated to extend the municipal franchise to women, allowing them to stand for local councils – the Women's Local Government Society, formed to this end, was active in defending women's existing positions as well as seeking an extension of their influence in local government affairs. This had mixed results. Despite evidence of women's good work in the latter part of the nineteenth century their position was still tenuous, demonstrated by the confusion over women's rights to stand in elections, which ended in 1899 with them being officially barred. Women were also abruptly dismissed when the school boards were abolished in 1902. British women could vote in local elections from 1888 and stand for local elections after the ban on women candidates was lifted in 1907.

The first women's suffrage societies in London and Manchester in 1865 were organised to generate support for John Stuart Mill's women's suffrage amendment to the 1867 Reform Bill. This and subsequent attempts to extend the franchise failed, but women's suffrage societies attracted an increasingly large number of women and succeeded in becoming an established focus of women's political activity and debate in the period.

In nineteenth-century Britain there was no political representation for the working-class. The main political parties were the Liberals and Conservatives, and MPs were drawn, of course, from those who could vote – men over 30. MPs had to pay their own costs and expenses so were mainly wealthy landowners and industrialists. Towards the end of the century working-class representation became a concern for many, with the growing trade unions viewing parliamentary representation as a way of advancing their aims. The Liberal Party was seen as the vehicle for doing this and in 1869 a Labour Representation League was established to register and mobilise working-class voters on behalf of Liberal candidates. The Fabian Society, founded in 1884, was committed to a policy of working within the Liberal Party and a number of 'Lib-Lab' candidates were elected as MPs by the alliance of trade unions and radical intellectuals within the Liberal Party.

This idea was not universally welcomed. Marxist socialists, seeing the inevitability of a class struggle between the working and capitalist classes, did not want to play 'second fiddle' to the Liberals. British Marxists set up their own party, the SDF in 1881. While other activists did not share the idea of a class struggle, they were also frustrated with the ideology of the Liberal Party and the lower priority given to working-class candidates. One of these activists was Keir Hardie, who worked with SDF members to form the Scottish Labour Party in 1888. There was a growing call for a new party of labour, independent from existing political organisations. In the general election held in July 1882 three working men were elected without support from the Liberals – Keir Hardie in South West Ham, John Burns in Battersea and Havelock Wilson in Middlesbrough. Burns was a towering labour figure and wildly popular, but had problems with the ILP's socialism; when Campbell-Bannerman formed his Liberal government in 1906, Burns was appointed to the Cabinet, the first working-class member. Hardie's critical and confrontational style in parliament led him to emerge as a national voice of the Labour movement.

A conference was organised in Bradford in January 1893 for advocates of an independent Labour organisation. It was the first conference of the ILP and Keir Hardie MP was elected as its first chairman. Others present at that meeting included George Bernard Shaw and Edward Aveling. In Hardie's keynote address he noted that the Labour Party was not an organisation, 'but rather the expression of a great principle'. The party called for a range of social reforms, including medical treatment and school feeding programmes for children, housing reform, measures to reduce unemployment and provide aid for the unemployed and welfare programmes for the sick, disabled, elderly, orphans and widows – all causes close to Charlotte's heart. It also campaigned for women's suffrage.

In 1896, when London was host to an international conference of socialists and trade unionists, Charlotte was among the delegates. She adopted the Marxist teachings of the SDF like a religion. The fortunes of the SDF had waned – Engels had remarked in 1894 that although a million people had passed through its ranks, only 4,500 remained, mainly due to dislike of founder and president H.M. Hyndman. Unskilled and casual workers were joining the trade union movement, while SDF members tended to come from the ILP and other socialist groups. Just before Charlotte joined the SDF its fortunes were improved with the return of three defectors – William Morris, Edward Aveling and his partner Eleanor Marx, daughter of Karl. Charlotte was a useful recruit, organising meetings, donating money and speaking. The hall of the Despard Club at 95 Wandsworth Road was put at the disposal of the socialists, and christened the Social Hall. It became the centre for working-class activities, including lectures and concerts. Charlotte tried to explain to all who attended the economic reasons that laid behind their poverty; she firmly believed that people had to be awakened for the country to be transformed. She was totally against any violence, insisting that there must not be 'any class bitterness', but she had not considered the process by which the ownership of property would be taken from individuals and given back to the community. She soon became frustrated by the lack of progress in improving the lot of the working classes, but then personal matters intervened.

Charlotte was close to Eleanor Marx and Edward Aveling. They shared her love of Shelley and had published a paper showing how his ideas linked with socialist theory. In January 1897 Aveling organised a concert at Social Hall and fell in love with a young actress, Eva Frye, who sang at the concert. They secretly married and in 1898, learning of the marriage, Eleanor committed suicide, apparently with prussic acid provided by Aveling. This destroyed Charlotte's belief that members of the SDF must be of a higher order since they were in pursuit of a great truth. There was a rumour that Aveling rushed to Charlotte for comfort after discovering the suicide, but on this she was silent. No longer looking through rose-tinted glasses Charlotte began to see the SDF for what it was. There was also a social problem for which the SDF did not have a solution. All working women were likely to have to seek poor relief at some time, perhaps because their husband was too ill or old to work or had lost his job, but often they were alone and so most in need of help. Charlotte called them 'my sister women', deeply disturbed by

> those struggling with social problems, and those who slave all their lives long for the community – shop, factory and domestic slaves, earning barely a subsistence, and thrown aside to death or the parish when they are no longer profitable – mothers, bearing and rearing children, seeing them go forth ... and spending their own last years, lonely and unconsidered in the cheerless wards of the workhouse.

The laws of society saw women only in relation to men; a husband's absolute power also meant he had absolute responsibility for his wife's maintenance. Common Law left women defenceless and the Poor Law Act gave them no protection. Charlotte railed against the injustice. 'I tried to help, tried all I knew but alas! how futile were my efforts. Turn which way I would, I knocked my head against a law to which neither my sisters nor I had consented. The thought of all this nearly made me wild.'

Despite the law, men deserted their wives, often for sound reasons – desertion was cheaper than divorce and a wife was not responsible for her husband's debts. He may also go off to look for a job – once a man was forced into the workhouse he could not leave even to look for employment without taking his family with him, so it was easier to abandon his family to the workhouse while he searched on his own. Wives could only enforce husbands' responsibility through the courts; a deserted wife with no money had to turn to the parish so the Poor Law board could sue for maintenance on her behalf – if they could track down the missing husband. If working mothers had a job in a shop or factory, the ten- or twelve-hour day made childcare essential but the weekly wage was not enough to cover that and all the household expenses.

The Poor Law was harsh. The relieving officer would visit the home to make sure a wife had no valuables – even wedding rings had to be pawned before the parish would give relief – and she had to have a 'home worth preserving' – clean children, swept floors, no cohabitation. This would determine whether she could receive relief or be sent to the workhouse, where her children would be taken away (it was not a suitable place for a child) and she would not be permitted to visit them – until Charlotte won single mothers that right in 1898. If a woman received out-relief, cohabitation with a man not her husband was enough to withdraw the relief and, from 1889, when the boards were given the power to take children into care, it could be used as a reason for removing children. As the cost of divorce was impossible for the poor – in 1912 for those earning less than £2 a week the cost was £15–20 – and the wife had to prove both desertion and adultery, most simply took a common-law husband.

Charlotte tried to right the moral unfairness. 'I would rather be anything than a working-man's wife', she said more than once. One of her committees pressed the police into trying harder to track down runaway husbands while the board, somewhat reluctantly, hired detectives and offered rewards, but the size of the problem was just too great. She could not help single mothers in the workhouse, who needed to find a job and a childminder before they could leave, because the board refused to look after children while the mother went to find a job. She did have a little success, however, persuading the board to take in some children from a large fatherless family until the eldest could start earning a living.

One of the applicants for relief at a guardian's meeting attended by Charlotte was a widow with six children, the eldest aged 11, whose husband had died two weeks before. There was sympathy for her until the chairman discovered that she had received £15 in life assurance – enough to live on for about two months. She claimed the money had been used to pay off old debts but, when pressed, admitted that more than half of it had been used to pay for the funeral. The chairman saw this as real extravagance and delivered a lecture on the madness of spending enough money to keep her and her family for six weeks. It made complete sense though to Charlotte, who saw it as an extension of the daily struggle – the funeral had given this woman's life dignity and meaning. The reaction of the board and general society was 'part of the battle which Shelley recognised as materialism against humanity, which Marx recognised as capitalism against the worker', and which Charlotte Despard recognised as patriarchal society against women and their dignity. This incident, according to Linklater, made Charlotte take up the banner of feminism, but perhaps this should be the cause of women, as she did not like the term 'feminism'.

Charlotte had seen socialism as an ally of women but realised it was not. Many working men were suspicious of women, seeing them as too ready to act as cheap labour and break strikes, and concluded that they would use their votes to maintain the status quo in politics.

Although equal rights for men and women was adopted as part of the Second International policy in 1891, the European Social Democratic parties were more concerned with the principle than the practice. The Austrian, Belgian and Swedish parties abandoned the women's vote in order to gain a wider male franchise, while in France and Germany it was hardly a serious demand. The SDF at least made clear its hostility to the enfranchisement of women until every man had the vote.

Angry, Charlotte joined the Women's Liberal Federation and in 1901 formed a women's suffrage group whose aim 'was to make the vote the first plank in the women's movement'. She soon discovered they were 'Liberals first and suffragists second', unsupportable because her opposition to the Boer War was far more extreme than the Liberal Party's, and she had forsworn the politics of capitalism. When the group decided to affiliate to the National Union of Women's Suffrage Societies (NUWSS), whose policy was to secure the vote on the same terms as men, this was unacceptable to Charlotte. For her the purpose of the vote was to help women in the workhouses or receiving poor relief, so within a few months she had resigned from the group and was once more seeking a direction.

In 1901 the trade unions and socialist groups which were prepared to work for workers' representatives in parliament formed the Labour Representation Council. The SDF refused to affiliate, unlike its rival the ILP, which was ready to use existing institutions such as the unions and parliament to achieve socialism. The lack of reality in the SDF finally persuaded Charlotte that the policies of the ILP were the right ones. 'I believed' she said, explaining the change, 'that the transition of capitalism to Socialism must be gradual. Industrialism must capture the government machine.' She always hoped that there would be some revelation in workers' minds, and when there were strikes she prayed that 'the people's eyes may be opened'.

She was convinced that socialism, which alone seemed to remember that the poor were the blessed, was the purest form of Christianity, and her spiritual language reflected this. 'I felt and saw how the poor and afflicted – those who were being trampled by the great rush of men – were, in a sense of which the happy cannot know, the true children of the Saviour of men.' Charlotte saw the degradation in the streets of Nine Elms as not a problem but a sin, blasphemy committed by capitalism, and she moved further from the rationalism that had been her husband's faith. At the turn of the century she had a new air of spiritual authority, which would later dominate her character. Margaret Bondfield, then a trade union organiser and later the first woman Cabinet minister, recalled staying with her at her cottage in Surrey in 1898:

> I woke very early and saw her already at work outside. On her knees, weeding her garden at sunrise, she seemed to me like a saint at prayer, and later at breakfast her face shone with the peace and strength she

drew from nature. It was these communings in the garden with God
that gave her her unique steadfastness.

Charlotte began to form new friendships within the ILP. She shared with
George Lansbury, a guardian in Poplar, a hatred of the Poor Law and
enjoyed 'the spirit of comradeship' which Will Crooks created around
him. She spoke and canvassed for Crooks in his successful campaign at
the 1903 Woolwich by-election and remembered it as a happy time: 'What
days they were! How we laughed at one moment and at the next choked
down a lump in our throats as he poured out his humorous and pathetic
stories.' Her closest friendship was with Margaret Bondfield who said in
her autobiography 'I loved [Charlotte] and cherished her friendship till
her death.'

It was through Margaret that Charlotte was introduced to the women's
trade union movement. They met in 1898 after a meeting at Social
Hall which had been organised to recruit new members to the Shop
Assistants' Union. No shop assistants turned up. The young organiser
was in tears, until Charlotte comforted her 'like a mother' according to
Margaret, reminding her not to confuse disappointment with failure,
because 'it was only the call to that increased effort which gives strength
for victory'. It was difficult to organise women whose jobs were generally
unskilled and insecure, and even if there was a union it was powerless,
without the muscle of the vote. Margaret had joined the Adult Suffrage
Society, the only suffrage group advocating the vote for all classes of
women, and Charlotte was persuaded by her example. 'I had seen,' said
Charlotte, 'that women would never make much progress until they were
acknowledged as citizens. Trained in a democratic school, I desired this
privilege to be as widely extended as possible.' She began to talk to the
women in the Nine Elms laundries and sweatshops and the jam bottlers
in the Crosse and Blackwell factories nearby about the benefits of the vote
and unions. A small number of women appeared at Social Hall, or her flat
above the Despard Club or went down to stay at her Esher cottage, which
Margaret Bondfield remembered was 'open to all the lame dogs and tired
workers needing rest and soul refreshment'. Although Charlotte was
unconventional in many ways, in others she was the archetypal Victorian
lady and for the shop assistants, clerks and factory workers it was, as one

said, 'our first introduction to good taste, culture and the kindness of our gracious hostess.'

In her work trying to provide school meals or boots for the poorest children, Charlotte faced many obstacles, further examples of the inefficiency of men's government and administration and lack of imagination. It seemed obvious to Charlotte that when children could not learn through illness or poor diet, the refusal to spend a little on food and nutrition, compared with the costs of staff and buildings, was a clear false economy, leaving her to conclude that women saw these things more clearly than men and were 'gifted with an intuitive faculty which much exceeds that of men ... They could place their finger on the political mistake or the economic fallacy which mars the usefulness of well-intentioned laws.'

Although the argument for enfranchising women was overwhelming, even the most optimistic adult suffragist thought it would take twenty years to achieve. Charlotte looked for solutions to the impasse and then for guidance – Mazzini did not let her down. With real excitement she took the results to Margaret Bondfield who thought they were 'interesting, but not convincing', but Charlotte was convinced that a clear message could be distinguished on her planchette among the random scrawls of the automatic writing. 'Great upheavals predicted,' she wrote '– and a Coming.'

'The history of the twentieth century will show the rise of two great movements – women and labour', she predicted, based on the notion that the Industrial Revolution had destroyed the independence of men and women. The replacement of cottage industries by mass production made men wage-slaves and women house-slaves.

> Compare our own days ... when much of the work done in factories was done at home, and done by women under the supervision of women, baking, brewing, curing meats, preserving fruit and vegetables, spinning and weaving ... Because industry belongs to man, because in an earlier era, he removed it from the home to the factory he is jealous of her presence there ... The soft fragile girl of the mid-Victorian era, who faded into the pale and submissive

housewife, was his creation. She made a fine foil to his strength, and she ministered to his glory.

For Charlotte it followed that women seeking to regain independence should unite with workers in the face of the common enemy – the patriarchal capitalist society – and her work was devoted to that end, but just as socialists betrayed the working class, so suffragists adopted the outlook of the middle class. The suffrage societies differed in often crucial ways but an important principle in and among Labour and Liberal women was an emphasis on equality and democracy, both in their internal practice and in claiming the rights of women.

A number of women began pushing the cause of women's suffrage in the Manchester ILP and, with the foundation of the Labour Representation Committee in 1900, in the Labour movement generally. The Pankhursts were especially insistent that the Labour Party should adopt the principles of women's suffrage, but they were becoming frustrated that support for their demands was not growing fast enough. In 1903 the ILP had a new meeting hall built for the party in Salford to be named in honour of Richard Pankhurst, Emmeline's late husband, but Pankhurst Hall was not open to women, not even the Pankhursts. Emmeline was understandably outraged. It was against this background that in 1903 Emmeline Pankhurst formed the Women's Social and Political Union (WSPU). The WSPU did not arise from a vacuum, as sometimes appears, but from a growing national movement. The NUWSS was founded in 1897 and the national *Women's Suffrage Record* had been launched in 1902. The WSPU was in direct conflict with the adult suffragists – one of its organisers, Teresa Billington, said that 'Margret Bondfield and Mary MacArthur laboured against us and made havoc of the support we had collected.' (p.103.) There was strong rivalry between the various groups, although on the face of it they all wanted the same thing. The 'adult suffragists' were believed to be heading towards the same action as their colleagues on the Continent and abandoning votes for women, while the 'women suffragists' were prepared to accept votes for women on the same basis as men, making it a right of property. Both the WSPU and the adult suffragists were hoping to convert the ILP, to which both were affiliated, and then the Labour Party. When the WSPU put forward a model Bill which would enfranchise those women who met the property qualifications of the 1884 Reform Act, it was seen by opponents as a rich woman's charter. In 1905 the ILP proposed to the Labour Party conference that women's suffrage should become party policy, but instead the conference voted for adult suffrage. Christabel Pankhurst did not accept this meekly. In October 1905 two senior members of the Liberal Party, Winston Churchill and Sir Edward Grey, came to speak at the Free Trade Hall in Manchester and Christabel and Annie Kenney confronted them with the question 'Will the Liberal government give women the vote?' There was no reply, they heckled and were ejected. On the steps of the Hall Christabel spat, or pretended to spit, at a policeman, which was technically assault. When she refused to pay the fine the magistrate had no option but to send her to prison for seven days; 1,000 people came to demonstrate at the prison, 2,000 to welcome Annie on her release and the Free Trade Hall was packed to hear Christabel speak. This was a turning point – Helena Swanwick, later president of the International Women's League, wrote 'I could not keep out of this struggle at this time. It bludgeoned my conscience.' Charlotte could see the prospect of change coming.

Although Charlotte was attracted by the WSPU, the partial franchise had no appeal and a brief meeting with Emmeline Pankhurst in 1905 emphasised their differences. With unemployment at its highest since 1894, George Lansbury organised a deputation of 1,000 working women from Poplar to put their case to the prime minister, Arthur Balfour, for parliament to pass an Unemployment Relief Bill. Part of the deputation was led by Mrs Scurr, a brushmaker and later suffragist, and two guardians, Charlotte and Anne Cobden Sanderson. The three women addressed the women at Caxton Hall before their audience with the prime minister. The speakers were joined by Emmeline Pankhurst, who urged the audience to use the opportunity to demand the vote. As few of the women present would have been enfranchised by the WSPU Bill, this did not go down well.

Keir Hardie was an old friend of the Pankhursts (he is thought to have had an affair with Sylvia Pankhurst) and a strong supporter of suffragism. At his instigation the ILP had conducted a poll among women who paid municipal rates (under the 1884 Act a ratepayer was defined as anyone who paid rent in a household rated at £10 or more and who possessed his own key), and would thus be eligible to vote under the WSPU Bill. This found that of the 59,000 women interviewed 83 per cent might be regarded as working class, a result that was hotly disputed, with opponents saying that the sample was small and the criteria vague, but Hardie was undeterred, seeing this as a defence against the claim of elitism. For Charlotte, Hardie represented all the qualities she respected in the working man – his bluntness, his integrity, his ability to rise above circumstances, his 'feminine' capacity for indignation (Linklater p.106). For her, as for most of the country, he *was* the ILP and when he argued that the WSPU Bill was a first step, not even Margaret Bondfield could dissuade her. His intervention resolved all Charlotte's doubts. He emphasised the results of the poll and the time needed to achieve adult suffrage. Most importantly he stressed that the WSPU Bill enfranchised widows, many of whom were working class, simply because working men married earlier and died sooner than any other class. Charlotte remembered the widow with six children who had applied for relief and wrote in an article: 'There is no class of the community to whom the vote would be more precious, no class who deserve it more than these working-widows' (Linklater p.106).

By the summer of 1906 her doubts had been resolved and she was ready to give all her energy to the suffrage movement. In 1903 she had given up 95 Wandsworth Road and resigned from the Board of Guardians as she no longer had a residence in Lambeth. She served on the Wandsworth Poor Law Board for another year but this was an enlightened board which she decided did not need her. This had brought her into contact with the Tammany Hall kingdom of John Burns, which controlled Battersea Council and the Poor Law Board, whom she regarded as the great apostate. She had the highest admiration for his public libraries, bath and housing, but of the man she would say:

> Just for a handful of silver he left us,
> Just for a medal to hang on his breast.

His defection to the Liberals – in the hope of a Cabinet post – had split the Labour Party in Battersea, but it was made clear that his political machine, which commanded votes and jobs, had no place for idealists. As she was denied local work, Charlotte concentrated on the wider issue of the vote, seduced by the idea of women working for one another:

> I had found comradeship of some sort with men. I had marched with great processions of the unemployed, I had stood on platforms with Labour men and Socialists ... I had listened with sympathy to furious denunciations of the government and the Capitalistic system to which they belong. Amongst all these experiences, I had not found what I met on the threshold of this young, vigorous union of hearts.

She was a supporter of adult suffragism because seeking votes for women on the same terms as men related only to middle-class and wealthy women. Early in 1906 Annie Kenney and Teresa Bilington-Greig, both from Manchester, were sent to Currie Street to recruit Charlotte to the WSPU. Teresa knew that her interests lay in humanism and over lunch at the Eustace Miles café asked wouldn't she agree that:

> The most distressed, the most denied must be uplifted first – if the whole was to be uplifted. To secure full humanism, feminism must take priority for women reformers. To such men as could realise that the human race was dual, the other so-called humanist reforms had often only emphasised the subjection of women. I said, 'women the first!' Were they not the worst sufferers in her little corner at Nine Elms?

It did not take long to persuade her. Charlotte saw herself as revolutionary and even though the suffragettes were only doing what others – the Irish and the unemployed – had done, these were respectable women and she found the idea of their militancy exciting. Charlotte wrote:

> I confess there was something in this society which, from the beginning, appealed to me. The youth of many of the members; the fact that they had come together in womanly frankness and love, not for political ends, not to further the candidature of party men for public place and power, but for social and political ends which would affect themselves and the world; the dashing courage of the

little band, their selflessness, their quiet endurance of the results of their lawless action – these things attracted me. Sometimes I asked myself, 'Can this be the beginning? Is this indeed a part of that revolutionary movement for which all my life long I have been waiting?'

After the victory of the Liberal Party in January 1906 the WSPU transferred to London. In February Annie Kenney and Teresa Billington led a great march of working women from the East End to Westminster to mark the opening of parliament – this was a novelty and became front-page news in the popular press. Less attention was paid to the street corner meetings and similar events, but the press was there again in April when members of the WSPU demonstrated in the Ladies' Gallery of the House of Commons, interrupting the debate with shouts and a shower of leaflets. Some of the headlines referred to 'the shrieking sisterhood', others to 'female hooligans', and soon almost everyone was using the *Daily Mail's* name of 'suffragettes'.

In June Sylvia Pankhurst, the WSPU secretary, resigned to continue her art studies. Charlotte was appointed in her place and, because of the demands of her Nine Elms work, shared the role with Edith How-Martyn, the first woman to receive a Bachelor of Science degree. Shortly afterwards the two secretaries were bypassed, Teresa was sent to organise branches in Scotland and Annie to the West Country. When she arrived in London Christabel Pankhurst stayed with Emmeline and Frederick Pethick Lawrence in their flat at Clements Inn. The East End work diminished and weekly 'At Homes' began, so that interested women could meet Christabel at Clements Inn. Clearly these were aimed at middle-class women and Alice Milne, a Lancashire textile worker, was shocked at the ladies present:

We found the place full of fashionable ladies in rustling silks and satins ... It struck me then that if any of our Adult Suffrage Socialist friends could have looked into that room, he would have said more than ever that ours was a movement for the middle classes and upper classes. What a fever our Union members in Manchester would have been in, if such ladies made a descent on us in Manchester!

In October Christabel revealed the new direction for the WSPU. Instead of supporting the Labour candidate at an upcoming by-election in Cockermouth in Cumberland, the WSPU would be independent of all parties which did not support women's suffrage. This caused considerable concern. Even Charlotte, a fervent Labour supporter, thought the WSPU should be politically neutral and not engaging in party politics. A bias towards the Conservative candidate emerged in successive by-elections as the WSPU policy of putting pressure on the Liberal government became support for the Conservatives. In the spring of 1907 Charlotte was too slow to realise what was happening and did not notice the suspicions and jealousies beginning to divide the WSPU. Defying social convention was, for Charlotte, an important part of the WSPU and an essential part of that was imprisonment. In her eyes Christabel's imprisonment had given her a moral dominance – prison was a rite of initiation, and Charlotte was keen to be involved.

In October 1906 she was invited to take part in a demonstration in the House of Commons which meant a good chance of arrest and imprisonment. She was disappointed to be told on the day before the WSPU officers should avoid arrest. She did not try too hard and when police pulled Mary Gawthorpe, a tiny suffragette, off the bench from which she had tried to address visitors and MPs, Charlotte took her place. She was hauled down and all the women were cleared from the Lobby, past an inspector who called out the names of those he wanted arrested. 'Take Kenney, take Billington, take the two little Pankhursts,' he called. Charlotte left the Commons but was really disappointed later to learn that Emmeline Pethick Lawrence, the treasurer, and Edith How-Martyn, her co-secretary, had pushed their way back into the Lobby and been arrested.

This incident led to huge publicity – meaning a wave of recruits and a lot of work for Charlotte. Never good at office work, another secretary, Caroline Hodgson, was appointed to help her, but she still felt that she could have served the WSPU better by going to prison. While the militancy was criticised, Emmeline Pankhurst defended the action,

> they have done more during the last twelve months to bring it [the movement] within the realm of practical politics than we have been able to accomplish in the same number of years.

On 20 November Charlotte returned to the Commons to address an unauthorised meeting. As she hoped, the police arrested both her and her companion, Alice Milne, and took them to Cannon Row Police Station. Only Alice was charged, even though she had not spoken a word to the crowd. Charlotte returned to the Commons and made another speech, but by then it was evening and there were few people left to hear her. When Alice appeared before the magistrate he said that the police had clearly been acting under instructions in letting Charlotte go. Presumably the Home Secretary wished to avoid the publicity which would follow the arrest of someone widely known for her Nine Elms work, and as the sister of a Boer War hero. The suffragettes preferred to believe that the government feared a riot in Battersea, while the newspapers reported a rumour that John French had threatened to resign from the army if she appeared in court.

It seemed unlikely that Charlotte would get her wish and go to prison, but another chance presented itself at the opening of the new parliament in February 1907. When MPs were assembling to hear the government's programme for the year, a 'Women's Parliament' of about 400 women was meeting at Caxton Hall to be addressed by the leaders of the WSPU.

Speeches made the case for women's suffrage, punctuated by reports of events in parliament. When the last message reported that the king's speech had made no mention of enfranchisement, Emmeline Pankhurst proposed that a resolution condemning the omission should be delivered to the prime minister; 'Rise up, women,' she called. Charlotte strode down from the platform before anyone else could move and led the assembled crowd into the drizzle of a February afternoon. As they walked towards Westminster they started to sing the Women's Anthem (to the tune of John Brown's Body):

> Rise up women for the fight is hard and long,
> Rise in thousands singing loud a battle song.
> Right is might and in its strength we shall be strong
> And the cause goes marching on.

They arrived in a column four deep and the police tried to split them into small groups. The women avoided them and carried on towards the House of Commons, led by the determined Charlotte, who was camouflaging her appearance in a thick motor-veil which streamed out behind her. Flourishing her umbrella, she led the women into Palace Yard, walking straight into the police line, her followers pressing in around her. Mounted police tried to break them up. 'Something like pandemonium ensued,' reported the *Daily Mirror*. 'The women began to fight like tigers and they received and inflicted many bruises. Over the whole extent of Palace Yard a dense mass of people swayed and heaved.' The police had been told to avoid making arrests and for a time they tried to push the women back, but then the order was given to make arrests. Charlotte was almost seriously injured when a police horse trapped her against the lines of police on foot, then one of them seized her so violently that the sleeve of her coat was ripped off. She was taken to Cannon Row police station, formally charged and arrested. 'I am heartily glad to have done it at last,' she told reporters later. Her brother was distinctly cool. He was sorry for any injury she had suffered but '… if she insists in joining in with these people she must expect it. We have tried all we could to keep her from mixing up with these foolish women … They are all vain and some of them are a little mad I think.' When reporters asked if her arrest would provoke his resignation he replied 'What has it to do with me? I wish she wouldn't do these things but I can't prevent her.' Charlotte took this to be just his public manner, and on her release from prison wrote to congratulate him on his appointment as inspector-general.

On 14 February, having refused to pay the 40 shilling fine, she was taken with thirty-one others to begin her twenty-one days in Holloway in the second division (suffragettes had argued that they should be first division, or political prisoners). Her cell was 'dirty, dimly-lit … with a strange, sickening smell in it. It was stone-paved, and there was a narrow stone bench in one of the angles. Nothing else except a barred window high up in the wall.' There was a spyhole in the door and the prisoners were kept in solitary confinement apart from half an hour a day of communal exercise, when they were forbidden to talk. She was alone but there was no peace, with the sounds of keys, boots and the shouts of the wardresses. After a week she was unable to sleep or concentrate. She had taken three books with her – Shelley's *Collected Poems*, Mill's *The Subjection of Women* and Thomas à Kempis' *Imitation of Christ*. In the

Kempis she had marked herself a passage for guidance: 'For Thy life is our path, and by Holy Patience we walk unto Thee who art our crown.' She found prison irritating – as she did some of the prisoners. 'One may have too much patience,' she remarked, *'they* have.'

When she left prison in March, Charlotte no longer saw it as glamorous and the stature she had given to those who had been in prison was diminished. When other ILP members were concerned about the political direction the Pankhursts were taking, she now felt qualified to be involved. With Edith How-Martyn, Anne Cobden Sanderson and others, she said she would not engage in any activity which would damage Labour's interests and a message to this effect was sent to the ILP conference in April. They said they would support the party and would refuse to work in any by-election where a Labour candidate was standing. It was a mild statement but was taken as a serious challenge to Christabel Pankhurst's leadership.

The Pankhursts had tried for three years to persuade the ILP to support women's suffrage. When the message was read out at the ILP conference Emmeline, who was present, took it to be a pledge never to be at a by-election except to support a Labour candidate. She immediately came to her feet and said: 'We are not going to wait until the Labour Party can give us the vote. It is by putting pressure on the present government that we shall get it.' They resigned from the ILP and Christabel was soon in correspondence with Arthur Balfour, leader of the Conservative Party.

Charlotte and her colleagues tried to stop the move towards the Conservatives but found there was no way of influencing the Pankhursts. In the early days everyone's voice could be heard, but the WSPU had grown exponentially. The executive structure had not altered – the Pethick Lawrences controlled the administration and finance, and Christabel, as organising secretary, was responsible for tactics. Emmeline worked closely with Christabel and between the leaders and the membership was an invisible wall.

After Emmeline, the most popular person in the WSPU was Teresa Billington-Greig (who married in 1906 and added her husband's name to her own). She was a good speaker and excellent organiser – she had set up the largest branches, in Scotland and London. Before the WSPU moved to London she had suggested it should adopt a constitution based on the ILP's and, receiving no enthusiasm, drew up a constitution herself. At the October meeting to discuss the Lobby demonstration it had been accepted without question, but its significance had disappeared under the various events. Teresa and the ILP, not for the same reason, decided it should now be brought into operation. The WSPU had autonomous branches attached to a central headquarters and the constitution proposed adding an annual conference, to which branches could send delegates to approve broad policy and elect officers. The conference was due to take place in October 1907.

Charlotte and the other ILP members were reluctant to openly oppose the Pankhursts and so cautiously put their case to the branches. Their proposal that policy should be democratically decided was widely accepted. Teresa was busy recruiting in Scotland and after setting up new branches in almost every major city in July, she set up an elective semi-autonomous council to regulate activities.

The threat could not be ignored and Christabel wrote to Emmeline 'Teresa Billington is a wrecker … we have just to face her and put her in her place. She has gone too far this time.' It was not just Scotland – it soon became clear that the majority of branches intended to send delegates to the conference to question the WSPU's political leanings and perhaps to elect new officers. The triumvirate of the Pethick Lawrences and Christabel mounted a counter plot that it was the constitutionalists who wanted to divert the WSPU from its political neutrality. They suggested that other motives lay behind the declaration that Charlotte and friends had pledged to support only Labour candidates – to gain control of the WSPU, modify the policy of independence and change the methods of work. They were accused of spreading suspicion and disaffection. Emmeline was summoned back from speaking engagements in the north of England and, without hesitation, she decided to do away with the constitution. The Pankhursts were the WSPU and those who would not follow them were seceders.

At a committee meeting on 10 September Emmeline announced that the conference would not take place. The constitution had been annulled, she said, and a new committee would be elected by those present – herself, Emmeline Pethick Lawrence, the two secretaries Charlotte and Caroline Hodgson and five paid organisers. Charlotte was furious and demanded to know on whose authority the changes had been made. Emmeline replied that she was responsible; a new organisation, the National Women's Social and Political Union, had been formed and no one could serve on its committee unless they were in complete accord with her. She read out the names of the new committee, with a pledge they each had to sign: 'I endorse the objects and methods of the NWSPU and I hereby undertake not to support the candidate of any political party at Parliamentary elections until women have obtained the Parliamentary vote.'

As expected Charlotte refused to sign, and said she would wait until the pledge had been approved by the conference, but Caroline Hodgson did sign, undermining the fiction that they had seceded. That evening a meeting of the London members most loyal to the Pankhursts took place at Essex Hall. Emmeline spoke about the plots that had been hatched under the cover of the new constitution and dramatically held up a copy of the document. To shouts of approval and protest she tore it in two. A sense of rightness galvanised the constitutionalists: seventy of them gathered on 14 September to plan their strategy and resolved to follow the rejected constitution. To strengthen their claim to legitimacy they elected the secretary of the original WSPU to the chair of a new committee which would organise the conference, and thus ensured that Charlotte was at the head of the new movement.

The conference met as planned on 12 October, attended by delegates from a majority of branches. There was an angry demand that the Pankhursts should be sued for the return of funds, literature and offices which belonged to the WSPU. Charlotte showed her leadership, persuading the conference that the importance of their work should not be overshadowed by a desire for revenge, and the Pankhursts were left alone. Teresa Billington-Greig later wrote: 'There was little to be expected from a society that commenced its separate existence by making a free gift of the funds, name, prestige and achievements, which had been acquired by the efforts of all combined.'

Chapter 6

Dare to be Free

After the split in the WSPU in September 1907, the emergence of the new and distinct organisation, in which Charlotte was to play a leading role, was clouded in confusion while two national committees battled over which was the original WSPU and therefore should keep the name. A provisional committee including Charlotte, Teresa Billington-Greig and Edith How-Martyn claimed that they were the WSPU, saying they had adhered to the constitution, whereas those who cancelled the conference had acted unconstitutionally and were not qualified to speak for the WSPU membership. This may well have been true but other factors stopped the provisional committee assuming control of the WSPU, particularly the fact that the Pankhursts kept the offices in London's Lincoln's Inn and maintained control of the finances. The provisional committee had no permanent office and little money – they had only managed to stage the conference through strenuous efforts and generous donations. Charlotte guaranteed a year's rent and expenses amounting to £100 for their first headquarters at 18 Buckingham Street, but on the day after the split they had only two guineas in the bank and all their furniture had to be donated by members. Ten years later Marion Holmes said they began to almost live in Buckingham Street:

> What jolly 'scratch' teas we had on the bare office tables, and what startling plots and plans we hatched round them! Everyone took a willing hand in the cleaning and washing up, and it was no unusual thing to see Mrs Billington Greig or Miss Irene Miller, or some other favourite orator suddenly down her broom or tea-cloth and rush off with a belated memory of an expectant audience.

There was youth and excitement in the air as they began to reorganise – Charlotte, approaching 70, said 'I was older at twenty than I am now.'

There was press interest in the WSPU split. On 13 September the *Daily Chronicle* reported 'There is trouble in the suffrage camp ...' and recorded the attempts of Christabel to play it down. 'Please don't call it a split,' she said '... there has been no particular row ... it is more of a parting of company' – remarks in contrast to the antagonism which had surfaced, especially between her and Teresa Billington-Greig. The provisional committee tried to play down the extent of disagreements for the national press, to prevent any lasting damage to the suffrage campaign.

During September and October there was a furious exchange of letters between the two committees, with a move to encourage women to support one side or the other. In September 1907 Maud Arncliffe Sennett received letters from both Charlotte and Christabel asking her to speak at *their* WSPU meetings. Once the bitterness had died down they did cooperate, joining together for a meeting in Edinburgh. There were now two organisations calling themselves the WSPU – although some in the original WSPU started calling themselves the National Women's Social and Political Union – and there was a growing desire to end the conflict, which still attracted press attention.

In November the new committee decided it needed to choose a new name. Surprisingly none of the shortlisted options – Women Emancipators, Women's Enfranchisement League, Women's Association for Rights, Women's Freedom League – included any reference to suffrage. Teresa Billington-Greig implied later that the reason for the formation of the new organisation was motivated by a desire 'to make the militant movement what it ought to be', i.e., a movement to liberate women from all aspects of oppression. She claimed in later years that the source of her disagreement with Emmeline Pankhurst in 1907 was a difference of opinion over militant tactics, saying that the WSPU actions were not directed sufficiently towards institutions and practices that reinforced women's lack of equality, which was more important than internal democracy. She was strongly in favour of the name Women Emancipators and wrote in 1911:

No more potent explanation of what we hoped our rebellion might lead to can be quoted than this: when the name of the society came to be changed this little central group gave unanimous support to the title of 'The Emancipators', and the dreams we dreamed were as big as the title to which we aspired. (Billington-Greig, 1911)

Despite the apparent executive committee preference, the branches voted for Women's Freedom League. The new organisation's colours were green, white and gold; 'gold the earliest suffragette colour and colour of the dawn, white for purity of purpose, green for the promise of spring', its motto: 'Dare to be Free.' The telegram address was 'Tactics, London.'

The precise number of WSPU members who joined the WFL is unknown – Rosen estimates about 20 per cent, while Edith How-Martyn claimed over half the original WSPU joined the new organisation, which is high as the WFL seems to have begun with only twelve ex-WSPU branches. There was also a national branch for 'unattached' members. At the 13 October conference the democratic constitution was ratified and it was clear that the new organisation still saw itself as the official WSPU. A new national executive committee (NEC) of twelve was elected, with Charlotte as treasurer, Edith How-Martyn as secretary and Teresa Billington-Greig as organising secretary. It was decided not to create the post of president although this decision was reversed in 1909 and Charlotte was elected as the first president. Writing fifty years later Teresa Billington-Greig still had doubts that this was a good choice:

I suppose she was the best figurehead we had. Everyone loved and respected her – she was the sort of person who, though she could get very angry ... was incapable of doing anything mean or spiteful.

The problem with the choice of president was not her temper but the strengths of her character – her generosity, enthusiasm, idealism and intuition. She was so against the idea of authority that she refused to give a lead to a discussion or rule comments or irrelevancies as out of order. Debates would drag on until the original point was lost or she misunderstood a point of detail for a matter of principle, took a side and drew everyone else into the argument. When all was lost in confusion she would demand: 'Now what *is* the will of the committee? Surely this is a time for action not debate.' Every member of the committee threatened to resign at one time or another, none more so than Charlotte herself. She was not able to compromise on a principle or position that she felt was right, and the other members of the committee were repeatedly forced to back down rather than lose their president.

Stella Newsome, a member of the WFL, published *The Women's Freedom League 1907–1957* and explained the mission of the WFL:

> The policy was to secure for women the Parliamentary vote as it is, or may be, granted to men. Militancy was directed solely against the Government. Private property was never attacked and human life and property were always respected.

The question of exactly what was meant by 'militancy' was to be a matter of continuing debate.

After the split the priority was to develop the WFL's standing as a distinct national organisation and build up its strength outside London. The commitment to regional representation was shown by the opening of the Scottish headquarters of the WFL in Gordon Street, Glasgow, and later the election of a Scottish committee. The WFL was strong in Scotland, with about half the membership, because Teresa Billington had worked there for the WSPU and some branches followed her into the WFL. In many ways Scotland was ahead of England, including allowing widows guaranteed provision from their husbands' estates and allowing women graduates to be awarded degrees. In Scotland members tended to be linked with non-militant organisations. Charlotte said, on one of her frequent visits to Scotland, 'There is a special vitality, an unwavering sign of hope among the Scottish members.'

Teresa Billington-Greig was born in Lancashire and, with no qualifications, managed to get a job as an assistant teacher, going against authority when she refused to give the prescribed religious education to her pupils. She founded, and was first honorary secretary of, the Manchester branch of the Equal Pay League, the first feminist pressure group within the National Union of Teachers. Teresa joined the WSPU just after it was founded and in 1905 was asked by Emmeline Pankhurst and Keir Hardie to become a full-time organiser for the ILP – the second to be appointed and the first woman. In 1906 she became a paid organiser for the WSPU and in June that year led a deputation to Asquith's home, was arrested and sentenced to two months' imprisonment, although an anonymous donor paid her fine and she was released. Her status as the first suffragette prisoner in Holloway to become a member of the WFL was commemorated in June 1910 when she carried a special banner and walked at the head of the WFL Prisoners' section in the coronation procession. Teresa was voted chair of the first two conferences – Charlotte did not feel this was a role for her – but spent most of her time in Scotland, so members were more used to dealing with Charlotte, who shuffled across England and Wales, her life a succession of telegrams, railway journeys and speeches.

In the public mind there was still little to distinguish between the WSPU and WFL. The WFL wanted to change this and the conference on 1 February 1908 was the first display of the successful launch of the WFL as a democratic militant women's suffrage society. In her opening address Teresa Billington-Greig proclaimed:

I think we can congratulate ourselves upon having accomplished the real foundation work of our constitution, and organising and preparing ourselves to go forward into the militant suffrage campaign which cannot end except in success.

Wide-ranging discussions during the conference demonstrated the diversity of opinion of members and showed the beginning of the democratic organisation. Discussions considered the advocacy of militant policy, the principles of a women-only organisation, the question of absolute independence from political parties and the question of admitting men as full members. Views were firmly expressed that women had taken up the principle of separating their concerns and demands from those of men. Those opposing the motion argued that men brought party politics into every situation. Others argued that men should be allowed to help but women would be crowded out by men, especially married women, who would be disadvantaged because husbands would go to WFL meetings, forcing wives to stay at home. One delegate asked whether dual membership of the WFL and ILP was allowed. Teresa Billington-Greig, who by then had resigned from the ILP, stated that if women were also members of a party the only requirement was that they put the WFL first, although her comments were a direct contradiction to the WFL constitution which required strict party independence. Charlotte, perhaps recognising that a number of members still belonged to the ILP, as she did, argued

> ... we do not altogether call that a political party. You can be a member of the ILP without touching upon Parliamentary strife at all... As a member of the ILP I believe that you can keep your loyalties to both. You must not, of course, take part in any Parliamentary contests.

The issue of divided loyalties was a theme which ran through the WFL for decades.

At the 1908 conference the big debate was militancy – still a key issue for the WFL. Some were expressing reservations that militancy was no longer as successful at drawing attention to suffragette demands. Teresa Billington-Greig said actions could be 'as militant as you like, anything from Police Court protests to the blowing up of the Houses of Parliament'. In 1906, while in Holloway Prison, she had argued:

> To be shut out from the rights and privileges of law is to be an outlaw. An outlaw must be either a rebel or a willing serf. Anyone who believes in human liberty and self-government is forced to rebel. There is no other way. It is either servile submission to tyranny or rebellion against it.

This became enshrined in the constitution – the purpose of their actions was to demonstrate widespread refusal to be governed by instruments of male authority until women were granted equality. Until women were enfranchised they were outlaws, and thus justified in breaking laws which were instigated by men. It was agreed that militancy should continue to be part of the WFL's policy but there was a difficult discussion and it was pointed out that not all members could engage in militant actions, especially if they did not live in London, had family responsibilities or relied on paid employment. It was also agreed that members would not condemn any military action taken by the WSPU, in order to show a united front. It was clear that not all delegates had understood the implications of militancy – some branches closed because they were unhappy with the decisions.

With a policy of militancy without harm to people or property, Charlotte had an idea of making a run on the bank's gold reserves, as men had done to win the first Reform Bill. It would never have worked – women did not control enough capital to make an impact, and the supply of gold was far greater than it had been in 1832. The WFL staged protests in police courts in London and Glasgow about the lack of justice for women in man-made courts and began a policy of tax resistance – members were urged to resist paying income tax, property tax and inhabited house duty.

Tax resistance on the grounds of no tax without representation came from the Gandhi idea of 'satyagraha' – winning a political reform by changing the views of the authorities. Tax resistance was a useful method of civil disobedience or passive resistance for those who were unable or unwilling to take part in more contentious militant demonstrations, but it had limited impact because only single women were responsible for the payment of their own taxes. Charlotte helped to found the Women's Tax Resistance League (WTRL), which lasted five years, with more than 220 women taking part in tax refusal, with many others giving support through joining in public demonstrations, making donations and assisting individual resisters. Most of the women were from the middle classes, women who were wealthy or independent enough to be liable for taxation, including the very rich such as Charlotte, and heir to the Knight's Castile soap fortune, Dr Elizabeth Knight. Twenty-three of the resisters were doctors and there were a number of graduates. At one point the secretary of the WTRL estimated that there were more than 10,000 resisters – not all suffragettes, a large number were women who ignored or disliked having to buy a weekly stamp for their servants.

> For it's woman this, and woman that, and 'Woman go away!'
> But it's 'Share and share alike, ma'am!' when taxes are to pay;
> When the taxes are to pay, my friends, the taxes are to pay.
> Oh, it's 'Please to pay up promptly!' when taxes are to pay!
>
> From *Woman This and Woman That*, WSPU 1910

Direct taxation – imperial taxes – was resisted. These annual taxes fell into two categories: 1) property tax – inherited house duty and income tax, 2) taxes and licences on dogs, carriages and motor cars, male servants, armorial bearings, guns and game. Taxes to which no resistance was offered included local tax such as the Poor Law or water rates – propertied women had the municipal vote and so had some control over the expenditure of local councils. Including dog licences allowed many more women, including the less well off, to take part.

Tax resistance was a long process – possibly up to eighteen months. After various forms had been ignored the Inland Revenue would send a notice threatening distraint in ten days and the resister would make an official statement explaining their refusal to pay. Bailiffs could enter the home to seize goods of value to cover the amount owed plus costs or money seized from a bank or stocks and shares. It was inconsistent, sometimes because officials could see the legitimacy of a woman's position or supported women's suffrage, and there was some evidence of class discrimination. Wealthier Elizabeth Knight and less well-off working-class Emma Sproson were both taken to court for non-payment of dog licences, but Emma Sproson's actions prompted the severest reaction of the courts – she was imprisoned twice for six weeks in the third division and her dog was ordered to be shot. Miss Andrews of Ipswich was gaoled in first division for one week for non-payment of her dog licence, but little action was taken about Princess Duleep Singh's refusal to pay for licences for her eight dogs. It could also be very trivial and revealed the absurdities in the law. After months of resistance Clemence Housman was imprisoned for refusing to pay 'inhabited house duty'. The taxi to take her to Holloway Prison cost 4s 2d (21p), the amount of the original debt. Dr Alice Burns' husband lived in New Zealand but she was deemed to be living with him in a legal sense and he was liable for her income tax, but since he was outside British jurisdiction the money could not be claimed from him. WFL member Dr Wilks sued for the return of property distrained to cover her unpaid taxes. She won her case on the grounds that her husband was responsible for the debt, but as a poor schoolmaster earning a quarter of her income he was incapable of paying the tax and had been imprisoned. The case aroused a lot of anger. George Bernard Shaw explained that it was impossible for a husband to force his wife to disclose her income, and equally impossible for him to believe her if she told him. The anger and ridicule persuaded the Inland Revenue to drop the matter and Wilks was released from prison.

If no funds were available to clear the debt, tax resisters were imprisoned automatically. Resisters were advised to surrender small goods like jewellery to avoid the costs of transporting heavy goods – Miss Lelacheur of Henley-on-Thames avoided transport costs by surrendering a cow. Sales of goods at auction, or bailiffs barricading doors could attract publicity and the attention of people who perhaps were not usually involved in the suffrage cause and by 1912 tax resistance seemed to be having some impact. Reports of sales in *The Vote* recorded that tax officials 'invariably acted with the greatest kindness and courtesy' (*The Vote* 20 April 1912).

Charlotte was threatened with imprisonment in 1910 over non-payment of taxes – she had consistently refused to pay some or all of her taxes since 1905. Her sole liability was for house duty – even she could not prevent the trustees of her husband's settlements deducting tax at source (*The Vote* 2 March 1912 p.227). The periodic visits of the bailiffs to her properties made good propaganda. When the resisters' goods were taken for sale at auction suffragists/gettes would often purchase their goods to help resisters, and Charlotte's piano, frequently distrained, was sold and bought by friends and became a standing joke in the columns of *The Vote* (*The Vote* 11 May 1912).

The most well known of the tax resisters was Kate Harvey, partly because she was so determined, but also because her gardener, for whom she refused to buy national insurance stamps, was called Asquith, the same as the prime minister, which was a gift for the press. When a distraint warrant was issued against her in 1912, she barricaded her home against the bailiffs. After an eight-month siege they forced their way in with a crowbar, but with a defiant 'I would rather die first', she built a better barricade. A year later she was still refusing to pay and the bailiffs had to use a battering ram to enter her house. The courts decided to make an example of her and she was sent to prison for two months. She became a cause célèbre with mass meetings in Trafalgar Square and at Caxton Hall on her behalf. When her goods were to be sold the crowd was so hostile and the event so chaotic, the tax collector had to give up, losing £7 over the whole process.

Kate regularly featured in suffrage papers and the local press. During 1910 Kate held garden parties in support of the WFL in the beautiful grounds of her house, Brackenhill, and continued to do so when threatened, with guests scaling the fence or creeping through a hidden gateway. Events were held in the local Bell Inn public house in wet weather. One siege lasted eight months, during which 'vigilant watch and ward' was kept whenever she went out, often to meetings about tax resistance, and her watchers 'left the enemy no door or window by which he could enter peacefully'. Eventually the bailiffs lost patience, broke the locks on the garden gate with a crowbar and proceeded to seize silver. The following year the summonses were repeated and the bailiffs again broke in, although this time they had to use a battering ram. One of the sieges led to a rhyme in general circulation:

> Brackenhill Siege will bring good cheer
> To those who hold freedom dear,
> And fight the good fight
> Far and near.

Kate Harvey, who was deaf, was born Felicia Catherine Glanvill in south-east-London. Little is known about her early life, except that her father was a clerk in the London Investment Company and her parents were comfortably off. Kate married Frank Harvey, member of a very prestigious firm of cotton merchants based in London and Madras, India. Kate visited India and was said to have impressed people with her medical abilities. They set up their family home in Kent and had three daughters – Marjorie, Phyllis and Rita. Before he died in 1905, Frank established settlements which left Kate and the children comfortably off for life.

Kate became a suffragist, attending local meetings of the Bromley branch of the National Society for Women's Suffrage, becoming area secretary by the first AGM. The branch did not last many years but activities started again with a branch of the NUWSS. By this time Kate had moved into Brackenhill in Bromley. Although she had no formal qualifications she described herself as a physiotherapist, a brave thing to do when physiotherapy was thought to be a euphemism for sexual activities. In response to the 'Massage Scandals of 1894', four nurses established The Society of Trained Masseuses, which later became the Chartered Society of Physiotherapy, to show that it was a legitimate medical profession. Brackenhill became a home for disabled children and she used her therapy skills with them and fed them on a vegetarian diet. Many of the children came from the East End of London and were funded by Charlotte; Kate met Charlotte while both were working with the poor of Nine Elms. Their friendship became very intense; they were both involved with the suffrage movement and Charlotte found comfort through Kate and her children. They celebrated the day they met, 12 January 1912, as 'the anniversary of our love'. Charlotte came to depend on, and perhaps use, Kate. According to Woodford,

> ... this deaf physiotherapist acted as press secretary for Charlotte, as well as attending demonstrations with her. On one occasion she held Charlotte round the waist while another lady (Rosalie Mansell) fought off the police who were trying to arrest her. They managed to escape in a taxi. It was Charlotte's vision of a spiritual crusade in which 'liberated women would liberate the world' that attracted this formidable combination of energy and efficiency that was Kate Harvey.

Kate accompanied Charlotte to various meetings, including those of the Theosophical Society and she organised Charlotte's activities, arranging speaking tours, the cars to railway stations, her correspondence and the Battersea accounts. In 1913 Charlotte, Kate and her three children had a holiday in Switzerland, which was much enjoyed. When Charlotte was ill in 1914 Kate nursed her at Brackenhill.

It is not clear whether Kate was born deaf or lost her hearing later. Despite her very full and public life, Kate appears never to have made a speech or been part of any discussion. She seems to have communicated using fingerspelling, a form of sign language. In 1914 the editor of *The British Deaf Times* reported 'There are deaf preachers, painters – even deaf potentates – and now we have a deaf suffragette!'

There were several newspaper reports of the sale of Kate's goods and it was from one of these (unknown) that the Editor of *The British Deaf Times* made his claim about the deaf suffragette. His article continues:

Mrs Kate Harvey … has earned some publicity by her refusal to pay the taxes as a protest against the withholding of the vote from her sex. On the 29th of November the authorities forced an entry to her house by bursting open a door, and the auction sale was announced for 3.30. A large number of suffragettes were present, and it was soon evident that determined opposition would be made. The proceedings partook of the character of burlesque – even farce – in fact, when it was over, people wondered whether a sale had taken place or not.

A rostrum had been improvised by placing a chair on a table in the dining-room, and upon this stood the tax-collector, who acted as his own auctioneer. The first article put up was a sideboard, and on the auctioneer calling for a bid, speeches in opposition were made, which delayed the proceedings for a time. At length, however, a bid was made, one penny!

This was followed by laughter, things went from bad to worse and after he had made nine guineas the auctioneer declared the sale closed. The sideboard stayed where it was but the tax collector would not give up his money.

Unfortunately during this comic-opera sale, some person went off with Mrs Harvey's pocket electrophone from the top of a cabinet in the sale room. As this instrument was the sole means of Mrs Harvey hearing anything whatever, it is hoped that it will be returned to her.

At the first of her trials Kate had said that 'she was only doing what every businessman would do, refusing to pay for goods she could not choose.' Then she was fined £1 for each of ten counts with costs and special fees, amounting to £16 17s. She was later tried again for refusing to pay the fines and was ordered to pay the taxes and fines, which now amounted to £22 11s, or go to prison for two months. As a result of this trial meetings of the WTRL and the WFL (Kate belonged to both) were held every Monday and Wednesday evening in the market square in Bromley.

There were increasing protests from members of the public and MPs about the treatment of suffragette prisoners in Holloway so the authorities waited until parliament was prorogued (the session was discontinued) before carrying out Kate's sentence, and did not arrest her until nearly two months after sentencing. On 1 September she went to Holloway. She was a sick woman and was placed in a prison hospital cell which was scrubbed daily, but the boards were left damp every day and so she became really ill. She requested, but was refused, her regular homeopathic medical attendant. This, with the treatment given to an older, deaf woman, infuriated her local friends and the suffragette movement as a whole.

The national papers published more about the activities of the militant suffragettes, who were burning down railway stations and private properties, ignoring the peaceful protesters like Kate, although the prime minister did say in a speech in 1913, 'though the militants were most in public view, the non-militants … continued an industrious and very possibly effective propaganda.' (*The Annual Register* 1913 p.193.) Suffragette papers tended to publish photographs and reports of the wealthy and well-known, but did not overlook others, there were poster campaigns, rallies and protest meetings on Kate's behalf. One report read:

> Under the auspices of The Women's Freedom League, a demonstration was held in Trafalgar Square on Saturday to protest against the sentence of 2 months imprisonment which Mrs Harvey is undergoing … Mrs Despard said the sentence was a vindictive one and was imposed because Mrs Harvey was a woman, a suffragette and a rebel.
>
> (*The Daily News* 15 September 1913)

Her fine was paid by Bromley residents. Kate had served only half her sentence, but was so weak she had to be carried into Brackenhill. She continued to suffer from rheumatic chills and gastric catarrh. Charlotte wrote in her diary about Kate's release: 'Then at last the dear face, it seemed changed, she has suffered cruelly … I was so glad it was all over.'

Women used historical pageants to draw attention to prominent women through the ages as part of the suffrage campaign. Kate helped stage a local pageant and later was responsible for one staged at the Chelsea Town Hall, acclaimed as 'perhaps the most important ever held by the Women's Freedom League, or indeed the Suffrage Movement.' (*Just Suffrage*,15 December 1912 p.35.)

In June 1913 Kate and Charlotte were delegates at the seventh congress of the International Women's Suffrage Alliance in Budapest. Kate sold copies of *The Vote*, of which she was now the Press Officer, to members of the 800-strong delegation. They visited schools, crèches and clinics and Kate reported on their visit in an article in *The Vote*.

Like Charlotte, Kate was a writer. Her plays included *Baby*, performed by the Pioneer Players in 1911, and dramatic versions of Longfellow's *Hiawatha* and *Courage* (1914). In 2005 Bonham's sold a medal inscribed: 'Given to Mrs K Harvey By Women's Suffrage After She Had Been In Prison For Tax Resistance'. With it was a newspaper reporting 'the eagerly expected performance of Mrs Harvey's dramatic version of Longfellow's Hiawatha ... a splendid welcome for Mrs Harvey, who appeared in public for the first time since her imprisonment and subsequent illness.'

When war broke out in 1914 suffragettes were divided over whether or not their activities should continue – Kate thought they should stop. In March 1915 the *Bromley and Beckenham Journal* reported that two ladies were holding a concert 'in aid of the estimable work being carried out at Brackenhill Hospital':

Mrs Harvey has given up her entire house for the purpose of a hospital not for wounded soldiers, but for the benefit of those poor women and children who, owing to the great use of the regular hospitals for the wounded, are unable to gain admission to those hospitals, or have to be discharged long before their time.

Kate did not work in the thirty-one-bed hospital herself but lent the house and paid for the fitting out, the garden work and many of the other expenses. Special provision was made for children and maternity cases, and French and Belgian referees were accommodated. Support came from many, including suffragette friends, and medical staff in nearby hospitals praised the high standards of care.

In 1916 Charlotte bought a property in Hartfield, Sussex, with a contribution from Kate. It seems to have been intended as a holiday home and there is little information, except that it was situated in 12 acres and in a quiet and pleasant setting near Gallypot Wood, according to Charlotte's diary. They named the property Kurundai (a sacred Indian tree) and initially made frequent visits, but their relationship was changing. Kate seems to have concentrated all her affection and energy on Charlotte and to have had few other close friends. Charlotte continued to be very active, despite her years, and resisted all attempts from Kate to make her slow down. At this time Charlotte had a very difficult ward, named Vere, and they disagreed on the most suitable way to deal with her behaviour. Their joint activities became fewer, and by 1921 Charlotte had made over her share of Kurundai to Kate, although she still visited frequently, using a room kept permanently for her, and Kate cooked her vegetarian meals. By 1921 Kate had sold Brackenhill and started another school in Hartfield. Charlotte moved to Ireland and when she was presented with a Roll of Honour aged 91, Kate was one of the first subscribers. Charlotte continued to attend some of Kate's educational activities. At the end of June 1929 an international fair was held, organised by the staff of Brackenhill open-air school, with Charlotte presiding.

Kate died in 1946, aged 83. Very little notice was taken of her death in the press, but the official paper of the WFL, *The Women's Bulletin*, reported:

> Another pioneer member, Mrs Kate Harvey, has passed away. Mrs Harvey was an early member and supporter of The Women's Freedom League. She worked a great deal with Mrs Despard in Nine Elms, and in close cooperation with her in The Women's Freedom League.

When parliament opened in February 1908, in a change from large-scale demonstrations, small groups of women picketed the homes of Cabinet ministers to remind them that women's suffrage had been omitted from the king's speech. Ten women were arrested and sentenced to six weeks in prison in the third division, reserved for prisoners of 'undesirable character', a really harsh punishment for a peaceful protest. In recognition, the WFL established its own Victoria Cross for extreme bravery and at the WFL conference Charlotte led the delegates in a minute's silence to honour the women.

Herbert Asquith became prime minister in April 1908. He was particularly hostile to giving women the vote and wrote: 'Women played very little part in my life,' although he enjoyed female company. In 1892 he had written that most women had no interest in getting the vote and were just 'watching with languid and imperturbable indifference the struggle for their own emancipation.' He returned to this theme often. In 1907 he said he would lift his opposition, 'the moment that I am satisfied of two things, but not before, namely, first, that the majority of women desire to have a parliamentary vote, and next, that the conferring of a vote upon them would be advantageous to their sex and the community at large,' (Rosen p.98). In January 1908 he told a deputation from the NUWSS that not only did they have to convince the majority of women, they also had to convince the majority of men, for an election to be fought on the issue, and to exercise patience. In February, a women's suffrage Bill was introduced and won a majority of 179. Women waiting outside to hear the results cheered and demanded that the government should enable the Bill to become law during that session of parliament. That was spring 1908.

When Muriel Matters arrived in London from Australia she hoped to be an actress, but had to find work as a journalist. She was particularly inspired by Charlotte Despard and joined her in 1907 in the breakaway WFL. Marion Holmes wrote:

It was in the very earliest days of the Women's Freedom League that Muriel Matters cast in her lot with us. She made her first speech at one of the 'At Homes' held in the offices in Buckingham Street, and I remember how eagerly we discussed her afterwards. Who was she? She had told us in her speech that she was an Australian, but for the rest we knew nothing. Then, in the usual cold-blooded fashion of NEC members we debated how we could best use her gifts – her enthusiasm, her eloquence, her wonderful magical voice – for the cause.

(*The Vote* Concerning Muriel Matters 19 Feb 1910)

Asquith had said that the majority of women needed to be convinced, so it was decided that the best way to do this was to set off in a horse-drawn caravan. Oxshott Heath in Surrey was a popular place for horse-drawn vans, and caravans were a regular sight from Charlotte's cottage. Charlotte obtained a caravan, gave it a smart suffrage makeover and provided furniture. Others donated a camp bedstead, lunch basket, kettle and maps (Liddington 2014). Charlotte wrote to a friend:

> A little note hastily at the end of an exciting day to say that I hope you will come to us on the 16th, when we are sending off the Women's Suffrage Caravan on its travels … as the times have been pretty exciting lately, there will be plenty to talk about.

Her excitement was caused by a recent joint tour of Wales with Millicent Fawcett. Wales was Liberal country with no support for suffragettes. They were shouted down in Cardiff, pelted in Swansea and in Pontypridd an angry mob burst into the theatre where their meeting was in progress. Audience and speakers retreated to the stage and hid behind the heavy curtains and Charlotte gave her speech in a hoarse whisper to the small frightened audience. Luckily Charlotte seemed to thrive on that kind of excitement.

On Saturday 16 May 1908 a small crowd of WFL supporters gathered at her cottage,

> … to witness the departure of the first Women's Suffrage Van on its journey … Before starting, everyone was allowed to explore the inside of the Van, which is most conveniently fitted up for the comfort of the pioneers.

(*Women's Franchise* 21 May 1908)

Charlotte and Muriel, Teresa Billington-Greig, and van organising-secretary Lilian Hicks, made short speeches, then it was time to go.

Some amusement was caused by the persistent refusal of the Van to go through the gateway of Mrs Despard's garden. This was attributed to the fact of one of the horses being nick-named 'Asquith'. So, naturally, he would feel a reluctance to advance the cause of Women's Suffrage. However the gate was lifted off its hinges, the Van got through, amidst enthusiastic cheers, and made its first official appearance on the King's highway.

(*Women's Franchise* 21 May 1908)

On Sunday 21 June 1908 the WSPU's demonstration in Hyde Park had a crowd of perhaps 250,000. The previous Saturday the NUWSS procession was a real spectacle, each contingent having beautifully embroidered banners. The WFL, the only militant society invited to join, was led by Charlotte.

For five months the van plodded through Surrey, Sussex and Kent, to a mixed reception. Margaret Nevinson wrote: 'We were greeted in these rural districts with a hostility and violence quite terrifying to the uninitiated. Yelling, shouting and musical instruments drowned our arguments; rotten eggs, fruit and vegetables ruined our frocks – obscenity unspeakable offended our ears.' The hostility they encountered, even in areas where there had been no militant suffragette activity, suggested that the young men were angered by the mere suggestion of equality for women. In August Charlotte rejoined the van, visiting seaside towns like Hastings. 'I am more and more convinced,' she wrote, that this is one of the best and least expensive ways of propagandum, and I hope we shall have several such caravans as this moving about the country,' *(Women's Franchise* 27 August 1908). When Charlotte took the van into the market square in Maidstone for a meeting in October, she was pelted by stones hurled by youths and one hit her on the forehead. With blood running down her face, she stood on a chair so they could see and hear her better There was a fresh shower of stones and the crowd surged forward, knocking her to the ground and smashing up the chair. She was helped to her feet and bravely climbed onto the caravan to speak again, but the caravan was attacked by people who hammered on its sides and tore off the tailboard. She finally admitted defeat and retreated inside, when the caravan was bombarded by rocks and pieces of granite. With amazing courage the women always returned the next day to places where they had encountered violence and usually discovered, as Charlotte did in Maidstone, that their audience was now subdued and gave their attention. In Sevenoaks she was pelted with clods of earth and fireworks, but the following day she was listened to quietly.

The vanning continued in the summer of 1909, with the WFL acquiring a second van. One travelled through East Anglia and the other left Hampton Court and went towards Salisbury. The NUWSS and the WSPU also used a caravan. In 1910 the WFL van went to Bedford, Buckinghamshire, and east to Felixstowe. Charlotte was proud of the vans – not just propaganda vehicles, but symbols of women's freedom.

In October 1908 the WFL captured the headlines in national newspapers with a night-time bill-posting campaign, when copies of the WFL's *Proclamation* were stuck onto hundreds of public buildings in London, Scotland and the provinces, including the wall of New Scotland Yard. One newspaper commented: 'Nothing could have exceeded the adroitness'. On 28 October 1908, WFL members Muriel Matters and Helen Fox chained themselves to the grille that separated the Ladies Gallery from the chamber of the House of Commons and attempted to address MPs. Simultaneous protests near St Stephens Hall led to the arrest of fourteen members. During 1908, twenty-nine WFL members were imprisoned.

The WFL had very little money. The responsibility for acquiring funds fell mainly on the treasurer – Charlotte, until she was elected president in 1909, then Sarah Bennett. Although the finances improved they were never as good as those of the WSPU or NUWSS and several times they had to rely on loans from members. Like the WSPU, the WFL was keen to open premises as shops and offices, to provide information, sell merchandise and have an on-street presence, although when windows were smashed and property damaged, this also left them open to retaliation. On 1 December 1909 the WFL shop opened at 302 Sauchiehall Street, Glasgow. It was described in *The Vote*: 'The centre is decorated throughout in colours of the League, white predominating.' (9 December). The hall served as tea room, meeting place and showroom for women artists' work. There was also an Artistic Goods Department where scarfs, ties, sashes, belts, blouses, buckles, hat-pins and pendants in the colours of the League were on sale.

After Dr Elizabeth Knight became treasurer in 1912 finances improved, through her own private income and the fundraising initiatives she started, which included, from 1913, the president's birthday fund to mark Charlotte's birthday, when branches and individuals were asked to donate. It was clear that many members of the WFL were not wealthy and so they needed to attract more supporters – from 1908 resources were channelled into organisers, and from October 1909 into the newspaper.

The Vote appeared in October 1909 following on from other suffrage newspapers – *Women's Franchise, Common Cause* (NUWSS) and *Votes for Women* (WSPU). Calls for a WFL newspaper increased after the success of *Votes for Women*, first published in October 1907, which became a weekly paper the following April. *The Vote* joined a long tradition of political journalism and woman-centred writing which emerged during the nineteenth century with the publication of journals directed specifically at women. Funding was discussed by the WFL NEC in May 1909 and it was decided to form a public limited company, with Marie Lawson as managing director. The Minerva Publishing Company offered shares to WFL members and received pledges for 2,570 shares, valued at £642, but by September 1909 only £108 had been received. The NEC, which already owned a large number of shares, faced the responsibility of providing most of the financial backing. Charlotte became the editor of *The Vote* in March 1911, replacing Mary Olivia Kennedy who resigned owing to 'pressure of private work', and worked closely with assistant editor Annie Smith, appointed in June 1911. *The Vote* was intended to appeal to women interested in enfranchisement, but clearly this was not the sole aim of the paper. Charlotte wrote in the first edition,

> ... we hope and believe that through its pages the public will come to understand what the Parliamentary Franchise means to us women. Now it will be both a symbol of citizenship and the key to a door opening out on such service to the community as we have never yet been allowed to render, and therefore it is our earnest hope that our paper will keep its place in the hearts of men and women long after the first victory has been won.

The Vote played a crucial part in the development of the WFL, providing an opportunity for readers to develop and share ideas and concerns.

Contributors were mainly from the WFL leadership and a number of male journalists.

Charlotte's comments marked the first public reference to a concern with the broader aims of the WFL and visions of a long-term future for the organisation. Its circulation was disappointing though, and the limited response to the offer of shares in the publishing company meant severe difficulties almost immediately. There was confusion over editorial policy and later outright complaints that it did not reflect the spirit of the League. Two months after the launch, Marie Lawson wrote to the NEC suggesting all editing should be done by the company editor, the WFL should contribute £2 a week to costs and should take 10,000 copies weekly. She also suggested the WFL should allow the company to quote for all printing requirements. The NEC turned down all suggestions except to contribute to costs and agreed to take only 1,000 copies, later increased to 2,000 – even this overestimated demand in London. After the early problems the NEC took more direct control, especially after Charlotte became editor. Writing for the first time in the new paper Charlotte said:

> We know that we can bring pressure to bear on the Government of 1910, and we must make it fear us ... it may well be that those in power may conciliate the women before they engage in another battle.

After strenuous appeals sales slowly increased and by December 1910, issues 53 to 59 sold in total 8,450 copies nationwide. It never rivalled *Common Cause* or *Votes for Women* (in April 1908 the circulation of *Votes for Women* was 5,000 per week), but generally WFL members did recognise the importance of their own paper in keeping members informed and generating a sense of a united organisation. Some branches were not happy with the paper, with the Manchester branch claiming it was 'useless for propaganda purposes' (NEC minutes 25 July 1910 p.226). *The Vote* was faithfully published during the war and every week through the 1920s and focused on issues deemed of interest to women. National treasurer Elizabeth Knight continued to make generous contributions which kept it afloat.

When parliament opened in January 1909 Charlotte led a deliberately small deputation to Downing Street to present the annual protest to the prime minister about the omission of the vote from the king's speech. Some of the women were arrested on the spot, and Charlotte followed them when she tried to take the group to see Asquith at the House of Commons. As she pointed out at her trial, publicity was not her aim:

> Had I wished to create anything in the nature of a riot, I could have done so, but as a matter of principle I tried in every way to keep my intention quiet. I am an old woman ... I simply wished to see the Prime Minister, and for this I was arrested.

Charlotte was then 64 and white haired and when she was sentenced to a month in the second division there was an uproar that continued until the court was cleared of protestors. One male spectator wrote:

> The deeply furrowed face, and the flashing, undimmed eye are photographed on my soul and I am moved to tears, but this court knows no compassion. Are we, who have not done for humanity a tithe of what she has accomplished, to enjoy our liberty ... while this freedom-loving spirit, this saint of God, is cooped up in a common gaol?

This was not untypical – her appearance tended to provoke a reaction. When she arrived in prison Emmeline Pethick Lawrence was in hospital, a casualty of a WSPU demonstration:

> I was thrilled to see that stately and commanding figure enter the ward, looking, if possible, more dignified than ever in the quaint uniform of a criminal. Her first act was a calm refusal to take the medicine which the doctor prescribed. 'I have never taken medicine in my life – I do not propose to begin now.' Her word was immediately taken as law. All the officers seemed in awe of her.

After five days the authorities discharged their difficult prisoner, on the grounds of ill health. She said 'as a matter of fact I was never better in my life', and that the rest had done her good. When she was released, early on a snowy morning in March, while waiting for a tram she saw a group of destitute old women under the arches and gave them all the money in her purse. With no money she had to walk two miles home through the snow and became ill with congestion of the lungs.

In 1909 patience with the government was wearing thin. It was clear that the impact of militant protest was declining and new actions were planned to emphasise the failure of government. Delegates from forty branches met at the annual conference in London and there were indications that the secretly planned and sporadic activities in London were not meeting the needs of the growing membership, although meetings with speakers such as Charlotte or Teresa Billington-Greig were always popular events in the branches. In June the WSPU decided to exercise the old right, given to all subjects, to petition the monarch through the prime minister and on 29 June a demonstration accompanied the petition into Parliament Square. Many women were hurt and 132 arrested. Later that day thirteen women began breaking windows in Whitehall in an outburst of anger. During the summer the WFL hatched a plan to saturate the area around Westminster with meetings, mainly where the unemployed would wait in the hope of work.

In the three weeks to 1 July they conducted 243 meetings around Westminster. That night they decided to send deputations to the Commons to protest against the prime minister's failure to receive the petition. The House was sitting late to discuss the budget, so a rota of women was set up to make sure they caught Asquith when he left the building. When they failed to catch him at any of the exits they returned the next day and the next and continued their vigil until parliament went into recess on 28 October. Their extraordinary patience attracted press interest and the peaceful picket was admired by many. The protest was unsuccessful and WFL members' impatience spilled over into disturbances and arrests – when the women failed to meet Asquith at the Commons they went to Downing Street and he had them arrested. Charlotte was also arrested but released when someone anonymously paid her fine. She wrote in a letter to *The Times*:

We wish the public would try to understand what this means. Women, politically unrepresented, have only one constitutional right, that of petition. This right is being denied by the head of the

Liberal Government who would rather send women to jail than treat them with ordinary courtesy.

In July Marion Dunlop of the WSPU had been imprisoned for the minor offence of posting proclamations and went on hunger strike to protest against being imprisoned in the second division rather than the first division, as a political prisoner. Others followed suit and in September, concerned about the effect of a suffragette dying in prison, the government authorised the use of force feeding.

The disappointments for the WFL in 1909 culminated in an attempt to destroy ballot papers in the Bermondsey by-election. On 28 October a letter was sent to Asquith informing him that as he would not receive a deputation, the WFL intended to 'invalidate a by-election by destroying ballot papers.' Two WFL members, Alison Neilans and Alice Chapin, entered the polling booths and used a chemical solution in the ballot boxes to burn the papers inside. Unfortunately some of the solution splashed into an official's eye and someone attempted to wash it out using ammonia, causing him agony. All attention was focused on this – the impact was profound, with the press coverage condemnatory and exaggerated. The *Pall Mall Gazette* on 28 October 1909 described it as an 'outrage unparalleled in English history'. Even though they argued that their solution was harmless, that their hands had been soaked in it with no ill-effects, Alison and Alice were found guilty of interfering with a ballot box and common assault and sentenced to three and four months third division imprisonment respectively. At her trial Alison Neilans said:

> If I have to go to prison as a criminal, then I am obliged to resist – perfectly peacefully – and that will mean forcible feeding, stomach tubes and other barbarous tortures inflicted by those in authority. Look at me. I am now strong, in two or three weeks I shall be a physical wreck.

To make matters worse, the chemical solution had not been strong enough to destroy the ballot papers and the by-election went ahead. This incident showed the antagonism of both press and public to militancy and strains in cooperation between the constitutional and militant sections of the movement. *The Times* reported that the WFL Burton branch had severed connections and decided to affiliate to the NUWSS because of Bermondsey. Although delegates at the next annual conference supported the action, a note of caution registered that future militant protests should not involve the risk of personal injury to others.

The atmosphere was tense, stones were hurled through windows, cabinet ministers jeered at, and Asquith assaulted. When it was known that two members of the WFL had been practising with revolvers at a shooting gallery, the threat of assassination led the government, in October 1909, to establish the Special Branch, to gather information on subversive groups like the militant suffragettes.

The ballot box incident gave the WFL a distinct identity which was 'firmly directed to the concept of a revolt of women against the barriers to their equality' (Eustance p.162), but this appeared not to be what the membership wanted and the number of militant protests declined. There was enough support for a number of spirited anti-government campaigns during the January 1910 election, causing difficulties for Churchill and Asquith particularly, as the suffragettes poured their energy into the election campaign. The WFL fought eighteen constituencies and, unlike the WSPU who opposed only Liberals, took care to campaign against anti-suffrage Conservatives too. The picketing and hunger strikes had clearly led to an increase in support. Returning from a tour of Liberal constituencies in Scotland, Charlotte wrote to an old friend: 'I have not been able to rest much – our work is so strenuous, fields white to the harvest and labourers few.'

In the four days before election day, Charlotte fitted in six major speeches and many smaller engagements in Liverpool and Birmingham, before returning to London to speak against John Burns in Battersea. The result was more than she dared hope for – in the new parliament the Liberals held just 275 seats, only two more than the Conservatives, and they were dependent for their majority on the support of eighty-two Irish MPs. Making a speech in Trafalgar Square Charlotte said:

Never perhaps in all history has there been so dramatic an illustration of the Nemesis which falls upon the perpetrators of injustice when the cup of their iniquity is full.

The suffrage organisations would have been sure that success was just around the corner, but we know now that it was to take many more years.

It became clear that without militant activities it was much harder to attract publicity and donations. The WFL continued to advocate passive resistance and much of its energy was devoted to supporting and encouraging tax resistance, but the difficulties caused by the differences of opinion within the WFL surfaced at the annual conference in January 1910. The outcome was a vote in favour of continuing to pursue a militant policy, but not to injure persons or private property. An amendment was added which required the NEC to 'initiate no undertaking involving risk of personal injury to bystanders.' The clear view was that delegates did not want another protest similar to the one in Bermondsey, despite Billington-Greig's message to the conference that the protest, which she had first suggested, had been a political act, and that in order to continue to be militant the WFL needed to be progressive. 'If you have continuous repetition, it becomes habit,' she argued (Eustance p.163).

The year 1910 also saw a diversification in WFL branch activities with meetings for specific groups – students or mothers and babies – a wider range of topics considered, e.g. food reform and the development of social networks with fundraising social events – described by one branch as mixing 'propaganda with pleasure'. Some branches chose theatre as a means to challenge inequalities, particularly successful performances of Cicely Hamilton's *A Pageant of Great Women*. Cicely Hamilton was a member of the WFL and the Women's Writers Suffrage League. *A Pageant of Great Women* was directed by Edith Craig and first produced at the Scala Theatre in London on 10 November 1909. The play complemented and enforced the WFL's basic claim that it was unjust and illegal to exclude women from citizenship. After success in London, Cicely offered to lend the props and costumes to any branch which wanted to perform the pageant, which a number did. Performances in Sheffield, Ipswich, Middlesbrough, Sunderland and Sussex filled the void in press attention and local interest which had developed in 1910 after the declaration of a truce. In Swansea the performance earned the grudging respect of the reporter from the Tory *South Wales Daily Post* who wrote '… mere man can and does admire the important part that woman has played in the world's history…'. He added that, '… the wisdom of giving votes to women is perhaps another matter.' (*South Wales Daily Post* 6 May 1910 p.5.)

Peaceful protests during 1910 in London included a John Stuart Mill procession on his birthday, 21 May 1910, ending with a wreath-laying ceremony by his statue in Temple Gardens. Reports of the event contained references to Mill's work around women's rights and the WFL campaign to continue what he began in 1867. This was hailed as a success and became an annual event for the WFL. Across the suffrage movement there was a sense of impending success and, especially for the WFL, this helped to stave off immediate problems regarding militancy because many believed it would not be necessary to resort to these tactics again. In June 1910 attention turned to preparations for the WSPU 'From prison to citizenship' procession. Hundreds of WFL members travelled to London and marched behind divisions – including graduates, nurses, cyclists, athletes, civil servants, pharmacists, shop assistants, factory workers, East End sweated workers, teachers – displaying the WFL colours of green, white and gold. There was also an international section, a section for prisoners and picketers, a Jiu Jitsu section and at the rear, a special detachment of motor vehicles for those members unable to walk the whole distance. This marked a change to public and collective demands – previously, secrecy had often shrouded militant protests. Although there was an outward display of unity between the WSPU, NUWSS and WFL, differences in military policy continued. There was no clear agreement between the leaderships on when or if to recommence active militancy. In November 1910, this highly volatile situation was ruptured by the decision of the WSPU to stage a militant protest outside the Houses of Parliament.

Aware of continuing debates in parliament on the Conciliation Bill, the WFL exerted political pressure in another direction – resistance to the census of April 1911, a proposal first outlined by Laurence Housman and an idea that was particularly attractive for Charlotte. The 1910 Census Act was public, but not the government's detailed plans. With a desire to obtain information which would enable the government to tackle health inequalities, 'State for each Married Woman entered on this Schedule', included questions on the number of children born alive to the present marriage, the number still living and the number who had died. The census schedule was to be completed by the 'Head of Family', usually the husband (or father or brother). Women were deprived of a voice – their experiences of childbirth were to be recorded for them by the 'Head of Family'. Data would also be sought about women's employment as the government was concerned about the effect of employment on women's fertility. Suffragettes had feared that future laws might limit women's economic freedom, particularly the right to earn a living. With the census in six months' time, Laurence Housman drew up a scheme for organised resistance 'and offered it first to the WSPU, which rejected it, then to the Women's Freedom League, who had already, I found, started a similar scheme of their own. So with them I worked.' (Housman *Unexpected* p.286-7.) The WFL's philosophy of passive resistance led to the idea for a census boycott, formally proposed in June 1910 and followed by a letter from the WFL to eighteen suffrage societies, asking them to join the protest alongside continuing frustration over the Conciliation Bill and tax resistance.

There was confusion over tax – married women could not be charged with income tax, so legally 'neither her money, her goods, nor her body may be seized', yet it was known that some cases had been brought against women and there was a muddle over whether husbands were liable for prosecution if women refused to pay. A letter was sent to David Lloyd George and received no reply, resulting in Teresa Billington-Greig writing an article in *The Vote*. Eventually Charlotte received a reply from a Treasury civil servant, stating that before receiving a WFL deputation Lloyd George needed, in writing, the proposed points that the WFL wished to raise; in other words, playing for time.

Interest in passive resistance in the WFL shifted in focus towards demonstrating the inability of men to govern without the consent of women. Edith How-Martyn responded to criticisms of the protest from *The Spectator*:

We cannot reiterate too often that our object is to give a practical example of the impasse which would be produced in our national life if women seriously began to refuse their consent to the autocratic government by men. Passive resistance against unjust authority is binding on those who believe in doing something to win their freedom. Until women win representation they are morally justified in demonstrating that their exclusion from citizenship certainly does involve national injury.

(*The Vote* 4 March 1911 p.226)

These were similar arguments to those from Gandhi. Although Charlotte made a number of references to Gandhi's model of non-violence, the WFL never fully developed along the lines he proposed.

All WFL branches were urged to take part in the census boycott and this was reinforced by numerous articles in *The Vote* and tours by popular speakers to branches. Housman said 'passive resisters were those women who are unable to act militantly so instead passively resist' (*The Vote* 4 March 1911 p.223). The WFL was planning a conference at Caxton Hall on 27 October. Teresa Billington-Greig drew up a briefing paper and there was an impressive list of a dozen organisations sending delegates including the national NUWSS, the Women's Cooperative Guild, with 27,000 members, the Conservative and Unionist Women's Franchise Association and the Union of Actresses, Artists and Writers. Conspicuous by its absence was the WSPU. Charlotte welcomed delegates, very pleased at the prospect of united action. There were various questions about legality, tactics and effectiveness, and it was agreed to meet again on 9 December. Charlotte, Teresa and the other WFL leaders knew though that it was important to involve the WSPU.

The WSPU was maintaining a truce while keeping up pressure on the government, which had asked the king to be prepared to create up to 500 new peers, in order to ensure the passage through the House of Lords of a Bill to abolish their veto. The king agreed, on condition that the question was first put to the country at a general election. Asquith announced that he had asked the king to dissolve parliament, which would be on 28 November, and until then government business would take precedence over everything else, including the Conciliation Bill. On hearing this the WSPU immediately ended their truce. Charlotte said to the WFL, 'Here came one of those moments, tests as I think of generalship, when it became necessary for your Executive to act on its own initiative.' The WFL was officially committed to militant action if the Bill failed, but the NEC decided there was no need for protest since the government was not to blame. Christabel Pankhurst decided that the election was an elaborate plot to prevent the Conciliation Bill becoming law and called for militant action. Asquith had already promised the Bill would be considered by the next parliament so her response was condemned by the Conciliation Committee as absurd and harmful to the cause. This was overshadowed by the brutality shown by the police at the demonstration in Parliament Square on 18 November, which later became known as 'Black Friday'. A deputation of over 300 women went to the House of Commons and there were 120 arrests, although the charges were dropped the following day on the orders of Winston Churchill. There were many injuries in the course of extreme violence against the protestors by the police. New, and shocking, was the sexual nature of the police roughness, with protesters reporting breasts and thighs being painfully gripped and beaten. It was estimated that three women died as a result of their injuries and further demonstrations in Whitehall and Downing Street followed.

'Black Friday' was a turning point in terms of tactics. 'I fear "the raid" is played out,' Charlotte wrote. The WSPU could not go back and the WFL had agreed there would be no destruction or risk of injury. According to Linklater (p.140), 'Hitherto it had been the smaller militant society; in future it would be the less militant.' The WFL NEC decided not to endorse an immediate resumption of militancy as there were hopes that the Conciliation Bill might be saved but it was evident some members of branches and the NEC supported the actions of the WSPU and resented the response to it by some, including their own national committee. Six members of Hackney WFL resigned after publication in *The Vote* of a letter from Lord Lytton, the conciliation committee chairman, criticising the WSPU actions and were not alone when they declared themselves disillusioned with the 'spirit of criticism' in the WFL (*The Vote* 17 December 1910 p.95).

Other members felt the WFL did not go far enough in distancing itself from the WSPU. An inconclusive attempt to mark out a distinct WFL policy in December 1910 was too little too late for Teresa Billington-Greig, who resigned from the NEC and the WFL, claiming to be thoroughly disillusioned with the militant suffrage movement. Internal difficulties were partly a result of the militant truce, because

WFL banner, designed by Mary
Sargant Florence, 1908–9. © *LSE
Women's Library collection*

Edith How–Martyn, Charlotte Despard,
Emma Sproson, date unknown. © *LSE
Women's Library collection*

The WSPU leadership 1906–7 (left–right) – Flora Drummond,
Christabel Pankhurst, Jessie Kenney, Nellie Martel, Emmeline
Pankhurst, Charlotte Despard, unknown woman. © *LSE Women's
Library collection*

WFL membership card.
© *LSE Women's Library
collection*

WFL Carnarvon office. © *LSE Women's Library collection*

Charlotte Despard and Emmeline Pethick Lawrence at a produce stall, 1930s. © *LSE Women's Library collection*

Ripple Vale, Kent, Charlotte's childhood home. Photograph taken in 2017 by kind permission of Ripple Vale School.

Teresa Billington-Greig. © *LSE Women's Library collection*

Katie (Katherine) Harley, probably 1917.

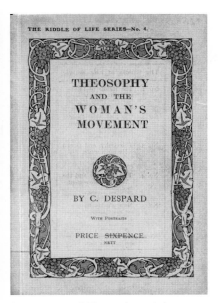

Front cover of *Theosophy and the Woman's Movement* by Charlotte Despard, published in 1913.

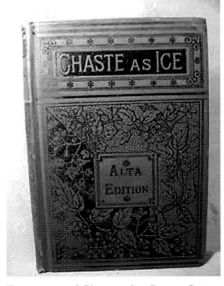

Front cover of *Chaste as Ice, Pure as Snow* by Charlotte Despard, published in 1874.

Painting of Charlotte Despard attributed to Charles Mendelssohn Horsfall.
© *National Portrait Gallery*

Left–right, unknown woman, Maud Gonne, Mary MacSwiney and Charlotte Despard outside Mountjoy Jail, Dublin c1922, possibly when MacSwiney was on hunger strike in support of prisoners.

Painting of Charlotte Despard by Mary Edis (Lady Bennett) exhibited in 1916. © *National Portrait Gallery*

Charlotte Despard by Mrs Albert Broom (Christina Livingston). © *National Portrait Gallery*

Charlotte Despard with Anne Cobden Sanderson at 10 Downing Street, August 1909.

VOTES FOR WOMEN.

MRS. DESPARD and MRS. COBDEN SANDERSON
Waiting for Mr. ASQUITH. Arrested August 19th, 1909.
WOMEN'S FREEDOM LEAGUE. 1, Robert Street, Adelphi, W.C.

Postcard showing Charlotte Despard with Anne Cobden Sanderson at 10 Downing Street, 19 August 1909 shortly before Anne Cobden Sanderson was arrested.

Charlotte Despard photographed by Lena Connell (later Beatrice Cundy) 1910s.

Charlotte Despard and Maud Gonne at the Dublin Horse Show, August 1922.

WOMEN'S FREEDOM LEAGUE.
1, Robert Street, Adelphi, W.C.

SUFFRAGETTES AT HOME.
(4.) Alison Neilans Cleans the Stove.

Alison Neilans cleans the stove, from the *Suffragettes at Home* series of postcards. © *LSE Women's Library collection*

Charlotte Despard and Maud Gonne, date unknown.

Edith How-Martyn, Mrs Sproson, Charlotte Despard and Miss Tite outside the WFL offices in the Victoria Institute. © *LSE Women's Library collection*

Charlotte Despard leading the Women's Coronation Procession on 17 June 1911. © *LSE Women's Library collection*

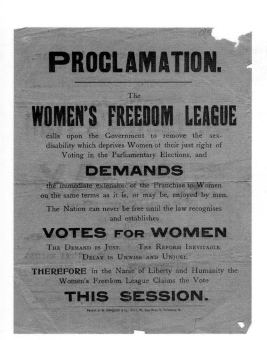
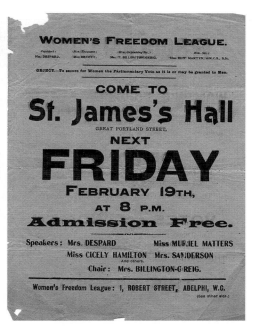

Call to a Women's Freedom League meeting on 19 February 1909. © *LSE Women's Library collection*

The WFL caravan on tour, 1908. Charlotte Despard and Alison Neilans at the window. © *LSE Women's Library collection*

Post Script

On 10 June 2018 women in Belfast, Cardiff, Edinburgh and London marched as part of the celebrations marking the centenary of the 1918 Representation of the People Act, which gave some women the right to vote. It was estimated that some 30,000 women marched in London. Wearing green, white or violet, the suffrage colours, the processions appeared as rivers of colour through the streets. These 21st century women carried modern banners, modelled on those carried by the suffragettes.

The Nine Elms Vauxhall Partnership took part in the procession, carrying a banner created by artist Ruth Evans and local women. Ruth said:

> 'Charlotte Despard was a truly remarkable activist and I'm looking forward to creating a banner in tribute to her. Many of the struggles she fought for continue today and I hope, through the process of researching and making with other women, to explore some of the historic and ongoing issues she campaigned for to inspire us into action.'

PROCESSIONS Banner, 2018.

Ruth Ewan
In collaboration with:
Devon Ingold, Katharine Hallgarten, Katy Holmes, Vanessa Matthews, Erenie Mullens-Burgess, Maritza Tschepp, Jo Tsagka and Amanda Waite
Supported by Jenny Pengilly and Rosie Hermon
Fabricated by Laura Lees
Commissioned by
Nine Elms Vauxhall Partnership
Part of PROCESSIONS, a UK-wide mass participation artwork to mark 100 years of women's suffrage, produced by Artichoke and commissioned by 14-18 NOW, based on an idea by Darrell Vydelingum

it represented the first real test of WFL efforts to generate a distinct policy and programme and clear image in the suffrage movement. In 1910 it became evident that in practice such a distinctive image was proving difficult to establish in minds of some members; whereas in the past there was flexibility, now members were increasingly being made to choose.

The general election was held in December and the WFL changed its meeting date to the 10th. At the meeting, chaired by Charlotte, several societies stayed away, scared off by the events of Black Friday. Charlotte talked about timing and it was agreed to announce the census protest when the text of the king's speech, due 6 February, was known. The speech said nothing about women's suffrage and Charlotte, at an 'At Home' a few days later, said that she would tear up her census form and hoped every other woman householder would do the same. An article by Edith How-Martyn in *The Vote* said:

> The Women's Freedom League ... now openly calls on women all over the kingdom to boycott the Census, to refuse all information about themselves and their households... We intend to do our best to make it unreliable and inaccurate.

The WSPU agreed to join the protest and the WFL Manifesto, 'No Votes for Women – No Census', was circulated under the names of Edith and Charlotte. The planned protest brought a countrywide debate about the boycott, putting accurate information against women's rights to citizenship. Key speakers including Charlotte and Laurence Housman toured the country, drumming up support. Charlotte spoke at Caxton Hall, telling her audience that she had 'everywhere met with success in persuading women to boycott'. She was planning a large house party on census night, urging others 'to get as much fun as possible out of this protest', hoping that none of the women listening would so 'lose her self-respect as to give information asked for on the Census forms.' (*The Vote* 4 March 1911).

Guidance on the census boycott

Suffragist Resistance to the Census
Passive Resistance

1. *Women Householders* – 1,000,000 will receive Enumeration Forms as heads of households. It is recommended that all suffrage societies combine to persuade Women Householders to refuse to fill [them] up ... to be endorsed with the phrase
    No Votes for Women; no information from Women.
2. *Women Residents not Heads of Households* ... It is recommended that:
    a)   women residents should refuse this information ...
    b)   ... should absent themselves from home for the night ...
3. *A combination of 1 & 2 ...*
    a)   A Woman Householder ... can throw open her house for the night of the Census to as many fellow suffragists as possible ...
    b)   ... run all-night entertainments and socials
    c)   walking parties could be organised for the hardy ...

Active Resistance
Destruction of Forms. This seems to be the only active course possible ...
Penalties ... to a maximum fine of £5.

Cooperation
... It is recommended that each society should work up the scheme among its own members and that local cooperation between branches should be advocated and encouraged.

WFL 27 October 1910

In the final two weeks Charlotte's caravan was brought into London to help with the publicity.

On Saturday 1 April, Charlotte spoke at a meeting in Trafalgar Square. She visited Sale in Cheshire to talk about the importance of the census boycott, and the next day went to Salford and Pendlebury. In Southsea on the south coast Charlotte 'spoke in her usual eloquent manner on the Census protest' (*The Vote* 11, 18 February and 4, 11, 25 March 1911).

Suffragettes, in many cases aided by their male 'Head of Family', boycotted the census by refusing to fill in the form and by being away from home on census night. Charlotte provided her name but nothing else – the register reads: 'Refused further information – a Suffragette'. In London, suffragettes spent the night walking round Trafalgar Square, there was entertainment at the Aldwych Skating Rink and the Gardenia Restaurant in Covent Garden stayed open. Emily Wilding Davison famously spent the night in a cupboard at the Houses of Parliament. There were overnight events in Manchester, Portsmouth, Cardiff, Bristol, Liverpool, Ipswich, Maidstone and elsewhere. Women walked on the Yorkshire moors; one woman wrapped herself up against the cold and spent the night in a cycle shed behind her house. There is not space to cover the many stories here (see Liddington, *Vanishing for the Vote*).

The government had agreed not to provoke matters by taking action against the protesters so no one was prosecuted. It is difficult, because of the nature of the protest, to know how many women (and men) were involved. According to *The Vote* the WFL could 'congratulate itself on having initiated and on being largely responsible for the carrying through of the most effective protest yet made by women against government without consent … The 1911 census has been made memorable by the organised revolt of women.' Charlotte, mocking her old adversary, wrote:

> Mr John Burns dare not allow the record of those who refused to register themselves in the Census of 1911 to be published. That is his mercy and magnanimity. 'For heavens sake,' I can hear him whisper, 'keep quiet! Assume that all is well and it will be well.'

> (*The Vote* 8 and 15 April 1911)

It took great courage to defy the census but some people were outraged. *Punch* joked: 'The suffragettes have definitely taken leave of their census.'

The move away from violent confrontation struck a chord with the membership and breathed new life into the campaign. It signalled a new emphasis on political protest which rejected violence to and against suffrage activists. Charlotte acknowledged this in a speech to a meeting in Portsmouth just before 1 April where the *Hampshire Times* reported she 'gloried in it because she realised that it would mean less suffering

to the individual woman than any other protest …'. She emphasised that
'…Women had suffered too much in the past, so now they were going to
have a real bit of fun and it was going to be the most effective protest they
had ever made, and a bloodless one …'. *Hampshire Telegraph* March 24
1911 p.2 (in Eustance p.174).

In the WFL annual report for 1911, of thirty-two branches sending in
reports, only eight did not mention the census and of these, three were not
in existence on census night. *The Vote* emphasised the numbers which had
taken part and declared: 'The census of 1911 has been made memorable
by the organised revolt of women …' (*The Vote* 8 April 1911 p.286).
Edith How-Martyn in *The Vote* said it was 'the most effective protest
yet made by women against government without consent', although one
enumerator in Brighton claimed the census protest had been exaggerated
by a 'few conceited, hysterical women and their effeminate supporters'
(*The Brighton Herald* 15 April 1911 p.10).

There was a real feeling of possible victory but some branch and
NEC members were concerned about the WFL's internal democratic
principles. There were now over sixty branches. The headquarters and
NEC were reorganised, a process which had begun in 1909 with the
formation of new headquarters departments, each run by an honorary
official elected by the NEC. Despite this, the task of coordinating
branches and responsibility for all militant and political work still fell
on the shoulders of Teresa Billington-Greig. She had always had great
authority and influence in the WFL but by 1910 her work had grown to
enormous proportions, leading to suggestions to divide her role between
two or three women. In the event she had a serious operation which kept
her away for most of the latter part of 1909, and returned in 1910 only to
be injured in a train crash in Ireland, followed by a nervous breakdown
which kept her out of touch with the WFL, until May. She threatened
to resign unless some of her work pressure was lifted, but the NEC was
concerned with other issues – treasurer Sarah Bennett was suspended
from her post in June 1910 and accused of disloyalty towards the WFL
because she had allegedly spoken to another society and was a member of
the WSPU. She was offered the chance to explain at the annual conference
in 1911 but failed to make any impression and resigned. The treatment
of Sarah Bennett revealed a nervousness among some WFL officials
about the extent to which some members still endorsed militant action,

heightened by the WSPU's brief return to militancy in November 1910. Some WFL members joined them, although the official policy was to maintain the truce until the government's actions were clarified.

Even while absent through illness, Teresa Bilington-Greig was still one of the main coordinators and directors of WFL militancy. She condemned the WSPU actions in an article in *The Vote* as 'inexpedient', and made clear her case for a continuation of the truce until the Bill had a clear future. Likely her comments would have been stronger but she was constrained by the WFL policy of avoiding criticism of the WSPU. In 1911 she published *The Militant Suffrage Movement: Emancipation in a Hurry*, giving her opinions of the WSPU, the WFL and militancy, with a number of damning criticisms of the WFL. She said the organisation was a 'failure', had failed to distinguish itself from the WSPU and weakened itself by refusing to criticise any other society. She claimed there were some who were so desperate to distance themselves from the old movement that they failed to do justice to the new movement by missing crucial opportunities to emphasise or publicise women's demands. Because the WFL comprised so many different opinions it failed to take a decisive lead and rather than allowing internal democracy to work, had merely ended up with red tape and stagnation – it had become no more than a weak echo of the WSPU. The split in the WSPU was not just a personality clash, but due to the WFL's democratic internal organisation – traditions of democracy associated with liberal ideals of citizenship and democracy. She linked criticism of the militant suffrage movement with the wider concept of feminist revolt against inequality and male power contending that militancy had become publicity and protest for its own sake. Teresa was not the only member to draw out links between the militant suffrage movement and the wider feminist movement, but others still believed that the WFL occupied a crucial position in the campaign for women's suffrage and emancipation.

Teresa's resignation led to gaping holes in the NEC and departments she had led, and contributed to the undermining of the WFL as an effective national organisation in the following few years. Changes in personnel led to further difficulties relating directly to the issue of internal democracy, which was made more serious towards the end of 1911 by the resurfacing of still-unresolved questions surrounding the WFL's militant policy. This centred on the amount of control in

Charlotte's hands as she continued as president. Particularly after the WSPU resumed active militancy in early 1912, the difficulties for the NEC on questions of militancy and internal politics threatened to cripple the effective working of the committee. It led to almost all members of the NEC threatening to resign, culminating in the decision to call a special conference of branches in April 1912.

Ostensibly the purpose of the conference was to lay down policies for the WFL in the light of another failed Conciliation Bill, but it began with a vote of confidence in Charlotte's presidency. Seven NEC members – Edith How-Martyn, Alison Neilans, Bessie Drysdale, Emma Sproson, Eileen Mitchell, Katherine Vulliamy and Constance Tite – who disagreed with Charlotte's actions, had jointly sent letters to all branches explaining that president was acting autocratically and blocking the effective work of the NEC. At the conference on 27/28 April 1912 the main point of debate centred on Charlotte's decision to hold a militant protest in November 1911, in direct contravention of the WFL's agreed policy of observing a truce with the government. They argued that the president had ignored the advice and opinions of fellow NEC members and so continuation of the WFL along the lines of democratic self government was under threat. Various members made reference to the WSPU split in 1907. Mrs Kathleen Mitchell, an original member of WFL, said:

> The WFL came into existence, in fact it owes its very name to this, that certain people including Mrs Despard, Mrs How-Martyn, Mrs Sproson, myself, and many others found it impossible to reconcile their claim for political enfranchisement of women with an autocratic instead of self governing society ... It is with the greatest regret that I have to tell the Conference that my own experience has proved conclusively to me that this principle is in danger of being fatally reversed.
>
> (*Minutes of special conference* 1912 p.15)

Others defended Charlotte. Miss Agnes Husband made the point that while Charlotte might be autocratic, so were other members of the NEC. She argued that this was held in check by the democratic organisation of the meetings – one woman one vote (*Minutes* p.37). The range of interpretations of democracy and autocracy continued when Charlotte explained her behaviour saying:

> I am a democrat. My views are very well known, long long before there was a WFL ... Now I am sorry to say that I am what I am. My opinion on these things is before you, and it was before the WFL when it elected me as President. I cannot be tied up. I cannot be told you must say this and you must do that. That is absolutely impossible for me. I must be myself ... I simply and solely do what I can to help the WFL, the case of women and of women's freedom and emancipation ... Make someone else your President, or have no President at all, which ever you choose. As I have said already, if the latter is your will, or the former, I shall go out of this room and out of this hall, and those who will, follow me, and we will continue to work for the suffrage as we have always done. But I am absolutely loyal to the WFL.

Her references to leaving the WFL may have decided the matter – most wanted to avoid another split in the organisation. Along with her undeniable popularity this ensured the vote of confidence was in her favour by thirty-five votes to eighteen. The following week the seven discontented members resigned from the WFL, which lost the skills of these committed women. No further rift occurred and the second day of the conference was filled with debates on future WFL policy – the branches having sent many suggestions and ideas – resulting in a firm commitment to maintain closer links between the branches and headquarters. But despite the affirmation of principles of self-government and internal democracy the NEC continued to hold enormous influence on the policy and national image of the WFL. Many of the women elected to the NEC after the April 1912 conference were strongly behind Charlotte, leading to a united front in the NEC which continued up until 1914.

In the last half of 1912, 500 new members were enrolled and seven new branches formed, with 1,200 new members and another eighteen branches in 1913. This was the largest increase in membership in the WFL's history, but in terms of income (£3,120 in 1913) and membership (about 7,000) it was still only about an eighth of the size of the WSPU (Linklater p.167).

By 1912 the WFL's identity as a democratic and militant society had gone through a long process of development and change; it had been acknowledged that democratic and militant principles could only be sustained if they were flexibly interpreted and enforced. This does not necessarily represent a failure of democratic militancy because the WFL succeeded in becoming an acknowledged part of the women's suffrage movement. The flexibility which characterised interpretations of the WFL constitution after 1912 allowed for incorporation of broader concerns and interests by membership. These moves began to bear fruit in discussions of the WFL's future and the ways in which to end women's unequal position in relation to men. When honorary secretary Edith How-Martyn wrote to *The Times* about WFL membership on 16 October 1909, she said, 'it must be remembered that we have a large body of sympathisers who will not become members because they cannot fulfil the very stringent regulations...'.

Ireland stands out as the largest single area where attempts to organise branches of the WFL met with almost total apathy, even direct resistance. In 1910 WFL organiser Edith Bremner undertook a campaign in Ireland, probably the result of Charlotte's personal interest, which caused her to push for WFL involvement. Although very committed, the WFL failed to break through in Ireland – Bremner realised this and asked to return to England, declaring that 'only Irish women could organise in Ireland'. The well-established women's suffrage movement in Ireland was dealing with specific issues around Irish independence and home rule, and both the WFL and WSPU failed to appreciate the complexities.

Married WFL members with families and domestic commitments were subject to the rage and anger of anti-suffragists more than other women. Their presence in societies seemed to threaten the stability of a family unit which depended on the authority of the male breadwinner in the public sphere, and the support of the mother confined to the private sphere of the home. Articles in *The Vote* defended the right of mothers to vote and argued that such roles were not the only province of women. The arguments of the 'antis' were challenged by married members who highlighted their status as wives and mothers to emphasise their demands.

Some branches had 'mother and baby at homes', which mothers were encouraged to attend and some officials involved their children – it was reported in the local press in Eastbourne how Alice Dilks' daughter had presented a bouquet to Charlotte at a meeting in June 1909. Other children helped by delivering leaflets and so on.

Wives and mothers '... workers age long and time honoured ...' Charlotte wrote, so they should be paid for their work (*The Vote* 6 May 1911 p.17) The debates about marriage, contraception etc. took place in an environment where women's duties as wives and mothers were constantly affirmed, but there was still renegotiation taking place on the meaning of motherhood and marriage for women. Cicely Hamilton (a well-known critic of contemporary marriage), Charlotte and Edith How-Martyn rejected women's powerlessness within the home which denied them economic independence and equal rights over their children and with no redress against violent abusive husbands. Charlotte was one of few WFL members to draw attention to the plight of working mothers, describing their position as 'worse than slaves' in two articles: 'Why we want the vote: the child of the wage-earning mother', and elsewhere demonstrating arguments for economic independence and a higher status for domestic responsibilities (*The Vote* 16 April, 24 June, 1 July 1911).

WFL members drew attention to the way women were discriminated against in their association of women with motherhood and caring, and nurturing instincts. One case was cited in *The Vote* (6 May 1911 p.14), where a couple were charged with child neglect and there didn't 'seem to have been a pin to choose between them', expressing outrage at the harsher sentence given to the wife for 'no apparent reason for the discrimination on the part of the magistrate other than the woman was a woman'. Charlotte wrote several articles on 'the unmarried mother', where she defended the woman and attacked the unscrupulous man who took advantage of her. In 1908 and 1911 Charlotte, Edith How-Martyn and other members took up the cases of two unmarried mothers, Daisy Lord and Daisy Turner, who were accused of murdering their babies (Turner's the result of rape), and the WFL was active in demanding leniency towards them, arguing they had suffered at the hands of corrupt men (*The Vote* 19 August 1911 p.206 and 4 November 1911 p.15). In

February 1912, *The Vote* developed a regular column about cases of sexual exploitation, abuse and the harsh treatment of women under the law. The title 'How Men Protect Women' was changed to 'How Some Men Protect Women', reflecting the need for a more complex understanding of male sexual double standards, the accompanying danger for women and broader issues of sexual politics.

Cooperating with party political organisations was officially banned under the WFL's constitution, but the ILP was largely excluded from this. In Middlesbrough after 1910, for example, links continued and by 1912 cooperation was so close that it was decided by ILP members to forego plans for a meeting to attend a WFL meeting. Similarly, Middlesbrough WFL members attended a number of ILP meetings including one addressed by Keir Hardie in July 1913. Links with the Labour movement were compounded in 1912 when the special conference endorsed proposals already introduced by the NUWSS to support Labour candidates in parliamentary contests. By far the greatest cooperation was with the ILP, but in Hackney in August 1911, for example, the branch was accused of supporting the Tory candidate against the Socialist in the Bethnal Green by-election, which was denied, but in July 1912 member Mrs Mustard spoke at a meeting of the North Hackney Conservative club on the need for women's suffrage. Members in Swansea and Glasgow spoke at Liberal meetings.

A number of issues formed the core of decisions about how the WFL could diversify its programme of political resistance – diversity and tensions among members was one, with recognition of the need to offset the decline in interest in women's suffrage which had built up over the year of truce. This decline could be seen on three levels: first, press attention had dwindled nationally and locally. This meant that, second, financial contributions to the WFL had declined by as much as 20 per cent during 1910 – as Charlotte reflected: 'It is proof of the sad love of mere sensation that funds fall off when there is no active militancy' (Linklater p.142). Lastly, the decline in a sense of urgency and struggle felt in WFL branches which searched for direction and motivation and lacked local suffrage or community networks to stimulate activity.

Inspiration for a conceptual and practical basis of militancy came from the leadership – Charlotte and Edith How–Martyn, assisted by Constance

Tite, Bettina Bormann-Wells and London members. Following the resignations after the 1912 special conference, Charlotte had a firmer hold on the direction of WFL militancy and was prominent in moves to incorporate further instances of passive resistance into the WFL's political campaign.

The June 1911 WSPU coronation procession included an impressive WFL and NUWSS contingent. *The Vote* later commented: 'Never perhaps in the whole history of our great movement was the spirit of comradeship so overwhelming evident'. *The Vote* of 24 June 1911 (pp.110–16) lists forty-four WFL branches in the procession – the first and last time when cooperation had been so publicly displayed. There had been increasing cooperation between the branches but a lack of agreement among national leaders. The growing divergence between the WFL and WSPU nationally hit home when the WSPU decided to call off the truce with the government in the latter months of 1911. As a result, spokeswomen for the WFL became less reticent about stating their reservations on WSPU militancy, particularly Charlotte:

> … as regards our future action and the principles on which we act, we are militant; and when the moment for effective, logical, well-considered militancy arrives, we shall find means of showing that we do not intend tamely to submit to the perpetual tutelage which a manhood suffrage bill would entail. Not a militant action which spreads itself over one day and is simply forgotten by the curious sensation-looking crowd, shall we initiate, if the worse comes to pass. A militancy rather the object of which will be to hamper Government action continually – through resistance of taxation and revolt against other legislation – and to show in certain striking ways the importance of women's place in the nation.

> (*The Vote* 2 December 1911 p.66)

Charlotte emphasises here that a distinct militant programme endorsed by the WFL would be put into action if they believed the government would not act on its pledge and legislate on women's suffrage in the new government-sponsored Reform Bill. Charlotte indicates that the WFL had finally broken its commitment not to criticise their sisters in WSPU and was forcefully striking out in an independent direction. This was demonstrated again early 1912 when Charlotte said:

> ...We occupy a unique and particularly difficult position, but a useful one ... we are in the middle of two opposing principles ... Militancy to the WFL is an elastic weapon ... we can use it or we can refrain. When we use militancy we put forward the logic behind it.
>
> (*The Vote* 3 February 1912 p.172)

Charlotte was by now editor of *The Vote* and so had overriding control of material which went into the newspaper and the public image of the WFL. Her methods as editor were raised as another example of her autocratic style by Alison Neilans at a special conference in April 1912, referring to an article written by the president which contradicted another article written and endorsed by the NEC.

Difficulties and tensions in WFL in the first half of the year were not just about the NEC. Militancy was becoming acknowledged as a multi-faceted policy of resistance:

> This multi-faceted nature was reflected in the affirmation of militancy as *various types* of resistance which contained aspects of passive resistance and active, confrontational protests against the law, male power, and sexual and economic inequality. There was a conscious awareness of a policy of resistance which had outstripped older boundaries of suffrage militancy, but which was still bound by reference to them.

At the special conference in April 1912 it was agreed militancy was to be any kind of protest involving the risk of imprisonment. This included tax resistance because, as Charlotte pointed out, women were suffering in prison because of it, but there was to be no violence towards persons or private property. There were plans to boycott goods sold and produced by opponents of women's suffrage but most WFL members did not support Charlotte's plans for a 'producers and consumers league', where members would only buy from businesses managed by women. She also suggested the purchase of a farm to be operated by women who would produce food for other women. Her ideas were opposed simply because it would take too long. 'We should be working for the vote for our great great grandchildren', said one delegate, and a less vocal argument suggested it was 'limiting free speech' (*Minutes* p.36). In a letter to *The Vote* 14 January 1911 (p.147) one member, signing herself as a housewife, said she was not able to help with propaganda and speeches, but every week she bought her coal from an advertiser in *The Vote*.

Even with broad agreement on the issue of passive resistance there were still those members who wanted militant action which would produce immediate results and raise the profile of women's suffrage. Publicity was a powerful force and there was strong support for high profile protests against the government, although most were against the WSPU window-smashing. As Charlotte said many wanted actions that were 'going to last' and would in some way 'upset the structure of society'.

For the rest of 1912 they waited to see the fate of the Conciliation and Reform Bills and made much of sticking to the truce while members carried on with tax resistance and publicity and propaganda work at by-elections and branches. Others seemed to ignore the truce – the police rushed to arrest any WFL member even at peaceful protests and crowds of the public showed their lack of interest in the truce as they interrupted meetings. The most outrage from the WFL was provoked by the wrecking of a WFL fair organised by the Montgomery Boroughs branch in July 1912. In the same month Constance Andrews reported how on her tour with the WFL caravan, they were met in one small village by a crowd of 1,500 hostile people who refused to let them speak and hounded them outside their lodgings until midnight. The following day they found their caravan had been wrecked.

By the WFL definition of passive resistance as militancy the WFL had never observed a truce, and continued claims that they were refraining from militancy demonstrate how they still relied on an association of militancy with outright law-breaking and large public demonstrations. Some members were keen to undertake large-scale active protests again, with a growing gulf between the WFL's apparent patience with government, the effect and reactions to WSPU militancy, and the assaults on WFL activities. The discontent was offset by a rhetoric masterminded by Charlotte which always threatened active militancy by calling for members to volunteer for 'danger duty' while always asserting WFL actions would be logical and considered (e.g. On Watch! In *The Vote* 14 August 1912 p.292). Charlotte's policy kept dissatisfied militant advocates in the WFL as well as reassuring those who were less eager to resume active militancy and calmed fears that the WFL might copy WSPU activities, which had now moved on to arson and widespread destruction. At the end of 1912 patience was wearing thin as the government continued to prevaricate on the issue of women's suffrage. There were moves in the WFL once more towards a more direct anti-government stance, with mass public demonstration and shock tactics, as Charlotte argued:

> ... we desire peace with our brothers ...the latest militancy can be explained and justified to a certain extent ... all use these tactics if they really believe it is right ... we are fighting for our freedom in our country ...
>
> (*The Vote* 7 December 1912 p.98)

This was the situation going into 1913. As the WFL looked set to return to active militancy Charlotte commented: 'We are "builders" as well as "fighters"' (*The Vote* 7 December 1912 p.98). The militant resistance of the WFL finally saw dual emphasis on building the militant campaign to incorporate different positions of their members and fighting the government in their refusal to do justice to women and acknowledge them as citizens.

In January 1913 WFL members were bombarded with reports in *The Vote* of the tax-resistance campaigns of fellow members and urgent requests that they buy goods from pro-suffrage businesses placing advertisements in *The Vote*. At the end of January the government Bill, which included an amendment on women's suffrage, was rejected in the Commons. This finally broke the truce. Shortly after, Elizabeth Knight and Charlotte led a protest march in London in the style favoured prior to the 1910 truce and were quickly and predictably arrested. In a statement to members it was declared that the 'WFL will once more resort to militancy.' Branches undertook more confrontational methods of protest and in the following months militant actions focused strongly on other protests which had characterised WFL political resistance prior to 1910, public demonstrations which culminated in arrests. The policy of non-violence was an important part of the WFL resistance but the WFL also capitalised on the violence meted out to and by WSPU demonstrators.

The emphasis on WFL militancy turned towards a balance of public protest and passive resistance and the WFL began to reap the benefits of long discussions on militancy. In 1909 the question of free speech had divided the WFL – by 1913 it served as rallying point and formed the focus of two large London-based public demonstrations in April and May. Speakers strongly protested against the denial of free speech to women rather than, as in 1909, debating its denial to Liberal politicians by suffrage activists (WFL *Annual Report* 1914 p.17 and *The Vote* 9 May 1913 pp.23–4).

This led to protests against treatment of women in police courts and custody, raising the issue of inconsistency between the sentencing of suffragists and other women for non-violent crime and sentences given to men guilty of crimes against women and children. There were also protests against the forced exclusion of women from courts when certain cases were discussed, often those with explicit sexual references. The resistance from WFL members had moved beyond law and government to the heart of sexual politics. While much activity centred around London, tax resistance continued apace in the branches.

The WFL continued the policy of 'war against law' policy of resistance. This drew in new members as the WFL stood between the passive NUWSS and the violent militancy of the WSPU but still posed a threat to government and male dominated society, with anonymous persons paying fines imposed on WFL members to prevent them going to jail. WFL members were angry about a decision banning them from meeting in the traditional London venues, Caxton Hall and public meetings in London parks, so the NEC met in secret from March 1913, perhaps because of fears of a raid on the offices like that on the WSPU.

From 1914 the policy of resistance continued, but a proposal for militant actions discussed at the 1914 conference was not carried out due to the reluctance of some members to plan for militant action with the possible outbreak of war. The WSPU ceased its activities but the WFL policy of resistance to tax and other laws seen as unfair to women did not disappear.

Humanism was key to Charlotte's understanding of change in society – she perceived progress as the time when men and women would join together and work for the good of humanity. Humanism was first used to define a set of beliefs in the latter part of nineteenth century and was used alongside feminism by Laurence Housman in his book *The New Humanism* (WFL London 1920), which envisaged cooperation between men and women. In Charlotte's article in *The Vote* (28 January 1911 p.163) she wrote:

> Progress! Here I boldly and fearlessly maintain that from the platform of the WFL, from its initiations until now, the one note has continually been sounded. Progress for all to be a part of longing for better conditions, larger possibilities for all, men, women, children, workers, sufferers from the injustice of society ...

She thought the first stage, the achievement of equality, would only be achieved if women organised separately. Charlotte's ideas give an important indication of the development of the meaning of feminism in the WFL, as one of the most prolific and influential exponents of ideas on women's status and change in WFL in the years 1910–18. In spite of her rejection of 'feminist' there were important connections between her ideas and those of Borrmann Wells, so some common ground. Charlotte's views were important because of the way she combined a strong commitment to women's rights with a commitment to socialist principles of economic regeneration, workers' rights and comradeship between the sexes.

Linklater argues that through her Catholicism and her practice of theosophy, Charlotte came to understand how her socialist beliefs and her belief in women's equality need not be antagonistic, because they were part of some spiritual force which would lead to a new and equal society for all. Perhaps Charlotte's interest in theosophy was responsible for her ability to sometimes reconcile class oppression and women's interests. Like Darwinian beliefs, theosophy is grounded in principles of inevitable change, but differs because followers believed change would be achieved through individual moral and spiritual development. Other WFL members were drawn to a theosophical belief of the gradual replacement of masculine traits with more feminine qualities. Marion Holmes and Kate Harvey were among Charlotte's colleagues in the WFL who also worked and waited for the coming of a New Order, where class and gender inequalities would be a thing of the past.

According to Eustance, Charlotte's arguments and ideas on social change, and the connections she made with changes in gender relations, is one dimension of the development of feminist ideas by campaigners for women's rights in Britain during this period. They existed alongside and often intersected with a variety of alternative arguments. Those expressed by other members of the WFL focused on economic regeneration, the uplifting of women's responsibilities and skills, an end to male sexual violence against women and children, liberal beliefs of individual rights. These were often crucially connected through the language used and campaigns adopted by WFL members at this time.

Charlotte's interest in the changing economic power relations touched a chord with members who, like her, had acquired early political experiences in organisations like the SDF and ILP; but those who did not espouse to theosophy could not easily overcome a sense of conflicting interests between classes and economic regeneration and freeing of womanhood. Also, Liberal women could bring in ideas and beliefs about individual rights, democracy and equality which fitted into the constitutional principles of the WLF.

American writer Charlotte Perkins Gilman's ideas were similar to those of members of the WFL. She rejected the feminist label, calling herself a masculinist, and said she sought to introduce a truly humanist concept. She argued that women had been forced to depend on men economically since their labour had been appropriated by men. While this had been necessary for evolution, civilisation now required the achievement of a balance which acknowledged female qualities such as cooperation and nurturing. The balance could only be attained if women led the struggle for their equality, which would reap benefits for the whole of society. She was a popular figure for the WFL and her work was regularly recommended in *The Vote*. She visited England in 1913 and spoke at WFL meetings in London and at Kate Harvey's home in Bromley.

There was a dual emphasis on women's rights as workers and their duties as mothers and carers. WFL member Crystal Macmillan demonstrated this in her contribution to *The Vote* series entitled 'Why I want the vote':

> I want the vote for women because they are different from men, different in the external accident of life, and in much of the work they do ... And I want the vote for women because they are the same as men, the same in those fundamental human qualities in virtue of which a share in self-government is given to men ...
>
> (*The Vote* 9 December 1909 p.74)

The WFL separated women into three groups – wives and mothers, workers, and victims of dictated sexual identity. These categories, and a shifting emphasis on equality and difference, formed the basis of the WFL's broader feminist programme of change which took them beyond the vote.

The WFL was involved with working women – a significant number of teachers were members from 1910, they ran campaigns at National Union of Teachers (NUT) conferences and liaised with/published reports of NUT and National Federation of Women Teachers. The WFL was also involved in demands for more women doctors and in 1914 the regulation and registration of nurses. Some WFL members, notably Charlotte, took the issues of women's work further and acknowledged that if the WFL wanted to alter women's lack of economic power and ensure equal access to employment, it needed to represent those working in industry and the newly emerging 'white blouse' professions. In September 1911 the claim was that the WFL had 'many workers – teachers, clerks, shop assistants and artisans' in the ranks (*The Vote* 16 September 1911 p.255), but not all women workers had equal influence and there was a difference in agenda, e.g. analyses of working-class women's experiences constructed by middle-class activists. This conflict of interest reached a peak in the 1920s, but in the 1910s members made real attempts to address issues of industrial working women through considerable coverage in *The Vote*, which increased after Charlotte – a long standing sympathiser with difficulties working-class women faced – become editor in March 1911.

Charlotte's influence was largely behind efforts to raise the question of women's working conditions and draw attention to, and welcome, the formation of trade unions which accepted and represented women workers. Powerful figures in the WFL continued to call for dialogue between the women's movement and labour organisations, reaching a peak following a spate of publicity around the attendance of Charlotte and Middlesbrough activist Marion Coates Hansen at the 1911 Trades Union Congress. Both women were critical of the Labour movement's lack of interest in equal rights for male and female workers, firmly endorsing the need for women to unionise and cooperate with working men (*The Vote* 16 September 1911 p.255 and 23 September 1911 pp.268–9, p.271).

It was due to Charlotte that the WFL continued to discuss how the different interests of women workers inside and outside the WFL could be handled. In *The Vote* (29 April 1911 p.5) she wrote:

> ... the woman worker knows that until women and men stand together in the state, as they do in the family, no such organisation will be. For woman is there, in the industrial arena, whether men like it or whether they dislike it. They cannot help themselves. The thing has come to pass, she is there. Her knowledge, her experience and her point of view are necessary if labour is to be redeemed from base uses and to reap the harvest of joy and beauty which awaits it. Over and over again men have said to me 'This is our question as well as yours. We want your help. For a new and juster order has to be built up, and in this work woman, the worker must have her share ...

Charlotte's arguments were an important factor in the extensive economic and class analyses forwarded by WFL members but her strong convictions do not obscure the conflicting opinions of other members. Arguably, before 1918 no one set of ideas on economic change was ever fully integrated into, or excluded from, WFL feminism. This flexibility placed the WFL in a useful position during the First World War to argue for improved wages and conditions for the female workforce.

WFL members had growing links with suffragists in other countries. Charlotte was concerned with international women's questions, reinforced through attendance at the International Women's Suffrage Alliance Congress in Budapest in 1913 with Kate Harvey. Early in 1914 they suggested starting an 'international column' in the Vote, stating:

> ... to join in one great international sisterhood, the women workers of the world ... Are we ready to 'dare' all things for freedom not only for ourselves, but for the women of all nations...

> *(The Vote* 2 January 1914 p.161)

The annual conference in 1914 discussed the exclusion of women from certain trades, differentiation between women and men citizens, injustices to married women, women's financial independence and whether these issues should become an official part of the WFL's programme. Charlotte differed from fellow members on some issues but spoke for the whole WFL when she said:

> ... friends and colleagues, we are still face to face with an immense amount of work if another generation of women is not to go down to the grave in the same condition as we are today ...

> (Annual conference 1914 minutes p.5)

The WFL declared members must intervene and prevent war if possible, a stance which existed in various forms across most of the women's movement on the eve of a declaration of war and led to the calling of the 'Women's Anti-War Meeting' on 4 August 1914 at Kingsway Hall, London. Charlotte, on behalf of the WFL, was among the leading figures present. Her views were uncompromising – her spiritual and socialist conventions provided the basis for arguments that until men and women worked together equally, the 'epidemics of armed strife' would continue. The war, she argued, was the decisive damnation of corrupt society (*The Vote* 7 August 1914 p.263). Charlotte's views carried her towards pacifism and the Women's Peace Crusade, which she founded with Helena Swanwick, Ethel Snowden and Muriel Matters, but not so for the WFL. An emergency NEC meeting was held on 10 August and the official course of action agreed and published in *The Vote* (14 August 1914 p.278):

> The WFL, feeling keenly the situation of the country at the present moment, have decided to abstain during the war from all forms of active militancy. The NEC of the WFL re-affirms the urgency of keeping the suffrage flag flying, and, especially now, making the country understand the supreme necessity of women having a voice in the counsels of the nation, and in view of the earnest desire prevalent in the ranks of suffragists to render service to their country at this critical time, the WFL are organising a Women's Suffrage National Aid Corps, whose chief object will be to render help to the women and children of the nation.

This showed the WFL was keen to respond to the national crisis and emphasises its primary interest in women and children, so building on ideas about women's important role as mothers and their rights as workers but stressing that suffrage was of prime importance to the WFL and would colour their actions throughout war. It makes clear that the WFL did not simply cease all activity for *The Vote* and rush into support for war, as suggested the Pankhursts did. Her role in the WFL and influence on the membership makes Charlotte's position particularly important. From the outset of war Charlotte showed her views in *The Vote*, using longstanding arguments asking members to remember 'fellow suffragists abroad', and 'treat them with special kindness and consideration' and to

> ... remember the truth of the life of the nations depends upon the women and workers of both sexes ... If these combine, if these hold fast to the truth, it will be in their power, perhaps in the near future to stop war ...

(*The Vote* 21 August 1914 pp.288–9)

Her influence spurred on attempts to build on the international spirit significant in the WFL since the 1913 International Women's Suffrage Alliance Congress Budapest, but moves towards internationalism were dealt a blow in 1915 when the NEC was informed that the WFL was ineligible for affiliation to IWSA because of insufficient membership numbers, perhaps not helped by an article in *The Vote* (15 October p.784–5 and 22 October p.801–2) by Nina Boyle attacking the editors of the IWSA journal *Jus Suffragii*. This condemned the journal's concentration on pacifism and refused to accept the response of an IWSA member that it took a neutral attitude and represented women of all countries. Boyle re-emphasised her belief that the paper was 'full of pacifist propaganda' and failed to prioritise the issue of women's suffrage (*The Vote* 5 November 1915 p.810).

By this time Charlotte had moved beyond international sisterhood towards a pacifist stance on war. Her views on the war worked their way into speeches at WFL meetings and her presence was often enough to associate the WFL with the sentiments expressed, but in 1916 and 1917 complaints by WFL members against their beloved president were openly voiced (*Minutes* 1918 pp.53–5).

In May 1915 Charlotte attended the meeting of the British Committee which was formed after the 1915 Hague Women's Peace Congress and, with other well-known suffragists, became a member of the executive committee of the Women's International League for Peace and Freedom. Later, her role in the Women's Peace Crusade, which attempted to raise support for an end to war through peaceful negotiation and campaigned for a peaceful halt to the conflict, distanced her even further from the everyday work of the WFL. Charlotte toured Scotland, Wales, the Midlands, Yorkshire and Lancashire on behalf of the Peace Crusade. The WFL 1915 annual conference was delayed until October, when debates centred on concerns that officials were making themselves known through speaking for other organisations and were doing a disservice to the WFL by clouding the agreed policy and ideals. Even delegates who strongly objected to the president's attendance at peace meetings could not bring themselves to force her to choose between the WFL and the Women's International League and in the event made a special case which allowed Charlotte alone the freedom she wanted (*Minutes* 1915 p.136). This decision to not restrict Charlotte's activities was the foundation of an officially neutral policy on war and peace until the next conference in February 1918 when a policy of neutrality was adopted.

The outbreak of war meant that donations were very difficult to obtain and the WFL's 1915 income was three-quarters of the 1914 level. It was decided to channel all available funds to *The Vote* to keep it going as a weekly paper, which meant no longer employing paid organisers, who had been effective in supporting particularly remote branches and keeping the NEC informed of branch events. Some branches stopped communicating with the NEC, but others disbanded as members faced particular challenges or wanted to join other societies; perhaps half disbanded before January 1918. This gave some remaining branches the opportunity to pursue their own paths and associate with other organisations. Others were dismayed at not being able to work with the NUWSS, who were pursuing hospital and other activities, and the WSPU, which had collapsed suffrage activity.

The WFL was increasingly isolated among the three main suffrage societies. After the Pankhursts became involved in the war effort in 1915, the much-reduced membership formed the Suffragettes of the WSPU, which aimed to obtain suffrage, but even with close links with the WFL, WSPU branches never reached pre-war levels. As the NUWSS was focused on aid work, the WFL felt they could claim to be the premiere suffrage society in Britain with a membership larger than the other societies and as they considered themselves to be undertaking the most work in support of female enfranchisement. The WFL continued to work with other women's organisations, such as Sylvia Pankhurst's East London suffragettes, and held meetings mostly in London.

After war was declared the WFL sought a role and decided to form the Women's Suffrage National Aid Corps (WSNAC) in branches, to give members a definite role and purpose, and encourage them to continue to hold branch meetings. Some branches were supported in setting up workshops to provide employment for women and also encouraged to set up aid programmes for needy mothers and children. Spurred on by Charlotte, by the end of 1914 three WSNAC workshops were set up in London's poorer districts – South Hackney, Edgware Road, Nine Elms – and in Brighton in 1915. They were initially successful, though all but one was closed as unemployment among women declined dramatically during 1915. The WFL continued to work for different groups of women – pre-war concerns for unmarried mothers, housing, prostitutes and protection for children from sexual abuse was re-emphasised during the war by the state and the WFL. The most striking example was the opening of the WFL Nine Elms Settlement in the East End in 1914, the brainchild of Charlotte, who gave her property in the deprived area of Nine Elms to the control of organisers appointed by the WFL. The settlement was originally designed to cater for the children of working mothers and deserted children, feeding them vegetarian meals and providing activities. This was so popular that by 1917 it had moved to bigger premises – it was feeding 150–200 children a day and housing up to twenty-two children in the guest house while their mothers were ill, confined or working, showing a greater emphasis for the WFL on community responsibility. A similar initiative was the opening of a fifty-bed hospital for women and children in Kate Harvey's home.

The WFL became increasingly involved in matters of equality as well as suffrage, such as the practice of banning women from licensed premises during certain hours while men enjoyed unlimited access. Charlotte believed women went into pubs for company rather than alcohol so the answer was to provide alcohol-free venues, inspiration for one of the most longstanding WFL projects set up during the war, and she made her views public – 'Mrs Despard on the public house' (*The Vote* 19 March 1915 p.537). In March 1915 plans were made to open premises in Albany Street, London, to allow women of 'poorer classes' to meet and discuss questions of interest. The plans were modified and the venue moved to more middle-class Hampstead. This merited the attention of *The Times*, which reported on the opening and plans to

> ... carry out Mrs Despard's ideas of a home where all comers may find refreshment and recreation. One of the aims ... is to redeem a name that has gone down, the name 'public house'.
>
> *The Times* 27 September 1915 p.5

The Despard Arms opened in September 1915.

In 1918 women over 30 were enfranchised, so some women now had a legitimate political identity – but there was still much to be done. A survey of the WFL immediately after the announced Bill, and in the last months of the war, demonstrates that the WFL was conscious not to let the progress in suffrage obscure other demands. A wide range of activities including equal pay and opportunities and equal treatment under the law were reported. Charlotte, who had a wider vision for change, wrote:

> The first phase of our battle is over ... let us say at once that it is with no exultation, no rapture of gratitude, that we acclaim our victory, rather with wonder that such an elementary act of justice should have been so long delayed ... They talk of reconstruction. We prefer the word construction ... To the man-woman commonwealth of the future we look for the building up of such a society as has never been in the world before ... The form our union shall take, its relation to other organised bodies, its constitution, and the principles by which it will be guided will be for the members themselves to decide ... whatever their decision may be, it will be worthy of themselves and of the Cause they serve.
>
> (*The Vote* 18 January 1918 p.116)

Others echoed her words with action. The 1918 victory conference provided an opportunity for dealing with longstanding questions such as male membership. The effect of partial enfranchisement was clear. Eunice Murray argued that the WFL should not impose its own sex and class barriers and that men should be admitted if they were prepared to work in line with policy. Others argued that they were members of a *Women*'s Freedom League focused on women's matters which men could not understand. The split was even with each side receiving nineteen votes. Charlotte resolved the matter in one of her last tasks as president by casting her deciding vote 'for the men' (*Minutes* 1918 p.161). Opinions had hardened towards Charlotte's pacifist links but this was influenced by her decision to stand down as president, saying her commitment to the Women's Peace Crusade prevented her from devoting herself fully to the WFL. Believing that no one could replace her, it was decided to let the position of president lapse (although some members were unhappy with this and Alice Schofield Coates became president in 1925). When Hanna Sheehy Skeffington wrote asking for help in 1918, Charlotte replied that as she was no longer president of the WFL or editor of *The Vote* her influence was diminished.

The general election was set for December 1918, with the rushed passage of the Bill enabling women to stand as candidates. There was hope of WFL candidates, but it became clear that the lack of both finances and a workable parliamentary programme ruled out the possibility. *The Vote's* editor began to list the women planning to run and was pleased to see no less than five past/present WFL members, including Charlotte. Members placed greatest hopes on Charlotte who, although no longer president, had the admiration and devotion of WFL colleagues. Standing for Labour in Battersea, where she had worked long and hard for residents, she was seen as a candidate with a good chance of election. Her election agent was John Archer, later elected Mayor of Battersea, the first black mayor in London. WFL members led by Alix Clark established their own committee rooms and spoke at her meetings. Members also set up rooms in Hendon and Chelsea where Edith How-Martyn and Emily Phipps were standing as independents. None of them were successful. Nineteen female candidates stood and only one, Constance Markievicz, standing for Sinn Féin, was elected and did not take up her seat due to rejection of the British government. Jibes directed at Charlotte's pacifism by her coalition opponent accorded with overwhelming support for candidates committed to winning peace. The victorious coalition government took 478 seats out of a possible 707. In January 1919 the *Irish Citizen* reported:

> Dublin leads in feminism and deserves congratulations as the only place that elected a woman candidate during the recent general election. All the British women candidates (and they ranged from Independents to Coalition and Labour) were rejected in spite of the admirable record of many, notably Mrs Pethick Lawrence, Mrs Despard and Mary MacArthur. Their rejection is but another sign of the present hopeless state of reaction prevailing in Britain.

The women were anti-war activists which adversely affected their support. The results suggested the party system was far more ingrained than had been thought so it was clear that it would take longer and be more difficult to break the party system and put forward a WFL programme.

By 1922 Charlotte's connection with the WFL was largely symbolic as she had no official post and had moved to Ireland to participate in the

Irish independence movement, but she spent periods in Britain every year and never missed the birthday celebrations held in her honour by the WFL each July.

The WFL continued, although without the passion and fighting spirit of before. When it celebrated its Golden Jubilee in 1957 many of the pioneers were there, including Teresa Billington-Greig, but there were no longer any young members or local meetings. In 1958, when the headquarters were moved from High Holborn to the Minerva Club, ran by Marian Reeves, there were suggestions that the time had come to close. Many years earlier Charlotte had said: 'Better close down at once rejoicing as you have every right to do in the victory you have gained, than creep on from month to month, a little society not attracting the strongest and best women.'

In September 1961 Marian Reeves, the last president, undertook a visit to Dublin to inspect the first president's resting place in Glasnevin Cemetry. A few days later she died, and with her the WFL. On 16 October 1961 a report in *The Guardian* read:

In the coming week its remaining 150 members will receive the last bulletin that the Women's Freedom League will ever issue, one that publishes the news of the passing at a special conference of a final and fateful motion, 'That the Women's Freedom League should disband.' Thus ends one of the great women's organisations of the century.

Chapter 7

Private Sphere

Charlotte was a wealthy woman, used to living in luxury, which made it all the more surprising when, in 1890, she left Courtlands, the home she had shared with Max in Surrey, to go and live in one of the poorest parts of London. At Courtlands Charlotte cultivated her garden, had visiting cards printed and gave 'at homes' with the finest teas, as befitted a middle-class lady of her time. Years later the comment was made that she might have become a leader of society 'for she has wit, charm, versatility – all that goes to the making of a brilliant social success.' She was sufficiently a part of society to be able to offer her niece Ethel a coming-out season in London, although Ethel, daughter of John Lydall, was unable to take up the offer due to her strict father.

A report from the Esher Local History Society reveals that Mrs Vera Ryder was a resident of Esher and wrote in her autobiography *The Little Victims Play* of

a formidable Esher figure in her youth, Mrs Despard, the suffragette, mentioned in awe as Vera and the other children were driven past her house, Courtlands, along the Portsmouth Road ... She had come with her husband, Max, to Courtlands in 1879. The house then had 15 acres of land sloping down towards the distant Mole from Esher's ridge. There was a large ornate formal garden and a wilderness with a small stream, where she loved to be solitary or think of the plots of the novels she wrote at this period in her life...

The late Gerald French, her nephew, corresponded with me towards the end of his own life and described an occasion when a great group of poor people from Battersea were invited for the day. Colonel French, as he was, living at the house still standing on the corner of New Road and Portsmouth Road, and his sons helped Mrs Despard, keeping her guests entertained. The excursionists brought their own barrel organ and hauled it up from Esher Station through the village, playing loudly all the way.

Her husband died in 1890 and she threw herself into work for the poor, mainly in Nine Elms, Battersea, at the suggestion of another Esher widow, the Duchess of Albany … She kept Courtlands for some years allowing her brother's family to occupy it or inviting her suffragette and socialist friends to rest there. Margaret Bondfield the first woman Cabinet Minister, recalled her in 1898, weeding in her garden at sunrise, 'like a saint at prayer.' Converted to a highly orthodox Catholicism, strongly opposed to the Boer War in which her brother made his great reputation as a soldier, involved in suffragette demonstrations, several times imprisoned and finally embracing both Irish Nationalism and Communism, Charlotte Despard shocked conventional Tory Esher. No wonder that she was a bogeywoman figure to little Vera Ryder's nurses and governesses and their charges.

On 13 June 1890 there was a burglary at Courtlands while Charlotte was away. The cook and parlourmaid described locking up the house:

I went round the house that night with a fellow servant—I saw that all was safe—that was about ten minutes to ten o'clock—the next morning, 14th June, I came down about 6.30. I found the dining-room door open, the pantry door open, and the smoking room door open—they had all been shut and locked the night before—I also found the kitchen window open at the top—that had been shut and fastened the night before by a catch—I found the scullery door unlocked and unbolted—on the previous night that had been locked and bolted—when I found this state of affairs I informed my fellow servant, and sent for the police—Mrs. Despard, my mistress, was away at the time.

Missing were a silver cup and a pewter cup, a soup ladle, two plated gravy spoons, six egg spoons and a sauce ladle belonging to Charlotte, and a small clock belonging to the parlourmaid. The thief was sentenced to twelve months hard labour.

Charlotte moved into Earnshaw Cottage, in the grounds of Courtlands while her brother's family lived in the main house. In summer the cottage (which would have had plenty of room for large parties and several overnight guests) was sometimes used for London branch committee meetings. When a small girl, Vera Ryder was sometimes taken to tea with family friends who lived near Earnshaw cottage:

> Perhaps the most exciting thing that came our way on our outings was the possibility of meeting a certain lady who lived further up the road towards Oxshott. She was a Mrs Despard, a militant suffragette. Occasionally the even more notorious Mrs Pankhurst, and her daughter, Christabel, came to stay with her.

The Ryder children could not understand why grown-ups disapproved and Nanny 'hurried us past the little house as though it were a fever hospital with germs jumping out of it.' Nanny insisted that Charlotte was 'a very dangerous person', while the children thought she was a witch.

Wherever she lived Charlotte took with her a bust of Max, which stood inside the front door and was dusted and greeted every morning. In her small two-roomed flat above the Despard Club in London, Charlotte had a Welsh woman called Davis and her daughter to look after her and cook her vegetarian meals, but the most important member of the household was Rosalie Mansell, a trained nurse who acted as secretary and looked after the clinic downstairs. She was spotted by Charlotte while working as a matron in the Lambeth Infirmary and when she came to work for Charlotte in 1898 she enabled Charlotte to branch out into other areas.

Charlotte had started the first school clinic in the country, ignoring the protests of the Poor Law Board that the law did not permit it and it could not be afforded; by employing Rosalie Mansell to examine and treat the children, and providing medicine and equipment from her own clinic, she could expand this work. Many of the problems suffered by the children came from malnutrition – from rotting teeth to rickets – so little could be done in the clinic, but it did pave the way for establishing similar clinics on a national basis six years later. It also forced Charlotte to the conclusion that this was further evidence of the inefficiency of government and administration led by men. Clearly women were better than men at seeing that children could not learn if hungry or unwell, so it made sense to spend a small amount of money on health and feeding rather than huge amounts on buildings and staff. Women, she thought, were 'gifted with an intuitive faculty which much exceeds that of men ... They could place their finger on the political mistake or the economic fallacy which mars the usefulness of well-intentioned laws.'

In 1911 when the WFL treasurer resigned and the editor of *The Vote* was ill, Charlotte took on both their posts for several months. She continued to speak at ILP branches and attend meetings of trade unions. Meanwhile, all the work in Nine Elms had to continue, which would not have been possible without Rosalie Mansell. Charlotte piled more and more work on to her – Rosalie, according to Teresa Billington-Greig, did most of the work while Charlotte 'queened' it. Rosalie acted as Charlotte's alter ego, as school manager and member of the WFL Executive as well as running the clinic, kitchen and club when Charlotte was absent.

In 1905, through the probable intervention of her brother, Charlotte adopted a baby girl called Vere, the result of a love affair between a cavalry colonel and a nurse towards the end of the Boer War. The demands of public life left her little time to attend to the child and she was guardian in little more than name. Rosalie acted as the child's foster-mother, but the pressure of all the responsibilities proved too much and the WFL was almost led into a fatal crisis by her slow collapse. Like many nurses at the time, Rosalie used laudanum as a tranquiliser but as the tensions and workload increased, she increased the dose until she was addicted. She was taking it intravenously and so openly that baby Vere developed a phobia of needles. Charlotte was aware only of an uncharacteristic and growing inefficiency which was confusing her already complicated schedule. Charlotte missing appointments and unforeseen absences from the NEC was making life very difficult for the other members. Her behaviour as chair had led five members to resign in six months, including Maud Arncliffe Sennett, who set up her own suffrage party in Scotland, the Northern Men's Federation. Her explanation of leaving was 'wearying of the waste of time, talk and mock procedure, and of the lack of grip at the head ... I resigned.' It was almost impossible for the executive to function with the president's indecision, made worse by her secretary's inefficiency, and in the autumn of 1911 her colleagues rebelled when she offered to resign on some point of principle. To the horror of the wider WFL her resignation was accepted. Letters and resolutions of support flooded in but in the end it was the new Conciliation Bill which persuaded her colleagues to reconsider. The Bill had received its second reading in May with a record majority of 255 votes to 88 and then it had been stalled by government business. When Lord Lytton protested to Asquith, the prime minister promised to make as much time available in 1912 as the Bill required to become law. With the Bill's success apparently assured, the executive decided they could allow Charlotte to remain in office for the few remaining months before women's franchise became law.

On 28 March the debate on the Conciliation Bill turned the previous year's majority into a deficit of 208 to 222. On hearing the news Charlotte rushed to Trafalgar Square, flanked by Rosalie Mansell and Kate Harvey. Before she could take up her familiar place below Nelson's Column the police moved in to arrest her. A constable held her by the arm but Kate held her round the waist while Rosalie tried to push him away. Rosalie was knocked to the ground but just as the police were about to drag Charlotte away, a group of young women pushed them apart and managed to put her in a taxi before the police recovered. Physically but not morally shaken, she appeared the next day at the official protest meeting organised by the WFL.

When Rosalie left to be cured of her addiction at the end of 1912, Charlotte became responsible for Vere, now a mischievous and emotionally insecure 10-year-old. A succession of schools had failed to control her behaviour and although Charlotte wanted to sympathise, she seemed only to be able to deliver stiff lectures on behaviour: '... you shouldn't boast ... never forget how much people have done for you ... do try to be a little more thoughtful.' Many years later Vere wrote:

> I can't say she felt motherly love for me. I never remember her hugging me or nursing me, though she may have done so when I was very small, but she gave the love and protection she knew of, and as I never had anything else I didn't miss it.

Vere became a source of friction between Charlotte and Kate – Charlotte was exasperated by the girl and bothered by her own impatience, and aware that Kate expected her to spend more time and attention on Vere's difficulties, but she was an old and busy woman, with important work to do.

The most bitter argument between Kate and Charlotte broke out in 1916 over the conflict between Charlotte's work with the peace movement and her responsibility for Vere. Vere was now a high-spirited girl in her teens – rather too high-spirited for Kate, who felt that her behaviour and liking for practical jokes was having an effect on her own daughters. She decided that Vere was lacking love and attention and told Charlotte this in a very direct way. Charlotte found her comments hard to take, although realised there was truth, telling herself, 'I must try more, only love will save my child,' but there were committee meetings to attend and work to do. When Vere became too difficult she was banned from Kurandai and packed off to school, friends, or her mother. Her mother lived in London and while Rosalie had been in charge it was agreed that her drinking made her a bad influence, but now Charlotte convinced herself that Vere would be better off spending more time with her mother. Kate did not agree with this and Charlotte wrote in her diary: 'She does not understand – I have my duty to the people.' Kate was provoked to say how good it must feel to be so popular with everyone at her feet and Charlotte was deeply hurt. 'All is dead between us,' she wrote, 'something beautiful has gone', but still, 'from my point alone I must be true to my duty.' She was prepared to give up her one close friend for her public life. Kate gave way, admitting that Vere would have to be sacrificed for the greater good, but at that moment in autumn 1916, Charlotte admitted the importance of her public work over her private life.

In her 60s Charlotte wrote: 'I don't think the good, conventional child has any conception of ... the gay spirit of adventure that attends the steps of the born rebel.' Fifteen years later she was writing about 'my poor rebellious Vere ... I had a painful scene with the poor child who is full of rebellion ... The outburst came when I told her to brush down her fringe.' Clearly Vere was a difficult child. She had not settled at any school and after her sixteenth birthday would not stay with any of the women farmers Charlotte had persuaded to employ her. Charlotte wrote, 'I am sad at heart for the poor thing, she should be having a joyous time', but did not blame herself. After placing her at yet another farm she wrote: 'I had not time for a long talk. Still, I fear that she thinks everyone is to blame but herself.' She put the matter of Vere from her mind because she had not time to worry about the demands of the child.

In Victorian times it was common for women to adopt children; relatives or children from the streets. It was often, but not always, middle-class women who took on a mothering role with their charitable work or public service. These were not always successful relationships – often the women had difficulty recognising the distance their work had carried them from conventional maternal feelings and behaviour. Vicinus (in Cieslakowska-Evans) identifies Charlotte as one who 'refused to give up any of her committee work and left the day to day care of her child to her secretary.'

In 1921 Vere visited Charlotte, who was living in Dublin. She was picked up by the police, who were looking for a victim, and taken to police headquarters. Charlotte insisted on riding with her in the back of the lorry, a sight which nearly set off a riot.

In 1922 Charlotte purchased Roebuck House in Dublin, an impressive early Victorian detached house with a garden of mature trees and 'full of promise'. Charlotte had her own bedroom and bathroom where she still had her daily tepid bath, and Maud had her own apartment. There were several servants including Maud's French cook, Mrs Meagher the housekeeper, Maggie the maid and Michael the chauffeur. At Christmas in 1923, 3,000 Irish prisoners were released so Charlotte had many visitors; there were mattresses in every room.

While where she lived was not important to Charlotte, her appearance clearly was. After Max died she wore plain, usually black clothes (she took to wearing dark clothes in later years), a flowing black lace mantilla and leather sandals, although she did wear boots in old age. She was always elegantly dressed and liked to wear jewellery. Every week she had a professional shampoo at an expensive hairdressers and was always immaculately groomed,

Teresa Billington-Greig mused how Charlotte always seemed at peace in the midst of turmoil, a 'picture of placid dignity. How her very clothing refused to be deranged – that uniform which called to mind the unity of a great Spanish Lady and a devout Catholic nun' (McPhee and Fitzgerald p.100), although a grand-niece remembered the horrified reaction as she shuffled down the aisle in her sandals and robes at a family wedding.

Vera Ryder wrote about the 'shiny white hair which shone through a flowing black chiffon veil' and sandaled feet peeping out from beneath 'voluminous black skirts', making her 'really most attractive for a witch'.

Sean MacBride remembered how she wore her sandals even in winter, but with woolly socks. She was always neat, always a lady. She liked to have a tepid bath every morning and Alice Schofield Coates, who went with her to the 1917 Labour Party conference, said she was 'not pleased' when their landlady responded to their request by running a hot bath. Charlotte is usually thought of as quite tall – Margaret Bondfield and Teresa Billington-Greig commented on her 'tall, straight figure', but when Charlotte was with Maud Gonne she was often described as a little woman, perhaps because Maud was 6ft tall or because, in her later years, she was becoming smaller.

Charlotte clearly had a presence and people remembered her speaking: she was a great crowd-puller. At a meeting in Hyde Park where she was a principal speaker a policeman commented: 'Some of the platforms, you see, have only got a handful but Mrs Despard has got a big crowd, but that's nothing … Mrs Despard – she always gets a crowd.' (Mulvihill p.77) She was standing

> Cassandra-like; the whole thin, fragile body seemed to vibrate with a prophecy, and, from the white hair, the familiar black lace veil streamed back like a pennon … the selfishness and materialism of the crowd, its indifference to its own improvement, its deafness to the misery of others, seemed to shrivel before this woman's look. (p.77)

Gretta Cousins commented that she was

> a leader of the highest quality, an aristocrat who was the most democratic of the political thinkers among us. She was one of the rare Catholics who were Theosophists. She looked as old as the hills and twice as wrinkled, but her heart was eternally young. She was a warrior – and a pacifist. Her type of mind appealed to me most of any of the suffragettes. (p.77)

Mary Colum said that 'the Pankhursts fought magnificently but when they made speeches they talked like lawyers and politicians. Mrs Despard's speeches had warmth and poetry, and that intellectual reality mixed with emotional intensity which I have always thought is a Celtic quality' (p.77). Although everyone acknowledged her warmth and good humour, not everyone liked her style. Teresa Billington-Greig was not always charmed by 'Shelley ad nauseum', and Helena Swanwick found an absence of directed logic in her mystical speeches. Hochschild (p.376) writes of an imaginary cemetery with

> the graves of those who understood the war's madness enough not to take part ... Like Sylvia Pankhurst, few in this imaginary cemetery would be saints or paragons of good judgement, but when it came to the war, even someone as indiscriminate in her enthusiasms as Charlotte Despard made a better choice than her brother and those who dutifully marched off to be slaughtered under his command.

In her diary Kate Parry Frye reports going to see Charlotte speak in Dover on 19 January 1913.

> Then at 8 Miss Burkitt and I went off to hear Mrs Despard on 'theosophy'. A very interesting lecture but only the very first steps in theosophy. Nothing I did not know – or do I seem to know it all without being told? I spoke to Mrs Despard afterwards and did a little talking to others about the meeting. (p.138)

Kate had also heard Charlotte speaking in March 1909 and found her 'a little too emotional' for her taste (Crawford).

In her diary Ruth Slate recalls attending a meeting organised by the Women's Labour League in Farringdon Street on 21 January 1909, when speakers included Mr and Mrs Ramsay Macdonald, Margaret Bondfield, George Lansbury and Charlotte.

> Need I say I was ready to fall down and worship Margaret Bondfield and Mrs Despard, especially Mrs Despard, whose face and gestures have been in my mind ever since. *How* she pleaded, speaking of the inadequacy of the feeble effort made lately in connection with the St Pancras workrooms and urging for wider scope and training for all women. It was a grand meeting, though so pathetic.

> (Thompson p.137)

In July 1909 Ruth wrote to Charlotte for advice on the best course of action to take 'in the women's cause', and received a helpful and sympathetic reply (Thompson p.108).

Louie Bennet, who would become leader of the Irish women's trade union movement, acknowledged the special appeal of Charlotte's 'type of personality' in Ireland. She organised the spring tour of 1912, which was so successful that immediately a Despard Fund was started to bring Charlotte back in September. On the last night of the spring tour she held her Dublin listeners' attention for nearly an hour:

> It was with deep regret that they saw the chairman remind her that her time was up and that she must bring her speech to a close as she had to leave to catch the Holyhead boat ... she left the Hall amidst a tremendous ovation of cheers and applause, many of the audience pressing forward to touch her hand as she passed ... her beautiful personality and beautiful selfless self has roused in us the spirit of hero-worship, and the opportunity for even a fleeting sight and sound of her is an inspiration and encouragement (p.96).

After the autumn tour 'Two Irishwomen' writing in *The Vote* refer to her vision of a free people: 'One of Mrs Despard's great gifts is that she can impart a dim impression of this vision and stir other souls in pursuit of it,' (p.97).

Such was her personal appeal, when Charlotte stood in the general election the *Pall Mall Gazette* reported that sentiment would be a deciding factor:

> Only to mention Mrs Despard's name in the poorer streets of the constituency is sufficient to draw a shower of blessings upon her for all the practical kindness and genuine philanthropy she has scattered through Battersea for years past. Then too must be considered the romantic figure she makes as she addresses the electors with her lace mantilla shading her fine head, her ruggedly beautiful cast of countenance, and her glaring eyes, her startling eloquence, and passionate intensity.

> (Mulvihill p.125)

Chapter 8

Charlotte in Ireland

Although, as Linklater suggests, Charlotte was no more Irish than she was working class, Ireland became very important to her. On 31 December 1920 she was visited by Dorothy MacArdle, Irish historian and member of Sinn Féin, who brought first-hand news of the worsening situation in Ireland, with a story of uniformed terrorists on one hand and young men courting martyrdom on the other. 'She fears, as I fear, something desperate, then a massacre, followed by the stifling of all spirit', Charlotte wrote. 'I promised to go if it would help' – words that would shape the rest of her life. While this set her against her brother, despite their differences brother and sister shared one belief – both were convinced they were, at heart, Irish.

For Charlotte, Ireland had been an ideal holiday, with frequent visits to the grand house belonging to Max's family and suffrage tours before the war; now she wanted to be Irish. When Charlotte met Max she was delighted that he was Irish – and by Ireland itself when she saw it for the first time on honeymoon. They stayed at Westfield house, near Castletown on the River Nore, a fine eighteenth-century building with a spreading view of the Kilkenny hills. For Charlotte it epitomised the beauty of what she now saw as her native country. She and Max frequently visited Ireland and she was very happy there, feeling refreshed every time she visited. 'Her Ireland was an ideal of a nation, warm, friendly and beautiful, tarnished only where English industrialism had taken hold,' (Linklater p.43). The Despard family estates were at Mountrath in the centre of Ireland. The Despard name was synonymous with rebellion and Max's father was a stipendiary magistrate in Queen's County, whose life had frequently been threatened by the Whiteboys and other secret societies.

After the Great Reform Act became law in 1884, Ireland dominated parliamentary affairs. Charlotte declared she had been 'a Home Ruler all her life', and supported Parnell, who seemed to be on the verge of achieving it. Charlotte saw herself as Irish in this context, bearing no ill will against the Irish party for voting against the Conciliation Bill, as did other suffragettes. 'For years I have longed for the redemption of my people', she said when the Irish Executive voted to oppose the Irish MPs at the next election in retaliation, 'no majority will ever make me oppose Home Rule' (Linklater p164). Her first purely political visit to Ireland was in 1909 when she spoke at James Connolly's Irish Socialist Republican Club in Dublin.

In summer 1908 women in Ireland decided to follow the English example and set up an organisation to campaign for suffrage, although working on independent Irish lines, and established the Irish Women's Franchise League (IWFL). The IWFL was led by Hanna Sheehy Skeffington, described as 'the most significant feminist in twentieth-century Ireland – an activist, writer and polemicist of the highest order' (Ward). In 1912 Hanna wrote, 'the leaders of the movement in England were invited to speak for us, and Dublin's and Belfast's and Cork's largest halls were packed to overflowing to hear them.' Emmeline and Christabel Pankhurst spoke and

> Mrs Despard, even then a veteran, was another persuasive and eloquent speaker who commanded attention and respect; many who came to scoff left convinced. The myth of the hard-faced man-hating spinster was dispelled; these women were charming, they made a pleasing impression; they showed courage and resourcefulness; they were ready to make sacrifices.
>
> (Sheehy Skeffington in Ward p.70)

When Hanna asked for help in October 1913 Charlotte replied:

> You will know that I am much interested in all you are doing; but, I am sorry to say I cannot help you financially at present. The League to which I belong and the other causes I have been helping take all my spare cash. The battle has been going on long now and some of our most generous supporters are becoming exhausted … For the year I have given and promised all I can. If it is possible I will help

you a little next year: but I cannot tell for certain. Meanwhile I send goodwill and good wishes.

The general election result of 1909 severely reduced the Liberal majority – in the new parliament they held 275 seats, only two more than the Conservatives, and they were dependent for their majority on the support of eighty-two Irish MPs. It was a situation any pressure group could profit from, but the most obvious beneficiary was the Irish Party, which could press for home rule in return for its support. Charlotte found it difficult to deal with political manoeuvring and tactics – she saw things in black and white and wanted rapid change – but had said about enfranchisement that 'the change will not come quickly as the English are naturally conservative … the Anglo-Saxon race lacks vision', but the Irish goal was change without delay and Charlotte was quickly absorbed into the struggle. After the Home Rule Bill was introduced in 1912, Charlotte campaigned throughout the country for 'the Home Rule of men and women together' – it was a good coincidence that the green, white and gold of the WFL flag were also the colours of the Irish tricolour. She was a speaker for the IWFL again in 1913.

On 22 September 1913 the king asked Asquith if he intended to use the army to put down disorder in Ulster. By then Charlotte's brother was Sir John French, commander of the army. His position was that he had no wish to see the army involved; he would not disobey orders, but argued against taking military action in Ireland. French doubted whether Sinn Féin had much popular support and was certain Ireland would be given home rule after the war. He wrongly believed that his personal connection with Ireland gave him a special insight into its problems; he thought martial law should be declared for the whole of Ireland and home rule abandoned. By spring 1918 French was re-established as one of the government's leading military advisers and became Lord Lieutenant of Ireland. Sinn Féin was declared illegal in July 1919, and on 19 December the IRA made an assassination attempt on French.

After conscription was introduced in January 1916 Charlotte began to be more involved with the peace movement – the Easter Rising in Dublin in 1916 triggered more serious militarism than she had feared. When George William Russell (known as Æ) wrote to *The Times* in April

1918 protesting against Irish conscription she commented: 'This country ought by this to be convinced that Ireland is and will be recognised as a nation' (Linklater p.213). Like most people in Ireland she had not fully understood the significance of the occupation of the Dublin Post Office and other key locations until after the revolt collapsed and leaders, including James Connolly, had been executed. It was news of the murder of Francis Sheehy Skeffington, pacifist, suffragist and husband of Hanna, shot down by a British officer while unarmed, that led to her saying: 'This is militarism' (Linklater p.189). She joined the Irish Self-Determination League and worked energetically for the release of Maud Gonne, imprisoned for anti-British activities and twenty-two years her junior.

Maud Gonne is one of the best-known names associated with revolutionary Ireland, described by Mícheál mac Lammóir as 'the nation's last great romantic heroine'. Like Charlotte, her links with Ireland were a little tenuous – although her father was of Irish descent her mother was English and she was born in Surrey. Her mother died when she was 4 and she and her younger sister were reared by governesses in Kildare and France. A third sister had died when only a few weeks old, which was said to have affected Maud deeply. When she was 16 her father, an army colonel, moved with his daughters to Kildare and Maud loved her life with the Dublin Castle set. Her father died at just 51, when she was 20, and according to Maud his dying wish was that he could have done more to redress the injustices he saw around him. Maud vowed to fulfil his wish, and took her place in Irish revolutionary politics.

Photographs apparently do not do justice to the 'beautiful wild creature'. Standing about 6ft tall with masses of auburn hair and fiery golden eyes, Maud was majestically beautiful. Poet W.B. Yeats, for whom it was love at first sight when they met in 1889, wrote of a 'beauty like a tightened bow, a kind / that is not natural in an age like this.' She seemed to be, he wrote, 'of a divine race', and people would stop and stare at her in the street. She was aware of this; 'I do not say that the crowds are in love with me,' she said 'but they would hate anyone who was!' In 1902 Maud gave an unforgettable performance as the personification of Ireland in Yeats' *Cathleen ni Houlihan* and, inspired by her, Yeats wrote some of the greatest poetry in the English vernacular. Maud had a great deal of charisma and used this to help her life's work – to free Ireland from English rule. She had an exciting voice, real stage presence and was a natural public speaker who was inspiring to others. Maud was brave, generous, passionate and sincere, but she had limitations: she was melodramatic, narrow minded and had an unpleasant tendency towards anti-Semitism. She admitted she was not intellectual, but she would go to almost any lengths to achieve her aims.

After her father's death Maud lived with an uncle in London, and disliked her guardian and England equally. An aunt took her and her sister to France where Maud fell in love 'at once and without any urging on his part', with the unsuitable Lucien Millevoye, a handsome but married patriot and journalist. Maud first became involved in revolutionary politics – for France – through Millevoye. Maud was back in Ireland by 1889 and determined to throw herself into the Irish nationalist movement but was blocked by members of the old guard, who did not trust women in politics. She managed to win the support of Arthur Griffith, future leader of Sinn Féin, and others who vouched for her. She was soon living in Dublin and presiding over a group of young nationalists, on the road to revolution. 'More and more I realised,' she wrote, 'that Ireland could only rely on force, in some form or another, to free herself'.

In 1887 Maud inherited a considerable sum of money and was free to live as she pleased. Her view of independence was over simple – she wanted to return to the traditional values of an Ireland before urbanisation and industrialisation, before British rule. She travelled around Donegal helping to mount resistance against the evictions of 1889 and 1890, sometimes actually rebuilding the burnt-out houses, and gave lecture tours in Europe and the USA. She campaigned vigorously for the release of the 'Treason Felony' prisoners in Portland Jail. She was very interested in parliamentary reform and her message was always the same – England has no right to Ireland and must be removed, by force if necessary.

In 1890 Yeats proposed marriage, as he did many times over the next twenty-five years. Maud turned him down; they were a perfect spiritual match but she needed to be free. Unknown to Yeats she was still continuing her affair with Millevoye, with whom she had two illegitimate children – her son Georges in 1890 and daughter Iseult in 1895. Georges tragically died when he was 18 months old and even though Maud had not been present for much of his life she was devastated by his death and carried his tiny bootees for the rest of her life. Being an unmarried mother would have made Maud a social outcast so she was unable to publicly mourn her son or acknowledge her daughter – she referred to her as her niece – but rumours abounded, and Maud lived the rest of her life under a moral question mark.

In 1897 the potato crop in Mayo failed again and there was threat of another famine. Maud travelled to Mayo to galvanise local support. She called a public meeting in Belmullet and addressed a crowd of 10,000 people, demanding food and money from the Board of Governors and intimidating the authorities into giving what she had promised. Her legendary status as the 'Woman of the Sídhe' (fairies) increased even further.

Maud founded Ireland's first women's nationalist organisation, Inghínidhe na hÉireann (Daughters of Ireland) in 1900 and met her future husband, Major John MacBride. He had just returned from South Africa where his Irish Brigade had been fighting the British in the Boer War. He was good looking, gallant, charming and passionate about Irish independence. Against all advice Maud married him in 1903. They had a son, Seán, but the marriage was unhappy from the start and lasted only two years.

Maud would not have described herself as a feminist, but she was frustrated by the way that women were ignored in politics. Inghínidhe na hÉireann ran Irish classes and promoted Irish goods but was also political. Its stated aim was Irish independence and it was vehemently pro-suffrage and anti-conscription. One of its first actions was the 'Patriotic Treat', a huge children's party planned to coincide with Queen Victoria's visit to Ireland in spring 1900, which successfully upstaged the government-sponsored festivities. In 1910 Inghínidhe na hÉireann battled malnutrition among Dublin's poorest children by setting up a School Dinner Committee, comprising their own members and members of IWFL. This finally led to a change in legislation in 1914 when the Provision of Meals Act was extended to include Ireland.

Maud moved to France and devoted herself to ambulance work during the war. She lived in France because she was afraid of losing custody of

Seán. This was resolved in 1916 when John MacBride was one of fifteen men executed by the British Army after the Easter Rising.

Maud returned to Ireland but she was less popular than before, some accusing her of basking too much in her ex-husband's martyrdom. She only started using his name after his death and wore black for many years, although she said this was for Ireland. She was unconventional and her 'grand romantic dottiness', as Michéal mac Lammóir called it, was less attractive in an ageing divorcée with a murky past than when she was young and beautiful.

In 1918 some seventy nationalists, including Maud, were arrested on the charge that they were in league with Germany against Britain. Maud was sent to Holloway for six months, where she shared her imprisonment with Kathleen Clarke and Constance Markievicz. Charlotte campaigned for their release. Having campaigned for many years for prisoners' rights, Maud found her imprisonment intolerable – Kathleen Clarke described her as like a 'caged wild animal … like a tigress prowling endlessly up and down.' She was the first of the three to be released, on grounds of ill-health.

At the 1918 general election, Redmond's Home Rule party was swept away and Charlotte was delighted when Sinn Féin won 75 of 105 seats, constituted itself as the Dáil and made Eamonn de Valera, the senior survivor of the Easter Rising, its president. 'To the ordinary thinker there is no issue. Russia is Bolshevik and Ireland is Sinn Fein', she wrote (Linklater p.213). The independence issue was disputed by many and most strenuously by her brother, now Viceroy of Ireland. French said at the time of his appointment: 'One must try to understand what the real Irish National aspirations are and how to get into, and keep trust with, them. But before one can even begin to put the garden in order, one must weed it out.' On arrival in Ireland he immediately arrested Sinn Féin leaders and banned the party. At the time Sinn Féin represented all those who wanted an independent united Ireland. He judged its declaration of independence in January 1919 as an act of rebellion. When the new republic's supporters began to raid police stations, he ordered further arrests and internment of suspects without trial. 'Jack is taking tough measures', Charlotte noted. With her ability to compartmentalise she still thought of him as 'my Jack Viceroy, mavourneen' (my darling), while actively supporting the Self-Determination League, Sinn Féin's front organisation in Britain. When Charlotte visited Dublin in April 1919 her brother was a virtual prisoner in Viceregal Lodge and she stayed with Maud Gonne. When Yeats visited he was apparently put off by the close relationship of these two kindred spirits and took care not to visit again while Charlotte was there.

By the end of 1919 the viceroy had dismissed the inspector-general of police, who opposed his hard-line policy, making it possible to recruit British soldiers to bring the police force up to strength. They began to arrive in March 1920 and were known as the Black and Tans. A new administration was installed in Dublin Castle, whose views were closer to French's, and the campaign became more obviously a running battle.

In 1920 Terence MacSwiney, Mayor of Cork, was arrested for being a member of Sinn Féin and began a hunger strike. He died on 25 October and it was his death that pulled Charlotte into Irish politics. Although she was caught up with Battersea politics and Austro-Hungarian starvation, the fast of MacSwiney concentrated her mind. With the success of the unions in preventing the government from interfering in the Russian invasion of Poland, her first instinct was to appeal to the trade unions 'to prevent, if even by direct action, what was going on.' The Labour Party was sympathetic and later in the year called for the withdrawal of the British Army of occupation, but there was a gap between sympathy and action and when her Commons friends fobbed her off she wrote angrily: 'There now seems little hope of stirring up B[ritish] Labour to take, as they should do, drastic measures, and so the horror continues,' (Linklater p.215).

As her interest became more public, messages arrived from Ireland asking her to intercede with her brother and it became more difficult for Charlotte to ignore his position. In September Maud asked her to use her influence with French to secure the release of her 16-year-old son Seán, but Charlotte's appeal to her brother met with cold silence. She reminded herself that he was now a mere figurehead, which was true, but mainly because new men were putting his policy into effect so the lord lieutenancy had reverted to its original ceremonial function. His silence was not helplessness, but from a bitterness that came from the creation of Republican flying columns to ambush police patrols in autumn 1920 and the reprisals of the Black and Tans. French found it impossible to ignore his sister's activities which, had they not been confined to England, were in his eyes open treachery. John and Charlotte had broken off all contact and on visits to Ireland he had her closely shadowed. 'The pore lady was niver foive minutes widout somebody followin' her about, though she doesn't know ut', an Irishman in Cork told a visitor from England (Hochschild 2011). Charlotte and Maud were speaking to a crowd of sympathisers when French roared past in his motorcade without stopping. He had the mortification of driving past a group of Sinn Féin supporters being harangued by two women – Charlotte and Maud, with whom it was alleged he had an affair (there is no evidence for this).

In the week following MacSwiney's death Charlotte was due to speak on Hungary and refugee children, but all her lectures turned to the martyr's death. When she returned to Nine Elms after her lecture tour she found three letters asking her to intercede with her brother against the execution of Kevin Barry, 'the young lad of eighteen summers who sought to free old Ireland', as the ballad describes him, but he was already dead. On her next tour her message was stronger: 'With all the force I could command … I indicted Lloyd George and his colleagues, Walter Long and Bonar Law, for murder most foul.' She joined demonstrations and spoke to huge crowds outside Wandsworth Jail where the other Irish prisoners were. Whatever the topic she was asked to speak on, her lecture was drawn to Ireland. She had not been back to Ireland out of deference to her brother's position, but on the last day of 1920 she was visited by Dorothy MacArdle.

Charlotte went to Ireland in January 1921 officially as a guest of the IWFL but her host was Maud. She was said to be on a tour of inspection, but it was a collection of evidence for the prosecution, gathering testimony about violence by British forces, with Maud as her guide. A few months earlier Michael Collins and his men had shot dead twelve British intelligence officers; on the same day some Black and Tans, searching for armed men in a football crowd, were fired on from the grandstand and, shooting back, killed twelve onlookers. In December part of the main street in Cork was set on fire by a company of Black and Tans enraged by the shooting of one of their number, and a week later one murdered a young man and an old priest in the street. The military authorities admitted that the troops were getting out of control, taking the law into their own hands; besides clumsy and indiscriminate destruction there was actual thieving and looting. Motoring through Cork and the south west, Charlotte and Maud took risks for the area was under martial law and soldiers and police were on high alert. They could not be regarded as safe but they had a trump card. Maud later wrote gleefully to a friend: 'With her I was able to visit places I should never have been able to get to alone in the martial [law] areas.' When they were stopped at roadblocks, 'it was amusing to see the puzzled expressions on the faces of the officers … who continually held up our car, when Mrs Despard said she was the Viceroy's sister', (Hochschild p.355). With this they could access the most sensitive areas, 'places I should never have been able to get to alone', Maud said. They found evidence of deliberate terrorism and destruction by military and police 'carried out scientifically', Charlotte told reporters, 'with the object of cracking the Irish spirit and Irish industry.'

The destruction of buildings suspected of housing gunmen had been officially authorised in an attempt to channel the destructive temper of the Crown forces. A Labour Party commission of inquiry later came to a similar conclusion, but her evidence had particular force – such a statement coming from the lord lieutenant's sister was a powerful piece of propaganda, recognised as such by both Sinn Féin and her brother. Unhappy that her brother should regard her actions as treacherous, Charlotte had reached one of her stubbornly certain moods that moved her from one cause to another. There was work to be done in Dublin – the children and wives of Sinn Féin prisoners were in a pitiful state and the White Cross, Maud's relief organisation, which supplied financial relief to the families of victims of violence, desperately needed help. Ireland and its people spoke to her and rather than be separated from them she chose to resign from Britain. For the next six months she passed back and forth between Dublin and London, cutting ties from one and weaving them to the other. She parted from her sisters with cold affection, their attitude strongly suggesting that exile was the right penalty for her behaviour. Although John had returned to England after retiring in May 1921, he refused to see her. Ties were cut with her many friends and associations among a sea of tributes. She also broke her ties with Kate Harvey, ties that were already weakened. 'We had many, many

lovely days of work and pleasure together and we have memories that
we may have roses in December. Ours have lovely colours and sweetest
scents', Kate wrote later in a letter to her. The house and her share of
the land at Kurundai were made over to Kate, and her house in Currie
Street was given to the Nine Elms Settlement until the council could
take it over. Her most difficult parting was from the people of Nine Elms,
where she had worked for thirty years. To leave caused her great sorrow,
she said, 'but the call of the native land is urgent ... the suffering there
demands my service for the years that may be left to me' (p.220).

Ignoring her Scottish mother, half-English father and all the years
of her life spent in England, Charlotte was now Irish. 'I have to go to
Ireland', she told a group of supporters who had gathered to celebrate
her birthday, 'it is the call of the blood, and cannot be denied' (Holmes
p.365). 'Mrs Despard is a most remarkable woman,' said Maud, 'and
intensely Irish in feeling' (Linklater p.220). Countess Markiewicz, née
Constance Gore-Booth, had also discarded her English heritage, but
for Charlotte it was a dangerous game – behind the idealism were secret
reservations that bewildered and almost destroyed her when they began
to emerge.

When she returned to Dublin in July 1921, staying at first with Maud,
the fighting had ceased and Sinn Féin and the British government were
beginning to negotiate a peace treaty. The 1902 Government of Ireland
Act had established two Irish parliaments, one for the six northern
counties and the other for the remaining twenty-six. Elections in May
1921 returned Republicans for almost every constituency in the south,
while in the north the Unionists captured thirty-eight of the fifty seats,
so Northern Ireland was in operation as an independent entity before
the status of the south had been established. The long drawn-out
negotiations with the British over the south's exact status split Sinn Féin.
In January 1922 de Valera resigned as president when the majority of the
Dáil voted to accept terms by which the republic would be known as a
Free State, but would remain within the British Empire. The question of
the boundary between north and south was to be settled by a Boundary
Commission but that was opposed by the IRA, which emphasised that its
oath of allegiance was not to the Dáil but to a united republic of thirty-
two counties.

To Irishmen and Women

Fully realising the responsibility we are taking and the risks we are incurring, for the sake of Ireland as a public duty, we make the following charges:-

Untried prisoners are being tortured to extract information.

Officers of the provisional Government, now the forces of the Free State Government, direct and, in most cases, actually participate in the infliction of the torture.

The chambers where the tortures are carried out are called 'The Interrogation Offices' or, in the more familiar language of the soldiers, 'The Knock-Out Rooms' or 'The Slaughter House.'

Some of the forms of torture reported in letters of prisoners which, in spite of all the sequestration precautions, have got outside the prisons are:-

Twisting the flesh with pliers
Pulling out the hairs of the moustache with pincers
Blackening the eyes
Twisting the arms
Shooting round the head
Beating with butt of revolvers and rifles and scabbards of bayonets
Breaking teeth
Repeated punching of stomach
Repeated electric shocks
Driving forks into the legs
When the 'patient' faints under the torture he's revived to be
    tortured again.

Some prisoners have been taken out to the Interrogation Room and tortured several times at intervals. Many had to be removed to hospital for treatment after torture.

From Wellington, Portobello, Oriel House and many other prison barracks and places of detention in different parts of the country these complaints have come.

We charge General Mulcahy and the members of the Provisional Government (now the Free State Government) with guilty knowledge of this ill-treatment of prisoners, and of taking measures to conceal it, but not to stop it.

The Provisional Government now the Free State Government have refused an enquiry into the matter.

They also refuse admission to the prisons to Visiting Justices and Sanitary Officers – and have forbidden all visits of relatives of prisoners, even when the prisoners are condemned to death.

They have refused admission of Solicitors to see prisoners.

They have censored the Press; the Editors of the three Dublin daily papers declare that they are not allowed by the Military Censor to publish any letters referring to the ill-treatment of prisoners.

Released prisoners have been threatened with 'plugging' if they reveal what they have heard and seen in the prisons.

We can and will supply the names of some of the official torturers and of some of the tortured prisoners to any Court or tribunal who can take the evidence of the victims <u>and ensure their subsequent safety.</u>

If the Free State Government still refuses a public enquiry, it stands self-convicted before the world.

For the Women Prisoners' Defence League
Signed – Maud Gonne MacBride, Hon. Sec.
Charlotte Despard, President

Postal Address – 71 St Stephen's Green
General Meeting Place – The Jail Gates
undated letter

In 1921 Maud was against the treaty but unusually quiet on the matter – Arthur Griffith supported it but her position hardened after his death in 1922, particularly because she hated Cosgrave's Free State government. She was disillusioned with Yeats due to his decision to serve in the Irish Free State Senate in 1922 and he wrote regret-filled poetry about how she had wasted her beauty and passion, notably *No Second Troy* in 1916.

Late in 1921 Maud and Charlotte moved from St Stephen's Green in Dublin to Roebuck House, a huge Victorian house about twelve miles north of the city, purchased by Charlotte. As well as the two ladies, Maud's son Seán and her daughter and son-in-law, Iseult and Francis Stuart, lived in the house, as well as Maud's pet dogs and a changing population of homeless prisoners, IRA gunmen and Belfast refugees. The house came to life at night and Charlotte, who had lived alone for thirty years, was often afraid when she awoke to footsteps and furtive conversations outside her door. She was less frightened when the secret purpose of the night visitors had been explained; 'these things affect me very little now', she said, but still woke often. Roebuck House was a popular haunt for IRA men on the run – both Seán MacBride and Francis Stuart had been imprisoned as members of the IRA and Seán was one of its senior staff officers and seen as a hero by hardliners – and also a target for police raids. At Nine Elms Charlotte had been used to being the lynchpin of activities, now she found herself an outsider, only partly understanding what was said about IRA activities. Both sides largely ignored her – she was irrelevant to the hunted and an embarrassment for the hunters. On one occasion the police arrested Vere, who was there on holiday, and Charlotte insisted on riding with her in the back of the lorry. The sight of her being taken to police headquarters almost started a riot, but like having IRA men in her house, the episode reassured Charlotte that she was in the heart of the battle.

The Free State came closer to civil war and Northern Ireland was racked by sectarian riots, the violence reflecting the Protestants' sense of vulnerability in their new province and the Catholics' confidence in help from the south. Since the beginning of the treaty negotiations IRA gunmen had come north in large numbers, while the Province had taken over from Britain the armed Special Constabulary. The 'B' Specials, 25,000 part-timers recruited from the Orange Order, were noted for the fervour of their Protestantism. Both sides claimed provocation for their actions – the murder of a police officer in Lurgan or the expulsion of Catholic workers from the shipyards, but in 1922, the first year of the Province's existence, over 200 people were killed and more than 1,000 wounded. The casualties seemed to be two Catholic to every Protestant and the semi-official harassment of Catholics sent a stream of refugees to the south.

Charlotte and Maud established a reception centre in Dublin where they tried to provide food and housing and help with finding work. The increasing numbers of refugees who appeared after the Special Powers Act in 1922 strained their resources to the limit. Angered by stories of Protestant discrimination, Charlotte went to Belfast to find out for herself, visiting Ballymacarett, a Catholic enclave around St Matthew's church in East Belfast, and Ardoyne, a similar community in the west of the city. In Ardoyne she witnessed the sort of incident responsible for Catholics leaving the city:

> Having visited many panic-stricken families and inspected their houses, riddled with bullet-holes, I stood talking with some of the women. Everything was quiet. The people stood about in little groups before their doors. The children were playing. Suddenly there was a pistol shot; it was fired from an armoured car. Panic followed, the children ran in to any open door. I was drawn by trembling women into the cottage of an ex-soldier – a man who had fought in Belgium and Gallipoli. Volley after volley, from rifles and machine guns, swept the streets, and this went on with brief intervals for an hour and a half.

Charlotte asked for an interview with Sir James Craig, the prime minister, but was referred to the Minister for Home Affairs, Sir Dawson Bates. Bates could not refuse to see the sister of the Earl of Ypres, Freeman of Belfast and enemy of all Republicans, but took the opportunity of telling her that she was a disgrace to her family. By way of revenge she published their conversation in an open letter to Craig:

> ... in spite of interruptions from himself and a gentleman in his office I told Sir Dawson Bates [what I had seen] and asked for protection for the Catholic workers.
>
> His reply was: 'We give protection to all law-abiding citizens.' 'Not to Catholics,' I said. 'Irrespective of creed,' he answered.
>
> I gave instances of the brutality of the 'Specials' and asked for their withdrawal. 'The 'Specials',' he said, 'are a fine body of men, who have been doing their duty under exceptionally trying

circumstances.' He then turned his back, and refused to say any more.

Even this brief paragraph shows some of the entangled divisions within the Province – Protestant and Catholic, dissident and police, worker and capitalist. The new province had no basis to give it stability and required a firm reinforcement of order, but measures like the Special Powers Act of 1922 only muddied things further. Charlotte told Craig in her letter:

Go on as you are doing. Give your legalized gunmen carte blanche to shoot, maim and insult their fellow-townsmen and to destroy their homes; keep thousands of men idle, and, as sure as day succeeds night, retribution in an awful form will come to you.

Before Charlotte had travelled to Belfast some members of the IRA had forcibly seized the Four Courts, Dublin's centre of justice, raising tensions in the south. They were allowed to remain there until the result was known of the election on 24 June to ratify the terms of the treaty with Britain. Less than a third of the electorate voted for Republicans opposed to the treaty, and four days later the newly elected government of William Cosgrave ordered the bombardment of the Four Courts. Immediately, Charlotte, Maud and Hanna persuaded the mayor to come with them as a peace committee and for a few hours the shelling stopped while they negotiated with both sides. The IRA refused to surrender their weapons and the guns began to fire again, the start of a year-long civil war where torture and assassination were commonplace on both sides. The war spread and de Valera and the anti-treaty Sinn Féin were drawn into the fight alongside the IRA. In response, Cosgrave passed the Public Safety Act, as draconian a measure as the Special Powers Act in the north. Some 12,000 suspects were imprisoned under the Act.

In 1922 Charlotte, Hanna and Maud founded the Women's Prisoner's Defence League (WPDL) for the 'help, comfort and release' of Republican prisoners. They all supported de Valera although they had been in favour of the treaty; they deplored violence and the focus of their actions was humanitarian. They helped to find jobs or provide financial assistance to prisoners' families and provided information – families often did not know where men were held and unless they had other resources faced the threat of the Poor Law. As Charlotte and Hanna had been suffragists they publicised the scandal of internment using familiar tactics. 'We had processions, poster parades, vigils at prison doors, letters to papers, home and foreign', wrote Charlotte. They also noisily interrupted the government's business. On 21 September Kevin O'Higgins, Free State Home Minister, was introducing a clause of the new constitution to the Dáil when, according to newspaper reports,

> Mrs Despard, standing at the rails overlooking the floor of the House, shouted out a protest against the alleged barbarous treatment inflicted on untried prisoners. The Home Minister, disregarding the interruption, continued his speech, but Mrs Despard also continued to address the Assembly, declaring that she spoke as an Irishwoman representing thousands of prisoners' relatives. The contest, which went on between the two speakers to the amazement of the many visitors in the Gallery, as to the whole House, brought the intervention of the Speaker who declared that, as Mrs Despard was breaking the rules of the House, he would have to order her removal. She retorted, 'I am breaking the rules of this house because of this system, and because it is impossible for the truth in regard to these prisoners to get out in any other way.'

After Charlotte had been removed, struggling and shouting, Maud rose, similarly made her protest and was removed, and Hanna did the same. Linklater (p.224) says it is impossible to measure the importance of their work – politically negligible, morally vital. Among the horrors of civil war, when captives were tortured and shot, or tied to a mine, when prisoners were sent insane, when the government executed hostages in reprisal for murders on the other side, the women reminded people of better times. It was difficult to see how their small efforts could have much effect in such an awful situation. 'Possibly if we had held our tongue things would have been even worse than they were,' wrote Charlotte. 'But we know the agitation has kept up the courage of our boys and girls in prison.' Even this small achievement was too much for the government and in January 1923 it banned the WPDL as an illegal organisation.

The women ignored the ban and continued to parade and held a regular Sunday meeting on the ruins of Gresham's Hotel in O'Connell Street to broadcast news about the prisoners. When the police drove them away they set up portable platforms until the authorities gave up, saying, according to Maud, 'those damned women make more trouble than the meetings are worth.'

The tall and gaunt Maud continued to lead placard marches around Dublin, her appearance now so eccentric that she was nicknamed 'Mrs Maud Gone Mad' (Charlotte was nicknamed 'Mrs Desperate'). In April 1923 Maud was arrested for her activities with the WPDL; her crime: parading with placards. Inside the notorious Kilmainham Jail she joined a hunger strike with ninety-one other inmates, while her close friend Charlotte maintained a solitary protest against her illegal imprisonment. 'I am dreading my watch,' Charlotte wrote to a Mrs Fowler, who had written to ask her for help. 'Moved by a sudden resolve, I waited outside Kilmainham,' wrote Charlotte, '– strange nights and days, bitterly cold … Oh the bitter cold and the *length* of those nights.' The 78-year-old Charlotte kept a constant vigil at the prison gates for almost two weeks before her friend was stretchered out, suffering from malnutrition but still defiant. The civil war was over by the time they had both recovered but Charlotte paid for her bravery for the rest of her life, with crippling arthritic pain in her shoulder and back which periodically incapacitated her.

Charlotte now had limited strength, but the demands of the WPDL did not lessen with the uneasy peace. Arrests and imprisonment without trial continued and those already behind bars remained there. With the rivalry between the IRA and Sinn Féin, the only pressure for their release came from the women; using the sort of non-violent militancy of the WFL they gradually moved the 'Free the prisoners' slogan into a huge and emotive movement, the suffragette tactics having an effect on the country at large rather than the government. In the autumn of 1923 the internees began to be released. Each train into Dublin brought numbers of confused, hungry, often wounded and homeless men. The WPDL set up a rota to meet the trains and the headquarters became a meeting and information centre for prisoners' families. Throughout the winter Charlotte met trains, collected food, money and clothing, comforted relatives and attended the Sunday meeting in O'Connell Street. The work sapped her frail strength but she felt bound to continue, emulating the younger Maud.

Their work earned Charlotte and Maud the title 'Madame'. This had first been applied to Countess Markiewiz, who was clearly foreign from her title and her upper-class English accent. It conveyed popular esteem and a conception that they were not Irish, which Madame Despard and Madame Gonne, as patriotic Irish women, must have been dismayed by. Worse, both fervent Catholics, they were generally regarded as Protestants. This did not diminish the affection felt for them by Catholic Republicans, but it did classify them as something apart and thus put an end to Charlotte's wish to take her place among the Irish people.

Maud was a dominant and compelling character who made Charlotte want to work to the limit of her remaining strength. She was beautiful and very charming. 'It is well for me,' said Helena Swanwick, 'that I have not spent my life within her orbit, for I have sometimes felt as if I might have committed any folly against my judgement if she had desired it.' Maud had star appeal, coupled with an air of vulnerability, that could silence a room. Both men and women courted her and she was known to have a recklessness, throwing everything into a cause, demanding total commitment in return, '… having thrown all she had, memories as well as dreams, into the cause she believed in.'

Charlotte used Maud as her guide through the complicated politics of Ireland, but it was difficult to assimilate the vocabulary and many years of experience. She was excluded at home and handicapped in public. She presided at the O'Connell Street meetings but she rarely spoke. In comparison with her work in England she was almost silent and when she did speak it was in small debating clubs, where she did not need to be able to talk about dead heroes to prove her point. She was more likely to spend her time having tea at the Ritz with Constance Markiewicz than making speeches. Maud was summoned to help with by-elections, while Charlotte visited prisoners in hospital, or sometimes read the English newspapers to see whether parliament would do what she considered to be the right thing: 'they seem to be moving towards reform, but whether to the real thing, the new order, one cannot tell.'

The sacrifice she had made to live in Ireland became clear when her brother died in April 1921. She had written to him but he would not forgive her and when she visited the hospital she was not allowed to see him. She had written to invite him to Ireland to meet her rebel friends but he was too unwell (even if he had wanted to accept the invitation). His death was 'a deep sorrow to me', she told her friend Mrs Solomon, but she was comforted because 'it cannot be long before I follow him'. Apart from her sadness over the death of her brother, she was deeply unhappy with her situation. She had cut herself off from England but was an outsider in Ireland. Being with Maud provided excitement and a sense of purpose, but she had to compromise her ideal of non-violence. Republicanism, which had seemed the high road of idealism, was now less clear.

On 16 July 1924 de Valera was released, and the following day Charlotte wrote:

> I went with Maud to [WPDL] headquarters to find out what was to be done in the way of demonstration, and we were told 'He has been here, and will be in again in half an hour.' We waited. I was just finding Maud to remind her of her White Cross committee when, at the head of the stairs, I saw a little group; someone said 'The President,' and then I was shaking his hand and saying as well as I could my gladness.

'The President' was de Valera, the title given to him by the IRA and supporters of the anti-Treaty Sinn Féin – the Republicans – who refused to recognise the Free State or any government which was not that of an independent united Ireland.

The 1924 harvest was the worst since 1879, and coupled with international economic decline it meant that Ireland suffered very badly. The only economic theory the Republicans could come up with was self-sufficiency, in the hope that cottage industries could help the unemployment problem. Charlotte set up her own industry, a jam factory. Her much-loved flower gardens were ploughed to grow strawberries and raspberries and for two years she worked as the business manager. There were up to fifteen employees in season, all Republicans, usually ex-prisoners or refugees from Belfast. Industrial relations were difficult; it was seen as a slur on honesty to be asked to keep accounts, or unnecessary criticism if there were fingerprints on the jars, and Charlotte had furious rows with them. After eighteen months she was disenchanted. Not just the rows and the fact that the factory needed large subsidies from her income to keep going, but the Republican approach to the problem was not working and unemployment continued to grow. Many others shared her view that 'we have not struck the right note in the country, more effort should have been made to find a solution to the economic distress.' Hanna described the 1927 annual exhibition of Irish goods held as usual at Christmas, patronised largely by Republican or Irish-Ireland supporters. Stall holders included Maud MacBride, 'whose shell-flowers are a beautiful and unique industry, creating things of beauty from Irish sea shells as ravishing as any from France, Mrs Despard whose jams and preserve factory gives much needed employment ...' (Ward p.235).

When the Boundary Commission split up in disarray in November 1925, with the boundary between north and south unchanged, de Valera dissociated himself from the IRA's policy of restoring unity by force. Six months later he left Sinn Féin and set up his own party Fianna Fáil (Warriors of Destiny). It had the same aims as the Republicans, but through political pressure from within the Dáil. Many Republicans joined Fianna Fáil and a smaller group promoted the idea that Republicanism's real ancestors were Wolfe Tone and the ideas of the French Revolution, with James Connolly and the theories of the workers' republic. This was more in line with Charlotte's views and she resigned from Sinn Féin, abandoned the Republican debating clubs and joined the Connolly Club, the centre of left-wing thought where Marxists met under the chairmanship of Connolly's son Roddy. People there associated the name of Despard not with suffragettes, but with Wolfe Tone's comrade in the United Irishmen rising in 1798 and she began to feel more at home.

Early morning on Saturday 28 June 1926, a group of Republican women waited outside Mountjoy jail to welcome Sheila Humphries and Bride O'Mullane. The group included Hanna, Maud, Constance Markiewicz and Charlotte, with members of the Defence League and other groups. Now over 80, Charlotte's physical strength was failing but she still had money. The 1926 dividend from Muir Mills was given to Roddy Connolly to set up the Irish Workers' Party and she purchased a printing press for its newspaper *The Workers' Republic*. Its slogan was

Connolly's phrase: 'Ireland free is Labour free, and Labour free is Ireland free,' which meant a policy of nationalising banks and appropriating landlords' estates. This was seen as a threat by the king of Irish Labour, Jim Larkin, and he set up his own Irish Workers' League. 'In the Labour world it is all hideous chaos – splits, suspicions, mutual recrimination everywhere,' said Charlotte. Dublin was the centre of Larkin's power so they tried to set up branches in the strongly Republican areas of Mayo, Cavan and Meath. Charlotte had purchased an ancient car and had a one-legged driver, Michael, who drove her across the country. She addressed meetings talking about the aims of the IWP and the economy. Addressing a small gathering of farmers and landowners she said: 'Pay no rent, pay no rates. The land is a God-given right. Farmers, to you gentlemen I say, you don't own your land. You have no call to it. Divide with your neighbour. Let Ireland be as the wild geese – fly in, fly out.' After her speech she had to sober up Michael for the dangerous drive home.

The IWP made few friends, but powerful enemies. The church thought it had anti-Christian ideas. By speaking in Republican areas the IWP was in direct competition with Fianna Fáil. Charlotte had hoped for an alliance between them, but this was impossible and when the IRA decided to support de Valera in the 1927 election, the IWP dwindled away from lack of interest.

Charlotte became deeply depressed. She felt she had lived too long, her life was without its purpose, all her causes and optimism had disappeared. For the first time she had to worry about money. The expense of running a large house full of guests, as well as subsidising the jam factory, had made a real drain on her resources. Her dividends had been given to the IWP but she still carried on feeding, housing and giving money to anyone who came to her door. When fishermen at Portacloy told her that lack of transport prevented them getting their fish to market, she bought them a lorry. When the Dublin Poor Law, overwhelmed by workers requiring relief, reduced the amount of benefit to 7s 6d a week and imposed a severe work-test, she helped set up the National Unemployed Movement to press for more generous conditions. The work-test was abandoned, but the rate of relief could not be increased; to supplement it, Charlotte organised and contributed on a large scale to the Unemployed Movement's emergency distribution of food. Things started to go wrong.

It was clear that savings would have to be made, a decision that was helped by the jam factory foremen disappearing with the reserves and a week's takings, and the factory was closed. Michael crashed the car and in his shame ran away, never to return. Her gardener refused to move out of a cottage which was needed for refugees and she had to pay for an eviction order from the court. Charlotte was betrayed on all sides, and she was beginning to doubt her sanity. 'Everything is sad and perplexing, and I have had difficulty in holding the balance of my mind.' Money went missing ('treachery I fear from some of those in my own house'), a leader of the National Unemployed Movement 'had played the traitor' and, she suspected, made off with her contributions; in the IWP, 'none of those who lead seem big enough for their big task', and she was distressed by her own helplessness in the face of all the starving people needing help.

Seán MacBride had disappeared in November 1925 after a spate of IRA violence. He was known to be alive and in hiding – it was hoped that he was out of the country. In July 1927, Home Minister Kevin O'Higgins was murdered coming out of church and MacBride was the first suspect to be arrested. He was eventually released, but the shock of his arrest for this violent crime was deeply upsetting for Charlotte and shocked her out of her acceptance of the IRA's tactics. It accentuated Maud's hostility to Cosgrave's government and Charlotte's alienation from her friend deepened her unhappiness.

Maud continued to lecture and tour for the banned WPDL throughout the 1920s and 1930s, until 1932 when de Valera released the prisoners on his accession to power, but he then began his own campaign of jailing Republicans. She started a newsletter and sent off many angry letters to the press, but her days as a political force were over and she had to watch as her son Seán took an active role in Republican politics. Maud was a legend in her own lifetime, one of the first modern female nationalists. She had the sad experience of outliving all her old friends and comrades; Charlotte, Hanna, Countess Markievicz, Yeats, Arthur Griffin. The free spirit became, as Maud said, 'a prisoner of old age, waiting for release.' Maud died in April 1953 at the age of 87 and was buried in the 'republican plot' in Dublin, holding her baby son's bootees.

Chapter 9

Final Days

Charlotte was old now and very frail; the pain in her shoulder a constant problem and her sight failing, so blurred that she could read only in the brightest light. At times she yearned for 'the body's end'. On her 80th birthday she wrote: 'I must not complain about this poor old body, though I begin to feel its limitations.' After being seriously ill with pneumonia, she reflected: 'It is curious to find oneself near the crossroads and to wonder what the passage will be.'

Each summer Charlotte returned to London for a month, to coincide with her birthday celebrations with the WFL. It was always an outpouring of love and something of a triumphant tour, visiting Nine Elms where her old home was now a municipal nursery, to Kurandai, where her bungalow was part of a school for disabled children, and the WFL. Particularly in comparison with all the difficulties in Ireland, she would be swept away by emotion, finding great comfort in old friendships and with all difficulties smoothed out by the efficient Florence Underwood and Elizabeth Knight. 'How is it I have such friends? May I become worthy of them ... Thanks, thanks for the unspeakable gift of human love.'

Her 80th birthday celebrations in June 1924 included leading a procession, in which Dame Millicent Fawcett and Emmeline Pethick Lawrence took part, from the Embankment to Hyde Park, continuing the campaign for all women to have the vote at 21. It was almost the last suffrage demonstration – her 84th birthday celebration was a victory feast to mark the achievement of their claim for women to have the vote on the same terms as men. When she spoke at the WFL celebration her old spirit had returned and she spoke with confidence:

I have seen great days, but this is the greatest. I remember when we started twenty-one years ago, with empty coffers ... I never believed that equal votes would come in my lifetime. But when an impossible dream comes true, we must go on to another. The true unity of men and women is one such dream. The end of war, of famine – they are all impossible dreams, but the dream must be dreamed until it takes a spiritual hold.

In Charlotte's eyes only one country had managed to turn the dream into reality. With her morale restored, Charlotte was determined to visit it. Her plans were delayed by a near fatal fall down the stairs of Roebuck House, but in the summer of 1930 she sailed to Leningrad with keen traveller Hanna, who had a BA and an MA in modern languages, specialising in French and German, and a delegation from the Friends of Soviet Russia (FOSR). The party included Helena Molony, Sheila Dowling 'and other radicals' (Ward p.268). A party of British communists was also on the ship and 'Hanna was, according to Charlotte Despard, active in putting forward an Irish republican view to the British comrades, as a result almost exhausting her stock of Irish revolutionary mementoes' (p.268).

For Charlotte, Russia represented the future, and she wanted to see that the future worked. Everything she saw gave her something to admire and a lesson for capitalism. The children she met in the kindergartens, schools and colleges enchanted her with their openness and confidence. 'No shyness at all,' she said, 'one could see that they had met with kindness only.' She enquired about punishment and noted: 'Punishments are taboo. In cases of insubordination, deprival of some dainty or treat, or, for a few short hours, isolation.' Even the Red Army, she found, inflicted no harsher punishments.

From Leningrad they travelled to Moscow and were taken on an exhausting tour of factories, craft schools and rehabilitation centres for prostitutes and minor criminals. Charlotte found it inspiring. Each of the institutions was run by an elected committee which set standards and solved problems There was no competition, compulsion or quarrelling and women were elected to positions of responsibility on equal terms with men. She attended a church service and 'could testify that the Soviet State is not a robber of churches', and a guide assured her that there was no hostility to collective farms: 'the poor peasant proprietor is being taken along gently – given really preferential treatment – and his opposition to collective farming has quite broken down,' she recorded. As she watched a youth rally, joy flooded through her at the success of idealism. 'Free, happy and rejoicing – I thought of Shelley and his *Revolt of Islam*, and breathed within myself a fervent wish that this grand nation – risen from the depths of humiliation – may not have her progress retarded by the capitalists and imperialists who are bent on her destruction.'

There was just one remaining question for this veteran prison campaigner – was there any serious crime, and if so how was it punished? They were not shown prisons and there was a long delay before she had a reply, but just before the end of her visit three legal experts replied. 'According to Russian law there are no crimes and no punishment,' she wrote. Death sentences might be passed in cases of treason but 'these are very rare. Other cases, and real incurables are sent to the island penal settlement. There, but that they must not leave the island, they are free to live as they will and practically govern themselves.' The picture painted of the island, known as Gulag, meant that she left the Soviet Union content.

Even then, three years before the Stalinist purges really began, Charlotte had been misled, although she had at least tried to find out. Her need to believe that everything was working in the Soviet Union was overwhelming – throughout her life she had wanted to be part of the socialist utopia prophesised by Shelley, that Marx and others had said would lead to a higher stage of civilisation. Her joy could only be expressed in poetry, the first she had attempted since her schooldays. With a frail hand and quavering strokes, she scratched out vast stanzas to celebrate the Soviet Union, the weak hand and strong words incongruous.

> The People want songs! I'll sing one to thee,
> Land of vast vistas, valiant and free,
> Seeing before thee a great destiny –
> 'Tis the land of the rising sun.
>
> Dear comrades, dear friends, across the wide sea,
> We meet you, we greet you in sweet amity,
> May the day soon arrive when all Nations shall be
> As the land of the rising sun!

The visit had made her more confident in the future. She was still working with the unemployed and the Prisoners' Defence League, and now she was on the Executive of the FOSR, and a vigorous supporter of Saor Éire, the Republican Congress, which was set up by the left wing of the IRA and inherited the aims of the IWP. She took to the hustings in the general election of February 1932, her chief targets the constituencies of Cosgrave's ministers, who used to find her urging their crowds to vote for de Valera. Her thin voice no longer carried and while still an embarrassment to her enemies, Charlotte was also becoming a liability to her own side. Desmond Fitzgerald, defence minister, shouted 'That woman there was on de Valera's platform – a member of the executive of the Friends of Soviet Russia and the Communist Party who seek to establish anarchy on the Russian model in this country in conflict with the teachings of the Catholic Church.' This line of attack would drive Charlotte from her adopted country.

In 1931 Hanna was arrested in Ireland and sentenced to be imprisoned for the duration of the war. She immediately began hunger strike and was transferred to Holloway where she met Maud and Constance Markievicz, also imprisoned for the duration of the war. She was temporarily released under the Cat and Mouse Act. There was outrage in Dublin at her arrest and Charlotte bombarded John French to secure her release. Also in 1931 the National Aid Association was formed to support Republicans forced out of employment. Maud was the chair and Hanna and Charlotte treasurers.

In 1933 a Marxist organisation called the Revolutionary Workers' Group emerged and the IRA, heavily influenced by Saor Éire, took a turn to the left, declaring that 'the reorganisation of Irish life demands the public ownership of the means of production, distribution and control.' To help matters along, Charlotte rented and later bought a house in Eccles Street which became the headquarters of the FOSR and a college for working–class members of the IRA. At first lectures focused on Marxist theory and life in Russia, but soon turned to the rise of fascism. The Army Comrades Association was an employment agency for former Free State soldiers and in 1933 it began to recruit men as a guard for Cosgrave's supporters against harassment by the IRA, wearing blue shirts as a uniform. Nearly a million people attended the Eucharist Congress in Dublin at Easter 1932. Religious feeling was still intense when, in his

Lenten letter for 1933, the Cardinal-Primate said communists were the enemy of God, and there was no room for them among the children of St Patrick. In Charlotte's eyes this was deplorable and she granted herself dispensation to ignore his words.

Catholic gangs began to attack left-wing speakers and break up meetings. A rumour spread that the Revolutionary Workers' Group had placed a consecrated wafer under the doormat of their headquarters, so everyone entering would tread on the body of Christ. Armed with knives and hatchets a mob, including members of the Blueshirts and the St Patrick's Anti-Communist League, besieged the house and set it alight. A week later Charlotte's Irish Workers' College was wrecked and looted and for a few hours she was trapped inside by the mob before she could escape through the backyard. She refused to be dismayed but it was soon clear even to her that Dublin could not be part of a communist world. In April, de Valera earned her contempt when he gave in to pressure and deported a communist, James Gralton, simply for his ideology. In June the Republican Congress, with a left-wing IRA group and the newly inaugurated Communist Party, assembled at Wolfe Tone's grave in Bodenstown to celebrate his birthday, but the day ended in a pitched battle. The IRA expelled members of the Republican congress and said that 'The movement which is known as Communism has become definitely associated with atheism and irreligion, hence any good or bad in the Communist economic theory is submerged.'

It had become impossible to be a Catholic communist in Ireland. Charlotte's political beliefs could not easily be accommodated even in her own house – Maud Gonne and Seán MacBride had joined her in the IWP, but the IRA's pronouncement made her beliefs an embarrassment. When she returned from her annual visit to England she moved out of Roebuck House to Eccles Street but there was nowhere for her to go. She was not at home in the Republican Congress as a communist, and could not tolerate the communist leadership's hostility to the Republicans. She thought about returning to England, or going to Spain. Her mind was made up by Hanna who had visited Belfast at the beginning of the year. Unemployment there had risen to over 20 per cent, leading to widespread rioting, but Protestant and Catholic workers had united in this capitalist corner of Ireland. Hanna had been arrested while trying to spread the message of communism, but she thought the sister of Lord French might achieve more. Charlotte did not hesitate. She gave her house in Eccles Street to the FOSR, Roebuck House to Maud and, with Lord French's portrait and Max's bust, set off for Belfast. She was nearly 90.

Charlotte seemed almost immortal. Frail, she reminded the WFL of unachieved goals. For some people Charlotte had been somewhere between sainthood and idiocy, but now she enjoyed a wider acclaim than before. With Mussolini in Italy, the Nazis in Germany and Franco's Falangists in Spain, she spoke in Trafalgar Square on an anti-fascist platform and was cheered as loudly as in suffragette days. When she told a *Daily Mirror* reporter that the discrimination against women was in danger of losing all the gains that had been made, it made the front cover: '"We must fight," says suffragette of 91.' Margaret Bondfield, first woman Cabinet minister, said: 'If I have won any laurels, I am proud to lay them at the feet of Mrs Despard.' Harry Pollitt, secretary of the Communist Party, said 'she has done more for Communism than any of us.' Her friend Lilian Baylis, now manager of the Old Vic and Sadler's Wells theatres, knelt before the crowd and kissed her hand at her 93rd birthday party. A roll of homage to her was signed by 2,500 people including suffragettes Teresa Billingon-Greig and Sylvia Pankhurst, politicians George Lansbury and Nancy Astor, vegetarians Bernard Shaw and Stafford Cripps, friends Kate Harvey and Margaret Bondfield, union members and many more. Missing names included Emmeline Pankhurst and Millicent Fawcett who had died, though younger than Charlotte, who commented: 'They pass and I remain, and indeed I sometimes wonder why.' Her beloved sister Carrie had also died, but Charlotte was not one for long periods of mourning. She liked to dispense her views about life and when reporters asked the secret of her long life she replied: 'If you want to live the happiest and fullest life, live with the people.'

Finally she returned to Belfast to be with the people and dedicated to them the poems she wrote:

> Long, long in grim darkness you've silently waited,
> Now to the Red Dawn your banner's unfurled.
> Bear it on body, who dares to withhold you?
> Forward! and onward! yours is the word.

She lived in Newtonards Road near Stormont Castle. Opposite the two policemen who guarded the entrance to the castle were two more, guarding Charlotte's front gate. She was still regarded as a threat to security – whenever she was driven off in her car, a police car followed.

With her secretary Molly Fitzgerald, Charlotte plotted the downfall of Bates, Stormont and capitalism. Struggling to read, she studied pamphlets from the Theosophist Society and the FOSR to draft another speech for a meeting of the unemployed. She had little personal contact with the people of Ulster apart from her doctor, John O'Prey, who shared her concern for the poor. Trying to make closer contact, Charlotte moved from Newtonards Road to a small house in Glenburn Park, nearer the centre of Belfast, but the gap was more than geographical. To raise morale among the unemployed, Charlotte thought it would be good to have a brass band, as miners and millworkers in the north of England do. She purchased the necessary instruments, at considerable expense. At first there was a lot of enthusiasm and the band could be heard practising or seen marching in the street, but soon a number of hardly used cornets and tubas appeared in pawnbrokers' shops. People agreed with her idea, but music had to go in the face of needing money to feed the children. Similarly workers' solidarity crumbled in the face of sectarian division.

The Women's Freedom League Bulletin of 5 April 1935 reported on a meeting at the Minerva Club in London, where members and friends listened to Mrs Sheehy Skeffington speak about her recent visit to Canada and the USA. Hanna was introduced as 'a very dear friend and one who had shared in our fight for Votes of Women'. The bulletin concludes with a message of love to Mrs Despard, 'whom we are eagerly looking forward to having with us in June, to celebrate the 91st anniversary of her birthday.'

In summer 1935 the worst riots yet took place in Belfast and the working-class unity of 1933 disappeared as Protestants raided Catholic areas. Even though it was guarded by the police, Charlotte's house was not considered safe, particularly because she had Roland Kidd staying with her, who was investigating abuses of the Special Powers Act for the National Council for Civil Liberties. His enquiries attracted the attention of Protestants and Charlotte was threatened and abused. She decided to move out of the city.

Charlotte's companions in Belfast were Molly Fitzgerald, an idealist who had worked as a secretary in Dublin, and Jack Mulvenna, former publican, who had been expelled from the IRA for his membership of the Republican Congress. They were both in their early thirties, vivacious, friendly and left wing. Although they were officially her secretary and chauffeur, Charlotte only ever referred to them as 'my dear friends'. She enjoyed their youthful energy and their Irish accents made her feel that she was still in touch with the people. Charlotte had been a beneficiary of the capitalist system she hated, as she lived on the income from the French and Despard trusts, but Molly and Jack were extravagant with her money and her fortune was less than in the past.

In 1937 she moved out of Belfast to a bungalow built for her on the clifftop above Whitehead. Before it was built, Belfast police searched the foundations for arms – in Whitehead there was little tolerance for Republicans. Charlotte had to borrow £3,000 from the bank to pay for her new home. She still had the interest on her marriage settlement, but Max's fortune had dwindled to less than £5,000. She had been extravagant in Dublin, including giving Roebuck House to Maud, and loans to her brother had not been repaid. She had asked him once about the debt, a few weeks before the assassination attempt and their estrangement, so she had never returned to the matter. Largely from a sense of justice, she asked the trustees of her marriage settlement – her brother's two children – to allow her to have some of the capital to pay off her debts. Suspecting the money would be misused they refused, and so, eighteen months later, when a further £1,100 of debts had been run up in her name, Charlotte was made bankrupt.

By then, as war approached, Charlotte was beginning to fade away and become confused, perhaps a little senile. The old pain in her back and shoulder worsened and she spent whole days in bed, drugged with painkillers and unable to move. On a fine day, local people might see her in her garden or hobbling down the road, but few local people entered the house, other than a nurse and Dr O'Prey, who came to visit and give her painkillers, and a priest, Father McCloskey, who could accommodate her communist ideas. Charlotte's days were very lonely – the outbreak of war in September 1939 cut her off from friends in England and she was an outcast in Whitehead. The passion and enthusiasm for her various causes had drained away, leaving a very frail and sad figure.

She was also beset by scandal. A newspaper report (*Weekly Irish Times* 4 November 1939) reported that the court was still dealing with her bankruptcy and it was said that 'too much of Mrs Despard's income had been going not for her benefit'. In September 1939 Charlotte made a new will, leaving the bulk of her estate to Molly Fitzgerald and Jack Mulvenna. Six weeks later she turned the wrong way coming out of the bathroom during the night and fell down a flight of stairs, cutting her head and dislocating a hip. She lived for three days but did not regain consciousness and died on 9 November. In the minds of local people there was little doubt that she had been pushed, but the evidence presented at the inquest pointed to an understandable accident. A frail 95-year-old woman, subject to dizzy spells and taking sleeping pills, would have been quite likely to stumble as she moved along a dark landing in the wartime blackout. Reluctantly the jury recorded a verdict of accidental death. Marion Reeve, then the President of the WFL, said that she could not believe Charlotte's death had been caused by an accident as she had people looking after her, people whom Marion thought would soon be separated from Charlotte because of the scandal. Technically the creditors should have been paid off and the residue left to Molly Fitzgerald and Jack Mulvenna, but it was an open secret in legal circles that 'no Republican would get a penny from the estate of Lord French's sister'. When the case was eventually settled in 1951, Molly had died and legal fees had drained away what money was left.

Charlotte had asked to be buried in Glasnevin Cemetery, the Republicans' resting place in Dublin, near Constance Markiewicz. Although the creditors' representative decreed the expense to be unjustified, Jack Mulvenna ensured her wish was fulfilled. The hearse carrying her coffin left Belfast on a bleak rainy morning followed by two cars. When they reached Lurgan there were five cars in the cortege, at Newry just north of the border twelve, and at Dundalk, the first town inside the Republic, twenty. Others joined along the slow journey until they arrived at Dublin at the head of more than fifty cars. The coffin rested overnight at St Joseph's Church, while a steady stream of people passed through to pay their respects and the following day a crowd of over 2,000 accompanied it to the cemetery.

Her pall bearers came from organisations she had wanted to unite in life – Peadar O'Donnell formerly of the Republic Congress; Roddy

Connolly, once of the Irish Workers' Party; Seán MacBride from the right of the IRA and Frank Hugh O'Donell from the left; Sean Murray head of the Communist Party; Mick Price, bitterly anti-communist chief of staff of the IRA.

At the graveside was Maud Gonne who spoke:

> Throughout her life she was like a white flame in the defence of prisoners and the oppressed. As President of the Prisoners' Defence League, she left her home to work all over the country for human liberty, and I, like many men alive today, owe my life to her. Because of her work the people of Ireland loved her, and especially the poor of Dublin, and to all of us her death is the loss of a great light.

Charlotte's many friends in England could not attend her funeral as it was arranged quickly and at that time they needed to apply for a permit to visit to Ireland. There was an outpouring of tributes and obituaries. One newspaper nicknamed her 'Grandmother of the Irish Revolution', while another (from the papers of Teresa Billington-Greig, not referenced) said:

> Mrs Despard, who has just died at the age of 95, was a remarkable woman. From her girlhood she was a rebel against injustice. Her energetic work in the service of the poor convinced her that women should have a say in government and she provided the 'Votes for Women' movement with one of its most vigorous and militant leaders. Where social progress and freedom are cherished causes her name will not quickly be forgotten.

Mrs Corbett Ashby:

> I was a great admirer of her because of her outstanding moral and physical courage, her entire unselfishness and her passionate desire to set wrongs right. The more unpopular the cause the greater her devotion to it. She was a leader who inspired complete confidence and great love.

Sylvia Pankhurst:

> She was one of our most courageous and devoted social workers. When I was in prison with her in 1907 and we used to walk round the hospital together, I was impressed by her truly magnificent courage. We shall remember her with love and admiration and gratitude for all the work she did with such fine spirit.

A memorial service was held in London, and a special service in Edinburgh, her birthplace, with readings of Shelley.

During her 95 years Charlotte saw many changes. She worked hard for much of her life to make things better for others. She fought for many causes and was an amazing woman who accomplished so much. It is tragic that after a life lived mainly in the public gaze, she died sad and alone, her name not widely known. As Marion Reeve said in a letter to Hanna Sheehy Skeffington in November 1939, 'We shall certainly not see her like again.'

Post Script

On 10 June 2018 women in Belfast, Cardiff, Edinburgh and London marched as part of the celebrations marking the centenary of the 1918 Representation of the People Act, which gave some women the right to vote. It was estimated that some 30,000 women marched in London. Wearing green, white or violet, the suffrage colours, the processions appeared as rivers of colour through the streets. These twenty-first-century women carried modern banners, modelled on those carried by the suffragettes.

The Nine Elms Vauxhall Partnership took part in the procession, carrying a banner created by artist Ruth Evans and local women. Ruth said:

> Charlotte Despard was a truly remarkable activist and I'm looking forward to creating a banner in tribute to her. Many of the struggles she fought for continue today and I hope, through the process of researching and making with other women, to explore some of the historic and ongoing issues she campaigned for to inspire us into action.

* * *

This volume serves as a small effort to remember Charlotte and her causes, highlighting how far we have come, and all that remains to be done.

Ireland notes

As with all conflicts, there are many different perspectives and points of view around Ireland's history. The following is intended only to give a very brief context to Charlotte's activities in Ireland.

Eighteenth-century Ireland was an overwhelmingly rural society with political, social and economic conditions that varied significantly by region. Farming practices were often outdated and there was recurrent famine, usually caused by bad weather or crop failure. As was common across Europe, the social order reflected the importance of land ownership with landlords at the top of the hierarchy then tenant famers then cottiers, who usually rented land on an annual basis and were most susceptible to economic downturns. The expansion of trade and industry produced a new social hierarchy, with growing numbers of merchants, industrialists and professionals showing that it was possible to make a living other than from the land.

A religious census in 1834 estimated that the population was almost 81 per cent Catholic, 10.7 per cent Anglican, 9 per cent Presbyterian. Around 99 per cent of Presbyterians and 45 per cent of Anglicans lived in Ulster and many Anglicans lived in and around Dublin, so they were strongest in the same area, which had implications for their cooperation against what were seen as Catholic threats to the Protestant constitution. Catholics were subject to a series of laws aimed at strengthening Protestant dominance of Irish society; for example, Catholics were banned from carrying weapons, and from teaching or managing Irish schools. An Act of 1704 made land ownership very difficult (although few could own land anyway, so this was not very significant) and those Catholics (and Protestants) who were eligible to vote were disenfranchised by 1728. Memories of Catholic insurgence in the previous century began to fade and tolerance increased. The penal laws began to be dismantled, and Relief Acts of 1778 and 1782 lessened the restrictions on Catholic land ownership, education and participation in the professions but restraints remained, so Catholic grievances were still a significant part of wider political debates.

About 95 per cent of Irish land was owned by about 5,000 Protestant families – the 'Protestant Ascendancy' which dominated politics, high society and the civil service. The crucial identifying feature of this group was its Anglicanism, which distinguished its members in crucial ways from Catholics and other Irish Protestants. Throughout the eighteenth century, Presbyterians extended their political and economic influence. The forced payment of tithes to the Church of Ireland and exclusion from public office until 1870 aroused bitter resentment among Presbyterians, especially as they felt they had proved their loyalty to the Protestant constitution. By the end of the century most legal constraints had been removed but a legacy of mistrust remained.

Until 1782 the Irish parliament had restricted powers and was subservient to Westminster. The legal and judicial systems were heavily based on the English systems. Domestic political power came from the Irish parliament in Dublin, but it was unrepresentative of the wider population, particularly Catholics, who were largely excluded from the civil service, judiciary and higher ranks of the police force. While the Irish parliament showed the distinction between Ireland and the rest of Britain, the Irish Executive showed its subordination. Appointed by and responsible to London, the Executive was based at Dublin Castle and presided over by the viceroy or lord lieutenant, assisted by the chief secretary from the House of Commons, who supervised Castle administration and oversaw the implementation of Irish policy.

Across the second-half of the eighteenth century, the population of Ireland rose sharply; the competition for political supremacy also increased. Defenderism emerged in the 1780s. Sectarian, its aim was to defend Catholics. The organisation had similarities with freemasonry and its secret signs and symbols, but Defenderism was more sophisticated and ideological than other groups. Defenders were involved in politics at national and international levels, with some following revolutionary events in France. Defenderism won support in towns and the non-agrarian population, and spread in the growing tensions especially in Ulster, with Defenders the perpetrators and victims of raids and riots. One of the most well-known was the Battle of the Diamond in 1795, a clash between Defenders and the Protestant 'Peep O'Day Boys', near Loughgall in County Armagh. Victorious, the Peep O'Day Boys reorganised themselves as the Orange Order, named for King William III and his victory at the Boyne in 1690, reflecting mounting concern about what were seen to be the advances of the Catholics and the consequent undermining of Protestant power and privilege.

Patriotism, too, had evolved during the second-half of the eighteenth century in the form of proto-nationalism, which emphasised the view that Ireland suffered through its dominance by the British legislature. Various groups highlighted economic issues, greater legislative independence, the rights of Protestants and the tendency of Catholics to seek redress from London. With British troops distracted by the American Revolution, fears of a French invasion increased and the Irish government responded by establishing volunteer corps across Ireland to undertake military and law-enforcement duties. Catholics were allowed to join the corps, but the involvement of Catholics in the defence of Ireland was too much for some Protestants. Despite the opposition of some volunteers, the organisation became increasingly sympathetic to the patriots and to the idea of greater legislative independence for Ireland.

The volunteers were radicalised and politicised. In 1782, legislative amendments granted Ireland a number of concessions, including some parliamentary independence – the English Privy Council still had the power to veto Irish Bills and the English parliament still presided over the Irish Executive. Inspired by the French Revolution the Society of United Irishmen was founded in 1791. Its support came mainly from Protestants, many of whom had a distrust of Catholics. Events in France and rising British panic about radical political activity in England and Ireland led to a series of laws aiming to curb such activity. The society re-emerged in 1795 – having been suppressed the previous year – as a secret, Republican and revolutionary organisation which, over the next four years, was restructured as a more disciplined and militarily inclined organisation. Links with other societies were established and those with the French were cultivated. In 1796 a French expedition set sail for Ireland – it had to turn back due to bad weather, but it sent waves of alarm through the Irish and English administrations.

Steps were taken to clamp down on seditious behaviour and martial law was declared in March 1798. The 1798 uprising involved about 50,000 rebels. About 30,000 people were killed. Insurgency continued even after the main violence ended and about 150,000 people were subject to flogging, transportation or execution. It was a traumatic episode in Irish history and exacerbated divisions. Well before 1798 there had been plans for Great Britain and Ireland to unite: Prime Minister Pitt thought a union would bring Ireland more firmly under Britain's control with a chance to push through Catholic emancipation, which would give a loyal Catholic population within the UK. Most Catholics supported the Union, because they had been led to believe Catholic emancipation would follow, but there was strong opposition from many quarters. This led Pitt to abandon plans for Catholic emancipation, which would turn out to be a grave error. The Act of Union was passed in 1800 and brought a number of changes, including new financial arrangements, the uniting of the churches of Ireland and England, the abolition of the Irish parliament and the transfer of Irish representation to Westminster.

After a campaign led by Daniel O'Connell and others the Emancipation Bill was passed in 1829. Although a general victory for Catholics there were still some senior positions closed to Catholics and the 40-shilling freeholders were disenfranchised. It gave Irish Catholics a feeling that change was possible and the socially and politically privileged could be toppled. It was also a political movement of global significance as it showed that democratic and non-revolutionary political associations could lead reform. Protestants were shaken by the Bill and the Orange Order developed further. Demands for repeal of the Act of Union grew and in 1840 O'Donnell established the Loyal National Repeal Association. Repeal was not straightforward, as it affected the fabric of British constitution. Against the background of a worsening agrarian crisis and international events, some organisations began to promote Irish separatism, and there was a brief attempt at rebellion in County Tipperary in 1848.

A pressing problem in Ireland was increasing poverty. The population grew from about 5 million in 1800 to a peak of around 8.2 million in 1841 but then declined, partly due to famines, to 4.3 million in 1911. This was unique in nineteenth-century Europe which experienced almost universal population growth. The rising population had a profound effect on rural life and the pressure on land. In 1841 only a fifth of the population lived in towns of twenty or more houses, and just under 85 per cent lived on the land in 1851. Although by 1914 the proportion of people living in towns rose from about a sixth to a third, Irish cities and towns expanded slowly in comparison with other urban centres in Britain and the industrial sector did not develop in Ireland as it did elsewhere.

While some Irish industries, such as shipbuilding, did really well, they could not provide enough employment to stem emigration or absorb the pool of surplus agricultural labour.

The Great Famine of 1845–9 was modern Ireland's worst catastrophe and the most severe natural disaster in nineteenth-century Europe. A fungus attacked potato crops, spoiling a crucial source of food for the Irish people. Half the 1845 crop was free from the disease, but the 1846 crop failed almost completely. It was not until 1849 that there was a near normal crop, a tragedy compounded by a spread of diseases. The Famine cast a long shadow. About 1 million people died through starvation or disease and around 1.5 million emigrated. At least 8 million adults left Ireland between 1801 and 1921, and Irish people were by far the most likely to leave Europe in the second-half of the nineteenth century. Some of those crammed into 'coffin ships' bound for America died and there was a decline of cottiers, already disadvantaged as the poorest of the agrarian hierarchy, leaving a legacy of bitterness. Between 1845 and 1851 a quarter of farms disappeared and there was a marked drop in the number of farms under 15 acres. Prime ministers Peel and Russell initiated schemes including the distribution of free food, but they could not solve the many problems. They were constrained by structural difficulties, inefficient organisation, incompetence and insensitivity and a serious food shortage in Europe. They also could not upset the economic status quo which it was thought could send the British and Irish economies into free fall. There was an error in suspending aid before the crisis had receded, and for many the relief was inadequate and slow to arrive.

For successive British governments the issue had been the improvement of Irish society to make it more easily governable, but there was no easy solution to the landlord/tenant problems. The settlement of the land issue was the central plank of Gladstone's mission to pacify Ireland but his legislation was watered down by cabinet opposition and Lords' amendments. The tide began to turn in the 1860s when the focus shifted to concerns of tenants. The 1870 Land Act did not legalise tenant right, but agreed it should be recognised where it already existed and introduced some measures for tenant land purchase. It was disappointing though, and by 1879 Ireland was suffering severe agricultural depression and a land war. The Land Purchase Act of 1903 established land purchase as the final solution to the land issue, inducing tenants to buy and landlords to sell. It took massive intervention from the British Treasury to accomplish this but almost 300,000 sales were accomplished between 1906 and 1908, and by the eve of the First World War, three-quarters of tenants were in the process of buying out landlords.

Calls for repeal of the Act of Union had disappeared during the Famine crisis of the 1840s, but it was followed by a period of intense debate about the relationship between Ireland and Great Britain, and what emerged was the increasing Catholicisation of the national question. One of the greatest threats identified by the Catholic hierarchy was the Fenian movement, which reflected much of the outlook of the wider Irish population. Fenianism came from the devastation of the Famine, the failure of the 1848 rising, and a volatile international situation where difficult relationships between Britain, France and America presented opportunities for Irish conspirators. Fenianism was a general term for organisations formed in Ireland and America in 1858/9 which were known as the Irish Republican Brotherhood (IRB), the Irish Revolutionary Brotherhood or 'the Organisation'. Secret and revolutionary organisations had a number of influences and objectives which focused on a hatred of Britain, disgust at self-seeking and ineffective Irish MPs, and a commitment to an Irish republic. There were international links, particularly with America. Most Fenians did not join in with the organisation's political activities, such as the Fenian Rising of 1867. Fenianism was anti-confessional, but the Catholic hierarchy condemned the IRB because of its secretive and revolutionary composition, which fuelled antagonism, but the key point of difference was the degree and direction of clerical involvement.

In 1873 the IRB's supreme council cleared the way for association with lawful political activity and agreed that insurrection could be postponed until (or perhaps if) this was approved by the Irish people. Fenian military planning had been on the basis that the British would be at war, with the French or Americans, and thus vulnerable, but by 1870 this seemed unlikely.

Protestant lawyer Isaac Butt believed Irish prosperity could only be guaranteed if the country retained its imperial connection and maintained that the Union had failed Ireland because of its misapplication. His task was, therefore, to persuade Britain to reform the Union and to convince Ireland that the Union should be maintained. Deemed too timid by some, but too radical by others, his long lasting legacy was the alliance he formed with Fenianism. A small element of Butt's party led by Charles Stewart Parnell transformed into a dynamic political movement.

In 1879 Parnell formed his first important alliance – a five-point pact with advanced nationalists. This 'New Departure' was the basis for constitutional nationalism, establishing itself as a potent force the British government could not ignore. The terms of the New Departure included a declaration in favour of self-government, vigorous agitation of the land question, the exclusion of all sectarian issues and an insistence that all Irish members vote together. The IRB's Supreme Council rejected the New Departure but agreed that individual Fenians would be permitted to take part in electoral politics. Plans for a revolutionary struggle and an Irish republic were put aside for the time being and Parnell agreed to work on the land question. In the process, he oversaw the transformation of constitutional politics into a national and implicitly Catholic movement.

Parnell became leader of the Irish Party in 1880 and until his death in 1891 was seen as the unchallenged leader of nationalist Ireland. Under his leadership the Party transformed into a tight political machine. In 1885–6 it formed an alliance with Gladstone's Liberals – the 'union of hearts'. Gladstone embraced home rule but it was to split the Liberals and send them into the political wilderness for twenty years. Gladstone was convinced by the Irish Party's claim to represent the will of the majority of Irish people, but his 1886 Home Rule Bill encountered strong opposition and was defeated in the Commons by 343 votes to 311.

Unionists responded to Gladstone's 'conversion' with alarm. Home Rule (or 'Rome Rule') was seen by Protestants as an expression of Catholic power. English Conservative allies like Lord Randolph Churchill encouraged collaboration and resistance, leading to an alliance between Conservatives and unionists that would keep Home Rule at bay until 1912. In 1898 O'Brien founded the United Irish League, an agrarian movement which tried to build on Parnellite traditions and encourage party unity.

The first twenty years of the twentieth century was a period of momentous change, with the formation of new groups, fluid alliances and everyone working for some cause or another, according to one observer. The Irish Party kept a firm hold over nationalist Ireland. The return of the Liberals in 1906 and the introduction of the third Home Rule Bill in 1912 stimulated widespread confidence in the inevitability of a national parliament, while unionism was mobilised in opposition to home rule. The First World War heightened existing tensions and created a charged political environment.

A number of events stirred nationalist opinion in Ireland at the turn of the century. Pro-Boer sentiment helped to strengthen ideas around physical force and join a number of individuals and organisations into an increasingly identifiable physical grouping, which eventually formed the nucleus of Sinn Féin. Sinn Féin (ourselves) was formed in 1905 by Arthur Griffith, journalist-proprietor of the *United Irishman,* who wanted to promote nationalist unity and saw in the Irish Party the reasons for Ireland's disarray. Griffith's attempts to construct an alternative between militant nationalism and constitutionalism were influential. Some of his views, such as a dual monarchy and his non-violent stand, meant that some republicans viewed him with suspicion, but many saw Sinn Féin as a vehicle for their positions. His organisations were dynamic and forward thinking, involving non-conformist women and Protestants, which was unusual – women activists were rejected by the Irish Party and most other political organisations. His central message was that Ireland should look within itself for self-respect and autonomy.

The Liberal landslide at the 1906 general election did not bring about the hoped-for legislation. The Liberals' showdown with the House of Lords led to two general elections in 1910 which left them with a reduced number of seats and requiring Labour and Irish nationalist support. In exchange they pledged to introduce a third Home Rule Bill. By 1912 unionism had become Ulster-based and unionists had begun to see that they could not hope to block home rule for the whole island, with some suggesting that the partition of the Ulster counties could be a solution. Many nationalists underestimated the extent of Ulster resistance and the social, political and cultural differences between north and south. Similarly, the Liberal Party's 1912 Bill had little consideration of unionist objections. Unionists had many reasons for opposing Home Rule, including a desire to maintain links with Britain, and a fundamental view that nationalism was Catholic and had little to offer Protestants.

The Ulster Volunteer Force (UVF) was established in 1913 to resist home rule. It attracted about 90,000 members and in 1914 distributed over 20,000 service rifles and 3 million rounds of ammunition. It was determined and disciplined. As political efforts to find a solution failed, the potential for militancy and confrontation increased. In 1913 the nationalist Irish Volunteers was established to protect the Home Rule Bill. This had strong links with the IRB and the involvement of the Irish Party stimulated recruitment – by the end of 1914 membership was estimated to be over 190,000.

Growing trade union membership and a series of strikes and lockouts by Irish workers in 1912–13 raised the temperature and the determination of employers to break the unions. The Irish Citizen Army, an armed force, was formed in 1913 to protect workers from the brutality of the Dublin Metropolitan Police during the Dublin Lockout of 1913–14. Its membership dwindled but it was revived by socialist and trade union leader James Connolly. The Citizen Army, like the Volunteers and the UVF, drilled, wore a uniform and was committed to military action if needed in pursuit of a workers' republic. Opposed to war it claimed to serve 'neither King, nor Kaiser, but Ireland', which presumably built bridges with the militant republicans, who in 1914 were making plans for an insurrection.

The suffrage movement also contributed to the instability of the period. Like its British counterpart the Irish movement was split along militant and non-militant lines, but the Irish movement was also divided along religious lines corresponding with the larger unionist and nationalist schism. The demarcations were intensified by the home rule crisis, with even staunch nationalists accused, usually by Republican women, of being pro-British because they lobbied the Westminster government and assumed women would be enfranchised under home rule.

The immediate effect of the First World War was to reduce internal tensions as the war was given priority and the Home Rule Bill was suspended until the end of hostilities. Over 200,000 Irishmen joined the British Army. The war accelerated militarism and constitutionalists maintained a hold over nationalist Ireland until at least 1916. Complicated and secret negotiations led to a decision to revolt at Easter 1916 – the Easter Rising.

On Easter Monday about 1,300 Irish Volunteers and 219 members of the Citizen Army seized a number of Dublin buildings, most famously the General Post Office which housed most of the Rising's leaders, and a provisional government was assembled. Sending in troops to quash the Rising led to fierce artillery bombardment and exchanges of fire. About 450 people were killed and over 2,500 injured, most of them civilians. The Rising was a complete surprise to most Dubliners, many of whom saw it as an insult to their men, who were risking their lives in Europe. The destruction and inconvenience did little to endear the rebels to the Irish public. The British government elevated matters by introducing martial law throughout Ireland, inconveniencing those who did not support the rebels but were furious at what seemed to be communal punishment. Fifteen of the rebels were shot and about 3,500 'suspects' were arrested, with 1,500 quickly released.

Neither Lloyd George nor a 1917–18 Irish Convention (boycotted by Sinn Féin and Labour) managed to find a resolution to the partition question. Nationalist opposition to the Irish Party strengthened. The Rising had not provided a political strategy or even a way forward but a combination of people laid the foundations for a new and formidable political movement, with Sinn Féin, joined by the Volunteers, emerging as a focus.

Sinn Féin's stand was non-violent and constitutional and challenged the Irish Party on its own territory. Sinn Féin had four by-election victories in early 1917, most notably that of Eamon de Valera. The highest-ranking survivor of the Rising, de Valera had been saved from execution by his American citizenship. In 1917 he was elected as Sinn Féin president and later of the organised Volunteers. He described his vision for Ireland's political future – a republic would be sought, but once secured, the Irish people would choose their own form of government by referendum. The stand on violence was imprecise, but it helped to win over a number of people, including increasing numbers of Catholic clerics.

The Irish Party had always opposed conscription but the most protest it could muster was walking out of parliament. The 1918 Military Service

Bill, to extend conscription to Ireland, delivered the final blow to the flagging party. All walks of people joined to oppose the Bill in an enormous opposition campaign, made redundant by the armistice. Sinn Féin had played a prominent role in opposition, the Bill providing proof of their predictions about British intentions. Their profile was raised by the arrest of most of the Republican leadership for involvement in a spurious 'German plot'. Michael Collins escaped arrest, going on the run and helping to plan resistance to British coercion of Sinn Féin or the Volunteers.

The end of the war brought different strategies, including drumming up international support for Irish independence and the first general election since 1910. Sinn Féin campaigned on a platform which tried to appeal to everyone. Aided by Labour's decision not to contest the election the result was a triumph for Sinn Féin – it took less than half the total Irish votes but increased its seats from seven to seventy-three. Twenty-six Ulster Unionists were elected, increasing their share of the vote, but the Irish Party dropped from sixty-eight to six, keeping a hold only in Ulster. In accordance with its policy, Sinn Féin did not take up its seats at Westminster but reconstituted itself as Dáil Éireann (the Parliament of Ireland) in January 1919 and declared Irish independence. De Valera, President of the Dáil Éireann and the Republic, left in April for an eighteen-month American tour. The Dáil managed to disrupt British government and administration.

There had been clashes between Volunteers and police before, but in January 1919 two members of the Royal Irish Constabulary (RIC) were murdered in County Tipperary. Some Volunteer units began to call themselves the Irish Republican Army (IRA) and there were uncoordinated raids on policemen and barracks, with large houses burned and public officials harassed. Many Volunteers were forced to go on the run, forming active service raids and relying on local communities to hide them as they evaded arrest, staging some of the most violent ambushes of the conflict. Michael Collins organised the systematic assassination of prominent security personnel and civil servants.

The government pursued an increasingly coercive policy but the police could not cope with what was effectively a guerrilla war. Extra forces were recruited, including the notorious 'Black and Tans', sent in to reinforce the police, and the Auxiliaries, a force of about 2,300 former officers. These extra forces were undisciplined and some engaged in shocking behaviour, including arson and murder. There was a vicious cycle of retribution, with 'retaliations' which cost innocent lives. At least 1,200 people died during the conflict and public opinion was outraged, especially in Britain, where the government was under pressure to restrain its forces. Although some areas of Ireland experienced limited conflict, moderate opinion in Britain and Ireland was increasingly vocal in its demand for an end to hostilities. A truce to begin in July 1921 was finally agreed.

There were May elections under the Government of Ireland Act, which created two Irish states, with twenty-six counties under Dublin and six under Belfast. The Belfast parliament started the business of government while Sinn Féin boycotted the Dublin assembly and returned 124 unopposed members to the Second Dáil, convened in August 1921. Four unionists were returned to the Dublin parliament established under the Act. The legislation failed – home rule in this form was clearly no longer acceptable to the nationalists.

Difficult negotiations preceded the signing of the Anglo–Irish Treaty in December 1921. De Valera had rejected Lloyd George's offer of dominion status on the Canadian model, with some safeguards on defence and security but Sinn Féin implicitly agreed to negotiate on the basis of twenty-six county dominion status. To the astonishment of many, de Valera remained in Ireland, leaving the negotiations to Collins and Griffith, who represented a party which was still divided on the issue of a minimum level of independence. Under much pressure the delegates signed the 'Articles of an Agreement for a Treaty between Great Britain and Ireland' on 6 December. The main sticking point was the continuing connection with the British Empire and the abandonment of Irish autonomy, with Lloyd George's insistence on an oath of fidelity to the monarch and the Commonwealth. The Irish public seemed to support the Treaty, or at least were happy with the cessation of hostilities. Within the Dáil, Griffith and Collins were seen as traitors to the Republican deal, although they insisted it was the best available compromise and the only alternative was a renewed Anglo–Irish war, which the Irish could not win. Partition was still an issue, many believing Northern Ireland would fail to function as a viable economic unit, leading to reunification. The various views had seemed to be held together by their opposition to the British, but this quickly collapsed under the strain of the Treaty debates.

In January 1922 the Dáil voted for the Treaty, by sixty-four votes to fifty-seven. Collins became chairman of the provisional government formed a week later but there was no hope of an easy transition to normal politics. There was savage and destabilising animosity between pro- and anti-Treaty Sinn Féin and armed conflict looked increasingly likely. At a general election in June the public endorsed the Treaty, with anti-Treaty taking 36 of 128 seats and the pro-Treaty Sinn Féin, fifty-eight. The other seats went to three parties which supported the Treaty, but a public mandate was not enough to convince the dissidents. Collins' supporters had become known as the Free State Army while the anti-Treaty IRA members were the 'Irregulars'. In April the Irregulars took up positions in the Four Courts and other significant and symbolic buildings in Dublin. Having refused an order to evacuate, the provisional government's troops fired on the Irregulars on 28 June, beginning a vicious war in Dublin between former fellow soldiers and friends, which spread to other towns and cities.

The Civil War lasted until the following May. The number of casualties is unknown – the government said 800 of its forces had been killed but the Republican death toll was higher. The insurgents who fought against the democratically elected government faced excommunication. While it was legitimately elected, the provisional government had sanctioned ruthless and brutal actions during the conflict, executing seventy-seven Irregulars and imprisoning over 10,000 people without trial.

The Civil War scarred Ireland for decades. The pro-Treaty party became Cumann na nGaedheal in May 1923. The anti-Treatyites remained as Sinn Féin until they split in 1926. In the immediate aftermath of the war, Ireland was effectively a one party state, only Labour providing some kind of opposition, as Sinn Féin refused to sit in the new lower house, remaining loyal to the Second Dáil of 1921. The early years of the Irish Free State were a disappointment. The priorities were order and stability and Cumann na nGaedheal established an unimaginative administration, with the legal and political systems continuing along British lines. In difficult times Cumann na nGaedheal governed effectively but without excitement or innovation. It failed to cultivate grass-roots support and earned a reputation for miserliness by cutting pensions and salaries and fostering economic alarmism. The main problem was trying to build on a settlement which came from an incomplete revolution. Republican aims and hopes had not been realised under the terms of the Anglo–Irish Treaty.

Charlotte's writing

Fiction:

Chaste as Ice, Pure as Snow (1874), London: Tinsley

Wandering Fires (1874), London: Tinsley

A Modern Iago (1879), London: Griffith and Farran

What the Shepherd Saw: a Tale of Four Moonlight Nights (1881) New York: George Munro, A collection of very short Christmas stories by Thomas Hardy, Charlotte Despard, and others. Despard wrote *The White Lady of Hillbury*.

Jonas Sylvester (1886), London: Sonnenschein

The Rajah's Heir (1890), London: Tinsley

A Voice from the Dim Millions; being the true history of a working woman. London: Griffith, Farron, Okeden and Welsh (1891).

Outlawed (1908) (with Mabel Collins), London: Drane

Songs of the Red Dawn (1932) Dublin: Odhla Printing (poetry collection)

Non-fiction:

Was it Wise to Change? London: Cassell, 1894. Reprinted from Cassell's Magazine.

Women's franchise and industry (1908)

Women in the nation (1909)

Women in the new era (1910)

Pamphlet issued by Home Rule for India League London: Pelican Press, 1910s. Written with George Lansbury.

The Needs of Little Children (1912) Report of a conference on the care of babies and young children. Papers by Miss Margaret McMillan, Mrs. Pember Reeves, Dr. Ethel Bentham, Mrs. Despard

Theosophy and the Woman's Movement (1913) London: Theosophical Publishing Society, Riddle of Life series; no. 4.

Vegetarian Messenger and Health Review (10) (1913).

The Christ that is to be (1917), notes of an address given at Queen's Hall, January.

Bibliography

Besant A, (1913) *Vegetarianism in the Light of Theosophy*

Billington-Greig T, (1911) The Militant Suffrage Movement: Emancipation in a hurry, reprinted in *The Non-violent Militant*, (eds). McPhee and Fitzgerald

Booth C, *Inquiry into Life and Labour in London*, 1886-1903, Interview with Charlotte Despard 4 May 1900 Booth/B/296 p.96-115 https://booth.lse.ac.uk

Broderick M, (2012) *Wild Irish Women: Extraordinary lives from history*, The O'Brien Press

Buettinger, (1997) Women and anti-vivisection in late nineteenth century America, *Journal of Social History* 30 (4) summer 1997 p.857–72

Cieslakowska-Evans A, (2005) *Adoption issues and the displaced child in mid-nineteenth century English culture*, PhD thesis, University of Derby https://researchportal.port.ac.uk/portal/files/6669493/Cieslakowska_Evans_Audrey_2005.pdf

Colum M, (1947) *Life and the dream*, Doubleday

Crawford E, (1999) *The women's suffrage movement. A reference guide 1866-1928*, London: Routledge

Crawford E, (2012) *Suffragettes and tea rooms*, https://womanandhersphere.files.wordpress.com/2012/09/simple-life1.jpg

Crawford E, (ed.) (2013) *Campaigning for the Vote: Kate Parry Frye's Suffrage Diary*, London: Francis Boutle Publishers

de Rousiers P, (1896, 2010) *The Labour Question in Britain*, p.101-2. https://archive.org/stream/cu31924032468823/cu31924032468823_djvu.txt

Despard C, (1890) *The Rajah's Heir: A novel*, Nabu Public Domain Reprints

Despard C, (1891) *A voice from the dim millions*, London: Griffith, Farron, Okeden and Welsh

Despard C, (1913) *Theosophy and the Women's Movement*, London: Theosophical Publishing Society

Despard C, (1913) *Vegetarian Messenger and Health Review* (10)

Digby A, (1990) Victorian Values and Women in Public and Private, in Smout, *Victorian Values, Proceedings of the British Academy 78* (1992) pp.195–217.

Eustance C, (1993) *'Daring to be Free' The evolution of women's political identities in the Women's Freedom League 1907–1930*, D.Phil thesis, University of York

Eustance C, (1998) *Meanings of militancy: the ideas and practices of political resistance in the Women's Freedom League 1907–1914*, in Joannou and Purvis

Goodland G, (2000) *From Old to New Poor Law*, History Review (38) December

Hannam J. and Hunt K, (2002) *Socialist women Britain 1880s to 1920s*, London: Routledge

Hollis P, (1987) Women in Council: Separate Spheres, Public Spaces in Rendall (ed.) *Equal or Different: Women's Politics 1800–1914*, Oxford

Holmes R, (1981) *The Little Field Marshal: A life of Sir John French*, London: Cassell

Holtby W, (1934) *Women and a changing civilisation*, London: John Lane

Hochschild A, (2011) *To end all wars: A story of protest and patriotism in the first world war*, London: Macmillan

Joachim M, (1908) *My Life in Holloway Gaol*

Joanou M. and Purvis J, (eds.) (1998) *The women's suffrage movement: new feminist perspectives*, Manchester University Press

Kean H, (2003) An exploration of the sculptures of Greyfriars Bobby, Edinburgh, Scotland and the Brown Dog Battersea, South London, England, *Society and Animals* 11:4

King S, (2004) 'We might be trusted': Female Poor Law guardians and the development of the new Poor Law: The case of Bolton, England 1880–1906, *Internationaal Instituut voor Sociale Geschiedenis 49*

Lansbury C, (1985) *The Old Brown Dog: Women workers and vivisection in Edwardian England*, Madison: University of Wisconsin Press

Leneman L, (1997) The awakened instinct: vegetarianism and the women's suffrage movement in Britain, *Women's History Review*, 6:2, pp. 271–87

Lewis G, (1988) *Eva Gore Booth and Esther Roper: a biography*, Rivers Oram Press

Liddington J, (2014) *Vanishing for the vote. Suffrage, citizenship and the battle for the census*, Manchester University Press

Liddington J. and Norris J, (1978) *One hand tied behind us*, Rivers Oram

Linklater A, (1980) *An unhusbanded life, Charlotte Despard: Suffragette, Socialist and Sinn Feiner*, London: Hutchinson

Lytton C. and Warton J, (2016) *Prison and prisoners: some personal experiences*, CreateSpace

Marlow J, (2001) *Votes for women: The Virago book of suffragettes*, Virago

McPhee C. and Fitzgerald A, (eds.) (1987) *The non-violent militant: selected writings of Teresa Billington-Greig*, London: Routledge and Kegan Paul

Mulvihill M, (1989) *Charlotte Despard: A biography*, London: Pandora Press

Newsome S, (1960) *The Women's Freedom League 1907–1957*, London: WFL

Oakley A, (2018) *Women, Peace and Welfare: A suppressed history of social reform 1880–1920*, Bristol: Policy Press

Pankhurst E, (2015) *My own story*, Andesite

Pankhurst S, (1932) *The Home Front*

Pankhurst S, (date unknown) *The suffragette movement: An intimate account of persons and ideas*

Paseta S, (2003) *Modern Ireland: a very short introduction*, Oxford University Press

Priestley L.A.M., (Mrs George McCracken) (1918) *The feminine in fiction: The love stories of some eminent women*, London: George Allen and Unwin

Purvis J. and Holton S. S., (2000) *Votes for women*, London: Routledge

Robinson J, (2018) *Hearts and Minds*, London: Penguin Random House

Rosen A, (2014) *Rise up women! The militant campaign of the Women's Social and Political Union 1903–1914*, London: Routledge

Ryder V, (1974) *The Little Victims Play*, Hale

Scurr J, (1917) The Beneficent Fairy of Nine Elms, *The Herald of the Star* 6(2) (February 1917)

Thompson T, (1987) *Dear Girl: The diaries and letters of two working women 1897–1917*, London: The Women's Press

Twigg J, (1981) *The vegetarian movement in England 1847–1981: A study in the structure of its ideology*, PhD thesis University of London

Vallely P, (2005) Women's suffrage movement: The story of Kate Harvey, *The Independent*, 24 November

Vicinus M, (1985) *Independent women: Work and community for single women*, London: Virago p.44

Ward M, (2017) *Hanna Sheehy Skeffington Suffragette and Sinn Féiner: Her memoirs and political writings*, Dublin: University College Dublin

Wiltshier A, (1985) *Most dangerous women: Feminist peace campaigners of the Great War*, London Pandora Press

Woodford D.E., (1999) A deaf fighter for the rights of women, *Journal of the British Deaf History Society* 2(3) April 1999

Journals:
The Vote
Women's Franchise
The Vegetarian News, November 1939
The Nation and Athenaeum (13) 1913
Anti-Vivisection Review (1) July 1909 – June 1910
A sainted lady in *The British Journal of Nursing*, 17 March 1917

Oxford Dictionary of National Biography:
Beckett I. F.W., *John French*
Mulvihill M, *Charlotte Despard*
Shepherd J, (2011) *George Lansbury*, ODNB
Toomey D, *Maud Gonne MacBride*

Websites:
https://www.ucl.ac.uk/bartlett/architecture/sites/bartlett/files/50.04_nine_elms.pdf
The Survey of London, chapter 4 Nine Elms

Esher District Local History Society
http://www.edlhs.co.uk/Newsletter per cent20Extracts.html

https://ipfs.io/ipfs/QmXoypizjW3WknFiJnKLwHCnL72vedxj
QkDDP1mXWo6uco/wiki/Lizzy_Lind_af_Hageby.html

https://www.thehistorypress.co.uk/articles/the-brown-dog-affair/

https://seanmunger.com/2013/12/10/londons-martyred-terrier-the-
amazing-story-of-the-brown-dog-riots/

http://www.navs.org.uk/about_us/24/0/286/

www.veganfeministnetwork.com

Katherine Harley
http://spartacus-educational.com/WharleyK.htm

http://www.shropshireremembers.org.uk/katherine-harley/
K Pybus

Stiles H D W (2018) A deaf suffragist – Kate Harvey 1862-1946 https://blogs.
ucl.ac.uk/library-rnid/2018/03/16/a-deaf-suffragist-kate-harvey-1862-1946/
16 March 2018

Primary sources:
Charlotte Despard's diaries and papers, The Women's Library, London and
    Public Records Office, Belfast
The papers of Teresa Billington-Greig, The Women's Library, London
Papers of Hanna Sheehy Skeffington and other documents, National Library of
    Ireland, Dublin

Index